Jan Ort

Facets of a Harmony
The Roma and Their
Locatedness in Eastern
Slovakia

CHARLES UNIVERSITY
KAROLINUM PRESS 2022

KAROLINUM PRESS
Karolinum Press is a publishing department of Charles University
Ovocný trh 560/5, 116 36 Prague 1, Czech Republic
www.karolinum.cz
© Mgr. Jan Ort, student Filozofické fakulty Univerzity Karlovy, 2022
Maps © Jaroslav Synek, 2022
Translation © Philip Jones, 2022
Set and printed in the Czech Republic by Karolinum Press
Layout by Jan Šerých
First edition

A catalogue record for this book is available from the National Library
of the Czech Republic.

This book was published with the support of grant no. 782218 from the
Charles University Grant Agency (GA UK) entitled "'Here is no difference
between Roma and gadže': Negotiating power, colour and gender in an East
Slovak village since 1945." The processing and publication of a comprehensive
ethnography of a selected village in eastern Slovakia was carried out at the
Faculty of Humanities and the Faculty of Arts of Charles University.
The publication is a detailed reworking of a thesis written by the author in
2017 and defended at the Romani Studies Seminar, the Department of Central
European Studies, the Faculty of Arts, Charles University in Prague.

ISBN 978-80-246-5068-5
ISBN 978-80-246-5127-9 (pdf)
ISBN 978-80-246-5205-4 (epub)
ISBN 978-80-246-5206-1 (mobi)

The original manuscript was reviewed by Dana Bittnerová (Charles
University, Prague), Martin Fotta (Goethe-Universität, Frankfurt am Main),
and Jan Grill (Univesidad del Valle, Cali, Columbia).

Contents

Acknowledgements   8

Introduction: A Village of Harmonious Coexistence   11
  Place   13
  Methodology   16
    Romani studies and anthropology among the Roma in Slovakia   16
    Positionality   19
    Methodology   22
    Writing of the Roma   24
  Being local Roma   30
    Silencing Gypsyness   30
    Locals but not indigenous   33
    Facets of a harmony   41

Chapter One: "Our Roma" and "our Gadže"   44
  The Roma in Slovakia   45
  Together but divided   48
  Asymmetrical relations   51
  A shared understanding of Gypsyness   54
  The language of Gypsyness   56
  Silencing Gypsyness   58
  "Our Roma"   61
  "Our Gadže"   62
  Still just a Gypsy   64
  Experience of the subordinate position   66
  Virtuous Roma and amoral Gadže   67
  Balancing the Gadžo way of life   68
  The narrative of social mobility   71
  The narrative of resistance   72
  Conclusion   74

Chapter Two: Housing and the Politics of Space   79
The territorialisation of the Roma in Slovakia   81
The asymmetry of post-war construction   84
Politics of the Gypsy settlement   85
Actors of territorialisation   88
The story of Jozef: a Gypsy in the village   91
Maintaining the settlement's size   94
Council flats for the Roma   96
Continuity of territorial stigmatisation   97
Covert discrimination   99
Territorialisation: the *Gadže's* perspective   101
Placing Gypsyness   103
"Jolanian Roma": local, but stuck in a place   105
"Amongst the *Gadže*": confirming Gypsyness   108
Creating a safe space   110
The settlement: discontinuity of material conditions   111
Beyond territorial stigmatisation   113
Conclusion   116

Chapter Three: Language of the "Rusyn Roma"   120
The Romani language in Slovakia   122
Language acquisition in Jolany   126
Slovak   128
Rusyn   131
Rusyn in the local authorities   132
"So the *Gadže* don't say..."   133
The Mayoress and Kaleňák   135
New domains of Romani?   136
Language as a tool of othering   139
Language and inter-Roma relations   141
Subverting linguistic dominance   143
Romani: the Roma's shared cultural code   145
Romani amongst the *Gadže*   147
"Original" Romani   148
Romani as a cryptic code   151
Conclusion   154

Chapter Four: Gypsy Economy in Jolany   157
The Roma and work in Slovakia   158
Historical overview of economic strategies in Jolany   161
"Gypsy work"   163
Non-Romani actors of the Gypsy economy   165
"Gypsy work" and inter-Roma relations   168
Being a trustworthy worker   170
Shifting the logic of adaptation   172

The Gypsy economy in Jolany 174
Visibility of the Gypsy economy 177
Migration 178
Roma as "(semi)nomadic Gypsies"? 180
Contesting Gypsyness through migration 182
Escaping everyday racism 184
Jolany as a safe space 186
Conclusion 188

Conclusion: The Roma as Locals 192
Harmony as narrative and social practice 195
"So the *Gadže* don't say..." 197
Place 200
Gender 203
Roma and kinship 206

Epilogue: Is Old Jolany Slowly Disappearing? 210

Bibliography 215
Index 225

Acknowledgements

The research and publication of this book has been supported over the years by the Erasmus+ programme and the Charles University Grant Agency.

Thanks are due first and foremost to all the residents of Jolany and several surrounding villages, who graciously allowed me to spend time with them.

Palikerav savore Romenge, že man prijiminde maškar pende, choc te dareka-na keravas diliňipena. Palikerav, že man sikhaďan kavka duma te del, že imar na phagerav e čhib. Palikerav, že mange phuterďan o jahka, že man sikhaďan igen but veci na ča pal o Roma, ale the pal o gadže a pal mande korkoreste.

I owe a huge debt of thanks for all of our meetings to Pišta and Jola-na, Peťo and Gába, Slávo and Ľuba, Ďoďo and Lída, Rasťo and Luca, Janek and Pavlína, Peťo and Renata, Rasťo and Káťa, Janko and Máňa, Peťo and Zuzka, Vašo and Marcela, Janko and Helena, Demeter and Helena, Peťo and Káťa, Peťo and Ivana, and all of their families. I would also like thank Ľuboš and Stela, Vašo and Dorota, and Jožko, Haňa and Miťo.

I arrived in Jolany having just been awarded a bachelor's degree in Romani studies. Seven years were to pass before I completed this book, during which time I began (but did not complete) a master's degree in General Anthropology at the Faculty of Humanities, Charles University in Prague, completed a master's degree in Romani studies at the Faculty of Arts of the same university, successfully defended my thesis, which was based on the research I had conducted in Jolany, decided to publish it, and gradually discovered that I would need to rethink the entire project and rewrite the book. This book is not only a report on a specific research situation, but also reflects the development of my thinking about Romani studies, anthropology, and research conducted among the Roma and the social implications thereof.

Over the years my thinking has changed and moved on considerably, for which I am eternally grateful to the residents of Jolany, to whom I was able to return throughout this period of my life, as well as to the many other people who encouraged, guided and rectified the way I thought about specific topics and relations.

I would like to say a big thank you to Helena Sadílková, who from the very beginning of my research read carefully and commented on all sorts of text, from the first notes regarding my thesis, via proposals for individual chapters of the book, to its manuscript, including translations from Czech to English. Helena also motivated me to express my ideas in book form and offered me her full support throughout the writing process.

Many thanks also to the reviewers of this book, Martin Fotta and Jan Grill, for their detailed and inspiring comments, as well as subsequent consultations regarding the entire text. Their feedback helped me clarify the narrative and argument of the entire book.

I would also like to thank Dana Bittnerová for her honest, inspiring appraisal, which she conducted for the editorial board of the Faculty of Humanities of Charles University.

I also owe a debt of gratitude to all of those who read the many different texts that resulted from my research in Jolany. Specifically I would like to thank Yasar Abu Ghosh, Jan Červenka, Petra Dobruská, Markéta Hajská, Tomáš Hrustič, Tomáš Kobes, Pavel Kubaník, Zdeněk Uherek, Matěj Spurný and the participants at his diploma seminar at the Faculty of Arts, Charles University, and finally the participants of Yasar Abu Ghosh's diploma seminar at the Faculty of Humanities, Charles University.

A special thanks to my parents for their unwavering support.

I would also like to thank Andrej Belák, Michael Beníšek, Renata Berkyová, Viktor Elšík, Markéta Hajská, Kristína Hamplová, Romana Hudousková, Zuzana Jarošová, Jakub Ort, Daniel Ort, Marie Palečková, Martin Pfann, František Pfann, Michael Polák, Jakub Raška, Štěpán Ripka, Eliška Ripková, Jaroslav Skupnik, Alžběta Trusinová, Tereza Virtová, Markéta Zandlová and the students on the Romani language course at Klinika for their support, stimulating discussions and shared observations.

Many thanks to Saša Mušinka and Lucia Segľová for the invaluable backup provided for the duration of my research in eastern Slovakia.

I would like to thank Lenka Badidová for her endless patience and the care she lavished upon me during my visits to the archive in Svidník. I would also like to thank the staff of the branches of the Slovak State Archive in Bardejov, Nižná Šebastová and Košice, and the Archive of the Office of the President of the Republic of the Czech Republic in Prague for all the help they offered me.

Many thanks are due to Adéla Petruželková, editor at Karolinum, for her patience, accuracy and assistance during the last stages of the book.

Many thanks also to Marie Kratochvílová and the editorial board of the Faculty of the Humanities of Charles University for the trust they placed in me.

Many thanks to Phil Jones, who took on the translation of the book from Czech to English with interest and enthusiasm.

Finally, I would like to thank my partner, Petra Dobruská, and our son, Jonáš, for their infinite patience and support during the finalisation of the book.

Introduction
A Village of Harmonious Coexistence

A newspaper report from 2010 depicted Jolany[1] as a village in which Roma and non-Roma lived side by side in perfect harmony.[2] The journalist intimated that in this respect Jolany was unique in Slovakia. The explanation she offered for this idyllic state of affairs was that the local Roma were more "civilised". They were, she wrote, regular readers of newspapers and did not overstep the socially accepted norm of three children per family. The report described Jolany as a functioning community in which the social roles of Roma and non-Roma complemented each other. The non-Roma tended to be older people, who would ask their younger Romani neighbours for help in the garden, thus providing them some much-needed extra income.

I reread this report in October 2014 while looking for a village in eastern Slovakia where I might carry out long-term fieldwork. Back then, the subject of my research was very loosely defined by questions pertaining to the sociability of the Roma and the negotiation of their position in a particular community. Leaving aside the irritation I felt at the patronising tone of the newspaper report, it did at least confirm to me that Jolany could be an ideal location for my research, since it subverted entrenched

---

1 Throughout this book I use fictitious names of villages (not cities) and people. For more on anonymisation, see below in main body of the text.

2 For the sake of anonymisation I will not provide a link to the newspaper article. In the interests of context I would merely point out that it appeared in a publication that styles itself a "Romani newspaper" (*noviny Rómov*). As well as the opinions of the Roma themselves, the article makes great play of the activities of the local mayoress, who pushed through the construction of the council flats for the Jolany Roma and was recognised for her outstanding contribution to the Romani community (see Chapter Two).

ideas of strictly segregated Romani settlements in eastern Slovakia (see for example Jakoubek and Hirt 2008, Scheffel 2005). Jolany is a small village that at the time I was conducting my research had a population of some 150, of which the Roma officially accounted for just over 30% (Mušinka et al. 2014). In reality the Roma accounted for approximately half of the total number of inhabitants. After my previously agreed accommodation in another village fell through, I set off for the northeast of Slovakia and the Svidník district near the border with Poland, where the municipality of Jolany is situated.

Upon arriving in Jolany I fell into conversation with a man who, after only a few words had been exchanged, invited me into the pub for a drink. The man was Peter, a Romani inhabitant of the village, whom I later informed over a beer of my intention to spend a longer period of time in the village. Perhaps recognising a certain interest in the Roma and encouraged by my knowledge of the Romani language, Peter was soon echoing the narrative of the report referred to above, assuring me that in Jolany "it's not like elsewhere in Slovakia – here we live side by side with the *Gadže*"[3]. Though I have always tended to take such claims with a pinch of salt, things did indeed seem genuinely different in the Jolany pub to how they were in some other places in eastern Slovakia, where racial segregation was very much the norm in local pubs. The practice elsewhere was for such establishments to have segregated areas for Roma and non-Roma, or for Roma people to avoid them altogether. However, in the small pub in Jolany we were gradually joined by other men, both Roma and non-Roma, who, upon hearing of my plans to remain in the village, concurred with what Peter had said regarding the harmonious relations that pertained there.

When emphasising those features that set Jolany apart from other places, these men, and later on other residents of the village too, touched on two separate topics that gradually formed the backbone of my research and, in the fullness of time, this book. On the one hand they spoke about people, namely, the relations between Romani and non-Romani villagers. And on the other they spoke about place, emphasising how important was their sense of belonging specifically to Jolany, which in this respect, they claimed, represented an outlier when compared to other villages in eastern Slovakia. This book addresses the following fundamental questions arising from these themes. Firstly, how might the narrative regarding the

---

3   Interview with Peter (b. 1953), conducted in Romani, 17 October 2014.

harmonious relations between Roma and non-Roma be read, and how did individual actors deal with the categorisation of people into Roma/ Gypsies? Secondly, to what extent has the concept of harmonious relations contributed to the construction of Jolany as a specific place? And finally, how did individual actors negotiate this sense of belonging to a given place in light of the categories "local" and "outsider"?

Place

Jolany is located in the Svidník District, a somewhat forgotten part of eastern Slovakia said to be the only region in the country without so much as a kilometre of railway track. The marginalisation of the area is bound up with the fact that the majority of its inhabitants were not ethnic Slovaks but Rusyns, a close-knit ethnic minority on the tripoint of north-eastern Slovakia, south-eastern Poland and Zakarpattia in south-western Ukraine. The ethnic composition of the population means the region also differs from the rest of Slovakia in respect of religion. The Greek Catholic Church predominates here (which under the communist regime was forced to be Orthodox). Like the rest of eastern Slovakia, at the time I was conducting my research (2014–2020) the region was experiencing a depopulation of rural areas, whose inhabitants were relocating in a search for work to larger towns and cities in Slovakia or the neighbouring Czech Republic, and even to the countries of western Europe. As I will show later in this book, these demographic changes also affected Jolany and created an important context for the functioning of relationships between the villagers.

The county town of Svidník only came into existence in 1944 with the merger of Nižný Svidník and Vyšný Svidník. However, a large number of local villages were also rebuilt that had been devastated during the Second World War, especially during the fighting that took place in the Battle of the Dukla Pass (the Carpatho-Dukla Operation) in autumn 1944. One of the municipalities most affected was Jolany, which was razed to the ground at the end of 1944. The only visible reminder of the pre-war period was a wooden church, a local landmark that had miraculously survived. When I began my research, in addition to the church there were around fifty other buildings in Jolany. On the hill on which the church stood was a small cemetery, in which the graves of the Roma were conspicuously segregated from those of the non-Roma. A path led down from the church to the village square, where a small grocery shop was connected to a room that served as a pub. Here you could buy bottled beer or a glass of lemonade and a shot of Juniper brandy or vodka. The shop sold basic foodstuffs and toiletries, though for anything else you had to travel to Svidník or to the Polish side of the nearby border. The shop adjoined the House of Culture, which had been built in the 1970s and now housed the municipal authorities. A stone's throw from the municipal office, on the other side of a stream traversed by a footbridge, stood eight council flats in two long blocks, which were part of the area known by the locals as the "(Romani) settlement" (cigánská osada [Slovak], vatra [Romani], vatrisko [Rusyn]). At the beginning of my research there were also three Romani families living in a built-up area alongside non-Romani villagers. This development lined the main road that passed through the village in the shape of an "L". The road was connected at one end to the busy highway leading from Svidník to Poland, and on the other disappeared into the woodland between the hills surrounding the village. One of the buildings right next to the main road had housed the school, but was now dilapidated and no longer fit for purpose. The village children attended school in the neighbouring Drevany.

The local chronicle, which contains both a brief history of the municipality and describes what it calls the "culture of the locals", is particularly illuminating in this respect. According to this text it was processing wood from the nearby forests that had traditionally served as a source of livelihood for the villagers of Jolany, an activity dating back to the 17th century and the very first mention of the village. In addition to a detailed description of the events of the Second World War, the chronicle devotes a considerable amount of space to a more general evocation of village life prior to the war. After a section on the development of education since the end of the 19th century, the author proceeds to organise her chapters along the lines of a glossary of folklore, in which she explains the individual terms pertaining to the culture of housing, alimentation, traditional costume and agricultural tools. The glossary comprises an explanation of Rusyn terminology, which itemises artefacts of the traditional village culture. The chronicle makes no mention of the Roma or their language whatsoever, even though, in a survey conducted by the Ethnographic Institute of the Slovak Academy of Sciences in the early 1950s, the Svidník District reported that the Roma had lived in Jolany since time immemorial (Jurová 2002). The chronicle also overlooks the diverse ethnic composition of this small "Rusyn" municipality, which censuses show was, prior to the war, home not only to the majority Rusyns, but also ethnic Slovaks, Jews, Gypsies (Cigáni) and, depending on the period,

Ukrainians and Poles (Majo 2012). At the time of my research, it was language especially that highlighted the diversity of the village population, with Rusyn, Romani, standard Slovak and local dialects thereof, and sometimes even Polish, Ukrainian and Czech to be heard on a daily basis. However, the chronicle ignores this historically rooted heterogeneity in its image of a unified local culture.

The chronicle makes no claims to represent a detailed history of the municipality and under no circumstances could it serve as the cornerstone of an analysis of local relations. All the more so given that it is a one-off record from 1988, in which the author retrospectively captured the entire previous period. However, the way the chronicle is organised basically corresponds to the impression given by the newspaper article that persuaded me to spend time in this particular village. In both cases the characteristics associated with the Roma were implicitly separated from descriptions of the way of life of the local population. The chronicle, which combines a certain type of event and information within a dominant aggregate of the experiences and lifestyles of the villagers, is silent on the topic of the Roma. In contrast, the newspaper report sets out to show how the Roma became part of the local community by means of the appropriation of certain characteristics of the "civilised" local culture.

The categorisations referred to above are thus clearly interconnected: on the one hand, the distinction between the Roma (or "Gypsies") and non-Roma (or *Gadže*: see below for a more detailed explanation of these appellations), and on the other, the distinction between "locals" and "outsiders". The Jolany Roma exhibited many characteristics that marked them out as locals, and others that branded them as "Gypsies" (*Cigáni*) and disbarred them from a normative "whiteness" (cf. Šotola et al. 2018). And so despite being perceived as members of the village community, in their capacity as Gypsies they occupied a subordinate position in its social hierarchy. These two modes of categorisation thus overlapped to a large extent – an identification with the category of Gypsy implied segregation from the local community, and to the extent that the Roma were able to participate in the local way of life, they did so *despite* their Gypsyness.

The ambiguity of Romani belonging to a given place is a theme that runs through this book. However, the individual chapters will not simply follow the dominant discourse, which distinguishes the Roma/Gypsies as somehow alien. I will not take this categorisation to be fixed, but more the result of specific historical processes and subject to ongoing interrogation and negotiation. When tracking these processes, I will focus on the agency of those who identify as Roma and are thus identified by their surroundings. Rather than examining the process of their exclusion and differentiation, I will examine how the Roma themselves understood their position within the local community and how they negotiated the categories referred to in their everyday dealings. Before introducing the topics of individual chapters and placing them within a broader theoretical and comparative framework, I would like to clarify the context and methodological basis of the research on which this book is based.

Methodology

Romani studies and anthropology among the Roma in Slovakia

There is a long tradition of anthropological research into the Roma of Slovakia. A central figure in this respect was Milena Hübschmannová, whose comprehensive interest in the Roma embraced the spheres of history, sociology, cultural anthropology, folklore, general linguistics, sociolinguistics, art, etc. (see *Romano džaniben* 2006). Hübschmannová, a qualified Indologist, explained the particularities of Romani culture largely by tracing it back to its Indian roots (Hübschmannová 1972, 1998). In anthropology, this emphasis on the origin of the Roma when explaining the dogged persistence of their distinctive culture was later dropped, and the authors of modern ethnographies of the Roma preferred to examine the context of specific European communities (see Stewart 2013; Olivera and Poueyto 2018). However, Hübschmannová, who began her research into the Roma in the 1950s, did not restrict herself to a diachronic perspective and the search for cultural and linguistic links with the presumed ancestors of the Roma on the Indian subcontinent. It is clear from her texts that she was attuned to the complex formation of the Romani identity in European society. For instance, she drew attention to the importance of power asymmetry in relations with non-Romani surroundings, the role played by the unquestioned dominance of non-Roma, and the various strategies deployed by the Roma to deal with their own marginalised and stigmatised social position (e.g. Hübschmannová 1970, 1999). It is in her emphasis on the agency of the Roma and her knowledge of the Romani language, not only as a vital mode of communication for research among the Roma but also the key to understanding their position in society, that her main contribution to the sphere of anthropology itself resides.

In addition to Hübschmannová, ethnographic research amongst the Roma of eastern Slovakia was carried out from the 1950s onwards by the ethnographers Emília Horváthová[4] (e.g. 1964) and Eva Davidová[5] (e.g. 1965). Even given the adoption of an evolutionary view of Romani culture,[6] their work remains important, above all as a relatively rich seam of ethnographic material and a secondary historical source. The British sociologist Will Guy then offers an ethnographically informed historical study on the basis of research carried out in the early 1970s in his compendious thesis (1977). A more widespread interest on the part of anthropologists in Romani settlements in (eastern) Slovakia can be observed around the turn of the millennium, since more broadly based research took place in individual regions (see Jakoubek and Hirt 2008, Kužel 2000).[7] The anthology by the Slovak ethnologists Tatiana Podolinská and Tomáš Hrustič (2015) presents the results of interdisciplinary research conducted among the Roma in eastern Slovakia.

It is against the backdrop of Czech and Slovak Romani studies and the focus of researchers from both parts of the former Czechoslovakia on the lives of Roma in Slovakia that this book represents a bold attempt to present a comprehensive ethnography of the Roma in one particular eastern Slovak municipality. For its objectives and theoretical starting points it draws primarily on the outcomes of long-term anthropological fieldwork in specific villages published in individual texts from the start of the millennium onwards (Belák et al. 2017, 2018; Grill 2012, 2015 a,b, 2017, 2018; Hajská 2015, 2017; Hrustič 2014, 2015a; Kobes 2009, 2010, 2012; Kubaník 2015, Skupnik 2007). Its diachronic sections (especially Chapter Two) are based on historical studies of the negotiation of inter-ethnic relations in specific communities (Grill 2015a,b; Sadílková 2017, 2020; Scheffel 2015; Šotola and Rodriguéz Polo 2016; Guy 1977).[8]

---

4   Horváthová also published under the name Čajánková.

5   Davidová also published under the names Zábranová and Davidová-Turčínová.

6   However, Horváthová's participation in the period discourse on the Roma was ascribed to censorship (see Mann 1996).

7   This interest was also connected to the humanitarian organisation People in Need (*Člověk v tísni*), which in the latter half of the 1990s provided assistance to Romani settlements affected by flooding (see, for example, Kobes 2017).

8   This list of writers who have been involved in anthropological research into the Roma in Slovakia is far from exhaustive. I cite those authors whose work I deem relevant, especially in

I attempted to spread my own research symmetrically between the Romani and non-Romani inhabitants of Jolany, which is not usually the case in this kind of work.[9] However, as I show below, I too was not always successful in this endeavour. On the contrary, many of the authors cited above (though not all) are linked by a knowledge of the Romani language and its use in their research amongst the Roma (or Romani speakers). I believe that not enough thought has been given to the implications of a knowledge of Romani when conducting anthropological research in Slovakia (and among Roma in general), even though it has a huge influence on the character not only of the data acquired, but also the relationship between the researcher and the research participants (Červenka 2000). At this point I symbolically return to the beginning of this section and admit to my own grounding in the tradition of the Romani Studies Seminar established by Hübschmannová at the Faculty of Arts, Charles University, from which I graduated in 2017. I later had the opportunity to supplement and confront this tradition while studying general anthropology at the Faculty of Humanities of the same university. As an active speaker of Romani I was able to use the language not only as a research tool (as it has also been embraced by many anthropologists), but also as a subject of research in its own right as I monitored its daily use and the language preferences of its speakers (Chapter Three).

An emphasis on language as a research topic is related to the multidisciplinary approach that Hübschmannová consistently promoted right from the establishment of Prague-based Romani studies (see *Romano džaniben* 2006). This approach is manifest here not only in sociolinguistic analysis, but also in the inclusion of a historical perspective (see Chapter Two especially). In contrast, the anthropological tradition provided me with a broader conceptual and theoretical framework than that offered by the multidisciplinary understanding of Romani studies. Finally, both traditions came together for me personally in the ethical and methodological imperative to respect research participants as full partners in the entire research process.

---

respect of a long-term focus on a specific location and an emphasis on the agency of the Roma themselves.

9   Of the anthropological studies of the Roma published up till now only Engebrigtsen, who conducted research among Roma and non-Roma residents of a village in Transylvania, Romania, has systematically attempted this (Engebrigtsen 2007).

Positionality

This book is based on research conducted over a long period in the village of Jolany, where I lived with one Romani family for ten months (from the start of October 2014 to the end of July 2015) and to which I regularly made shorter trips right up to August 2020. I arrived in the village as a twenty-three-year-old non-Romani student from Prague, a recent graduate with a bachelor's degree in Romani studies studying for an MA in the same discipline. I opted for longer-term research in order to acquire hands-on experience (which at that time I regarded as a precondition for entering into anthropological debates), to improve my knowledge of the Romani language, and to become acquainted in detail with the everyday lives of the Roma (and their neighbours) in a particular location.

My interest in the Roma inevitably led to a considerable disparity between the data obtained from the Romani and from the non-Romani villagers, and the research as framed in this way was ultimately one of the reasons the distinction between Roma and non-Roma was largely confirmed. During the research period I lived with a Romani family and the Roma were my key informants. I communicated with the Roma in their native language, Romani. I had only a passive knowledge of Rusyn, the first language of most of the local non-Romani villagers and often the main language for communication between all the locals. I communicated with the non-Romani villagers in Czech[10] and they usually replied in Slovak (i.e. not their native language but one in which they were fluent). However, these disparities of linguistic competence only explain part of the imbalance of the data acquired. I spent most of my research period in the company of Romani villagers, not only in Jolany and its immediate surroundings, but, in the case of young Romani men especially, in various Czech towns during their short work-based trips to the Czech Republic. In the case of the Roma I was able to use unstructured and semi-structured interviews as well as participatory observation as research methods, whereas in the case of the non-Romani population I relied mainly on more formal, semi-structured interviews arranged in advance.

---

10 For older generations of Czechs and Slovaks especially, the Czech and Slovak languages are completely comprehensible by both parties. In addition, the participants in my research were in regular contact with Czech (see Chapter 3).

Given the widespread belief amongst the Jolany population that I was there to study the lives of the Roma, the non-Roma may have felt that the research concerned only their Romani neighbours. At times I had the impression that some of the non-Roma were steering clear of more focused conversations in order to avoid becoming guinea pigs, as it were. In addition, during the interviews I conducted with the non-Roma, I often failed to relinquish the position of researcher interested in the Roma. Conversations therefore usually took place against the backdrop of the relatively sharp Roma/non-Roma dichotomy, and my presence often necessitated an explanation and defence of my position and relationship with the Roma in general and with my immediate Roma neighbours in particular. Furthermore, interaction between non-Roma and Roma villagers only took place sporadically. Apart from meeting Romani and non-Romani men in the local pub, I often found myself interacting more intensively with non-Roma in the role of escort to my Romani friends, often when they had been invited to do some work for a non-Rom.

As the duration of my stay increased, it became clear that the research conducted among non-Romani villagers would be crucial to an understanding of the complexity of local relations if I was to avoid a merely homogenising assertion of the presence of non-Romani dominance. At the same time, however, I began to feel more and more accepted by the Romani villagers and did not feel comfortable communicating with the non-Roma, to the extent of sometimes avoiding them. In addition, the latter group restricted their movements around the village and tended to remain in their homes and fenced properties. Although I gradually supplemented the limited number of more focused interviews with non-Romani villagers with interviews with representatives of local institutions (the doctor, school headmaster, the mayors of surrounding villages, and the coordinators of projects undertaken in the vicinity), I was unable to make up fully for this asymmetrical research structure.

However, the Roma themselves did not form a homogenous and clearly delimited group. Even within the relations that pertained between them I was situated in a certain way. During the course of my research I lived with Maroš and Katarína, whose family was one of those that lived outside the local Romani settlement in the immediate vicinity of non-Romani inhabitants. It could be said that this was the family with the strongest ties to the non-Romani inhabitants of the village, but also to other non-Roma in the surrounding region. Although I was in contact with all the Romani families to varying degrees (which at the start of my research meant a total of eleven households), the fact that I belonged, as it were, to one particular family determined to a large extent the form of the entire research situation. Inasmuch as I often place more emphasis in this book on families with greater social capital in the non-Romani world (either through their position in the layout of the village or via specific socio-economic relations), this is for two interrelated reasons. Firstly, it proved a more effective way of observing the dynamic negotiation of the characteristics of the category Gypsyness and the verification and possible transformation thereof via the stories and specific practices of the members of these families. In addition to being more often in direct contact with their non-Romani surroundings, the members of these families became more visible as individual Roma for both the surrounding world and for me as researcher by virtue of their attempt to stand out from the anonymity of the stereotypical and stigmatising image of the "backward Gypsy". However, the entire research situation can be looked at from the other side. From the very start, the negotiation of the significance of these categories as a topic in itself was interesting perhaps precisely due to my positionality within local relations, a positionality that had a great influence on what people I was in frequent contact with and how they behaved towards me. It was perhaps no mere coincidence that I found myself affiliated with Maroš and Katarína's family – those Roma with stronger links to the surrounding non-Roma world enjoyed not only greater social capital but also, from a purely pragmatic standpoint, offered a wider choice of accommodation to the newly arrived researcher. It became clear early on that there was quite simply no room for me in the low-grade council flats (see Chapter Two) in the Romani settlement. Moreover, the local mayoress at that time, responsible for managing the flats, came out against such an option. Instead, after several days of haggling, Maroš and Katarína were able to free up a small extension in their garden for me. My research objectives and my positionality within local relations were thus mutually supportive, both in respect of the distinction between Roma and non-Roma, and with regard to further differentiations between the Roma themselves.

Likewise, one is obliged to acknowledge the gender entanglements of the entire research situation. As a male researcher I participated at several social events that were aimed primarily at men. I met both Romani and non-Romani villagers in the local pub, where the presence of women was deemed inappropriate. Men and women were to some extent segregated even during Romani social events that took place at home – funeral receptions, christenings, birthdays, and even when dining. On these occasions I sat at a table with the men while the women attended to our comfort and sat nearby. I also participated in those economic activities that were almost (but not completely) exclusively a male affair, e.g. work in the informal economy for non-Romani villagers, work in the region as part of a European project, as well as meetings in Czech towns during work stopovers (see Chapter Four). The fact that my key respondents were male was because the role of men involved greater participation in public life, being the breadwinner, and being the spokesperson of the family or community. It was also because I am a man: it would have been inappropriate to have the kind of long conversations alone with women that I was used to having with some of the men.

Methodology

In addition to traditional ethnographic methods, especially participatory observation and interviews, I used historical research methods, in particular oral history and archive research,[11] in order to understand the diachronic perspective of local relations. As well as interviews with witnesses and the testimony contained in the municipal chronicle, I obtained data from both district and regional archives. Notwithstanding the practice of historical studies, in the text below I have opted to anonymise the village under examination (plus the surrounding villages), a common strategy in anthropological texts, though one that arouses mixed feelings. The anonymisation of the village not only protects my sources, but to some extent also gives an indication of the asymmetry of relationship between researcher and research participants. Though anonymisation is usually defended on the basis of the sensitivity of the data collected and the protection of participants' privacy, it can also be seen as offering protection to the researcher him or herself against the possibility of a rigorous confrontation with the content of the text, be this instigated by the inhabitants of a particular village or region or by other researchers. Having spoken with my host family and several other Roma in the village, and fully cognisant of the pitfalls involved, I opted to anonymise.

In an effort to minimise the risk of the text being misappropriated from the research participants, I attempted to discuss my research objectives and ongoing outputs on a regular basis with the local inhabitants.

---

11 The reason for linking up these two methods for historical research among the Roma was given in detail by Sadílková in her unpublished thesis (2016).

Right from the start of the project I explained to them that I was interested in the life of the Roma and, more broadly, in the life and times of the village, and that I was intending to write a university thesis based on my research. An idea took root amongst the villagers that I was "writing a book", which had not originally been my plan. I only decided to do so after successfully defending my thesis (Ort 2017). I discussed the main areas of my research in more detail with several of the local Roma. In addition to my host family, this mainly involved the Romani villager Zoralo, three years my senior, who drew my attention to aspects of the local relationships I had hitherto not noticed and picked up on an implicit bias contained in elements of my project objectives. Though I was unable to manage a collaborative writing of the resulting texts, not even in the case of this book, such discussions established an element of course correction and enabled me to reflect upon my own conclusions.[12]

Since the direction of my research had initially been prompted by a newspaper report describing local relations as harmonious to the point of idyllic, during the first phase of my work I was strongly driven by the endeavour to reveal their "true" nature and the power asymmetry that, I was convinced, must be concealed behind them. Like other researchers (Šotola et al. 2018) I focused on the dominant structures and discourses and their pivotal role in othering the Roma, and regarded the dominance of the non-Roma as representing an all-encompassing explanation of the social reality. In this way I also partially came to terms with the problematic legacy of the Prague school of Roma studies, the founder of which, Milena Hübschmannová, tended for the most part to explain the distinctiveness of "Roma culture" by recourse to historical developments (cf. Stewart 2013). I placed a similar emphasis on the influence of anti-Gypsy dominant structures in my thesis referred to above, which dealt with the spatial and social mobility of the Roma inhabitants of Jolany (Ort 2017).

The opportunity to publish my research outcomes in a more comprehensive ethnographic study persuaded me to re-examine the data. I returned to the conversations I had had with Zoralo and other locals. One of them, 50-year-old Churdo, had repeatedly reproached me for, as

---

12 On the topic of collaborative ethnography within the context of research among the Roma, cf. especially Gay y Blasco and Hernandez (2020), Silverman (2018). In the Czech Republic and Slovakia one issue of the peer-reviewed journal *Romano džaniben* was devoted to this topic (Hrustič, Poduška 2018).

he saw it, unnecessarily casting the Roma in the role of victims, and had been concerned that the book not be about "how everyone is hurtful about the Roma". My attempts to discuss the results of my research with the Roma themselves meant I tried to take the local Roma seriously and not to silence their testimony as representing the uninterrogated outcome of an asymmetric structure. And so this book is, inter alia, a search for answers to an ethical, methodological dilemma characterised by a dangerous ignorance of historically rooted inequality on the one hand, and the risk of the victimisation and silencing of the Roma themselves on the other.

Writing of the Roma

The call for academics writing about the Roma to reflect upon their own positionality and to check their privilege culminated in the formulation of a new approach known as Critical Romani Studies. In the introduction to the first issue of the journal of this name, a group of "activist researchers" drew attention to the hitherto unresolved colonial legacy of a certain element of academic debate from which the Roma themselves are excluded (Bogdan et al. 2018). In addition, criticism of the approach taken up till now to academic writing about the Roma is based on the theoretical and methodological challenge represented by intersectionality, which disrupts the pervasiveness of the differentiation between Roma and non-Roma and seeks to take into account the complexity of differential axes by carefully separating out race, class and gender (e.g. Corradi 2018, Fremlová 2018, Kóczé 2009, Jovanović and Daróczi 2015). The growing debate around the question of who should participate in the production of knowledge of the Roma and how (Stewart 2017) has spread to the Czech and Slovak academic world. There has been criticism of Czech and Slovak studies of the Roma for their allegedly deep-rooted reproduction of dominant discourses and their uninterrogated participation in the repositioning of the Roma as the colonial Others (Šotola et al. 2018). It should be noted that, within the context of the Czech Republic and Slovakia, the criticism thus formulated fails in reference to the work of specific writers and, with its emphasis on dominant structures, may paradoxically sideline the agency of the Roma themselves (a similar criticism was formulated within a European context by Stewart [2017]). Nevertheless, within the context of my research it is only right to give thought as to how the text of this book enters into the dynamic negotiation of relations in the community under examination and what language is used to talk about them.

In light of calls for an interrogation of the broader social anchorage of those individuals contributing to academic and more general social discussions regarding the Roma, I have indicated above my position within the social structure of the village and have set forth those assumptions that largely determined the focus of my research. Though I am convinced that the differentiation between Roma and non-Roma was pivotal for negotiating relationships in the village, an excessive focus on it might create the impression of two, clearly demarcated social entities. When writing about the Roma and non-Roma, I inevitably end up generalising the attitudes and opinions of the inhabitants thus categorised. In this book, however, I shall also allow the stories of individuals to be heard in order to highlight the diversity of life experience and trajectory, and the plurality of locally realised and situationally defined categorisations.

I endeavour to take into account the ambiguity of local relationships and the dynamic of their daily negotiation in the choice of language that I use to report on such relations. In this respect my first dilemma was whether to use the concept of *boundaries* when reflecting upon the social differentiation in the village. In the social sciences the study of social boundaries is inextricably bound up with the influential essay by Frederik Barth in which, in order to understand the existence of "ethnic groups", he transferred the emphasis from cultural content to the interactive aspects of ethnicity and the mechanisms by which the boundaries between "self" and "other" were formed (Barth 1969). However, the concept of boundaries was not accepted uncritically in post-Barthian discussions. Among other writers (e.g. Eriksen and Jakoubek 2019: 11, Eriksen 2019) it was Brubaker who observed in his critique of "groupism" in the social sciences that Barth's metaphor of boundaries continued to imply the existence of clearly demarcated groups (Brubaker 2002: 169). He was similarly sceptical in reaction to Wimmer's book *Ethnic Boundary Making* (2013), arguing that the spatial and physical connotations of the metaphor of boundaries (cf. Jenkins 1997: 21) implied a relatively constant, trans-situational and objective categorisation of relations (Brubaker 2014: 806).

I avoid using the metaphor of boundaries when analysing the situation in Jolany for similar reasons. Although I show that the distinction between Roma and non-Roma was deeply embedded and played a key role in the structuring of both local relations and, to a certain extent, space, my aim is to shift the emphasis from boundary-making as such (cf. Jenkins 2014) to the negotiation of the Roma's sense of belonging to the local community and to a specific place. In addition, I believe that it is precisely in its attempt to capture the far murkier (and far more situational) distinction between "local" and "outsider" that the concept of boundaries loses its strength. In my opinion, the pitfalls involved in a notion of demarcated groups do not disappear even if we accept a plurality of boundaries that can be negotiated, crossed, concealed or overlapped by different actors. Taking my inspiration from Brubaker (2002), I will therefore not speak of boundaries in the context of social identities and relations, but of categories that contain the potential for a certain degree of "groupness" (I have already indicated that there was a high level of "groupness" in the case of the Roma) and can form more lasting social ties and solidarity networks, but which at the same time can lead to the creation of physical boundaries.

I also deliberately avoid using the concept of *ethnicity*. Though this book can be understood as a contribution not only to academic but wider societal discussions about interethnic relations in Slovakia and other places, I believe that the concept of ethnicity would be a hindrance when analysing the dynamic negotiation of local relations. As I shall show below, the categorisation of Roma and non-Roma does not duplicate the ethnic categories of Slovaks, Rusyns, Roma and Poles. In the case of the Roma themselves, the situation is further complicated if we include the category of place. When the writers of the classic ethnographies of the Roma (Stewart 1997, Gay y Blasco 1999) set aside the concept of ethnicity, they did so due to its inability to capture the performative creation of Romani identity in the present without the necessity of relating to a distinctive place (Theodosiou 2004). In the case of the Jolany Roma, on the contrary, I set out to show that the relationship to place is important for their identification. However, this was not necessarily a relationship to a distinctive place, but to a place that to a large extent they shared with their non-Romani neighbours. Inasmuch as I avoid the concept of boundaries and ethnicity, I do so not with the aim of rejecting completely the relevance and applicability of these concepts in the social sciences. However, when focusing on the ambiguous status of Roma in a local community I believe that the utilisation of these concepts would not contribute to the process of analysing the multilayered nature of situationally negotiated categorisations, the meanings of which in any case change over time.

Finally, a word regarding the specific terms relating to the categorisations under examination. When I use the term Roma, I am not only drawing on the officially recognised designation of a specific national minority in Slovakia. I am also consciously responding to the term *Roma*, which in Jolany was a category of self-identification in the Romani language. In non-Romani language codes there is also the Slovak *Rómovia* ("Roma") or the more frequently used *Cigáni* ("Gypsies"), which I use in quotations, but also in order to emphasise the dominant social discourse. The utilisation of these terms corresponds to the distinction between what Olivera and Poueyto defined as the "Gypsy condition", i.e. the concept of the Gypsy as it was formed in European political and popular discourse (with reference to other writers I use the concept of Gypsyness, see for example Abu Ghosh 2008, Grill 2017, Horváth 2012, Kovai 2012), and "Roma culture", i.e. the formulation of a distinctive identity from the position of the Roma (Olivera and Poueyto 2018).

Nevertheless, as these writers point out, and as I indicated in the introductory paragraphs of this book, these categories of Roma and Gypsy operate on the basis of a dynamic relationship within which they only partially overlap. Sokolová, who examined how the popular discourse around Gypsies related to the politics of socialist Czechoslovakia, noted that "[w]ho counted as a 'Gypsy' in the eyes of the state had very little to do with one's putatively 'real' ethnicity but rather depended on how one was situated within officially sanctioned categories of the proper and improper, normal and deviant, and integrated and unintegrated" (Sokolová 2008: 43). Within a similar logic of the functioning of these categories I shall show that the Jolany Roma tried not to be identified as Gypsies, but, on the contrary, transferred this category over to certain of their Romani neighbours or other Roma beyond the borders of the village.

The use of the term non-Roma in this book is to some extent artificial, since the inhabitants of Jolany basically did not use it. I use it as an umbrella term for the various designations by which the Roma referred to the non-Roma and the non-Roma referred to themselves. This might be a good place to introduce the Romani word *Gadže* (general designation of the non-Roma) and its singular form *Gadžo* (masculine) and *Gadži* (feminine), which I use in order to emphasise its social connotations and the way the Roma themselves relate to the non-Romani world.[13] Notwithstanding the fact that there are several other designations that refer to the

---

13 When using this designation, which is deployed by the Roma in various forms elsewhere in the world, I use a mode of transcription specific to this part of the world, which at the same time accents its locally unique understanding (see Brazzabeni et al. 2015).

distinction in both academic and social discourse, it would be misleading to use these terms in relation to the situation in Jolany. Firstly, there is the difference between "Slovaks" and "Roma", or within the local context between "Roma" and "Rusyns". However, this distinction does not capture the dynamics of categorisation, since the non-Roma of Jolany included Ukrainians, Czechs and Poles, albeit in limited numbers. Above all, it overlooks the stratification of self-identification, in which the Roma and Rusyns regard themselves as Slovaks in certain situations and the Roma then think of themselves as Rusyns (or Rusyn Roma) in others.

In this respect one should emphasise that the designation "Jolanian Roma" (*Jolaňakere Roma*) is not a category I have invented in order to outline my research interest (as opposed to the term "Jolany Roma"), but above all a category that reflects the strong identification of the Roma with a specific place. Self-identification with the category Jolanian Roma did not therefore only refer to the village in which these Roma lived, but for the inhabitants of the wider region connoted specific attributes, e.g. a certain type of relationship with non-Romani villagers, the use of a particular language (or languages, see Chapter Three), a certain social status, etc. In addition, as I shall show below, (self-)identification with the category Jolanian Roma did not necessarily overlap with an individual's current place of residence, but was negotiated more situationally and dynamically. Some of the Roma living in Jolany declared that they belonged to a family (Rom: *fajta*[14]) that supposedly came from another village in the region, and defined themselves situationally in contrast to the Jolanian Roma (nonetheless identifying with them elsewhere). On the other hand, several Roma who had previously moved away from Jolany continued proudly to claim allegiance to the category of Jolanian Roma. This is again a good moment to point out that I do not treat the concept of place as being merely the demarcation of the subject of my study, but as a specific actor that participates in the structuring of the relationships under examination. It should therefore be noted that in the text I will use the term "Jolanian Roma" as a category of internal differentiation, and "Jolany Roma" as a general designation of the Roma in Jolany.

In certain texts, both academic and journalistic, one will find a distinction made between the "majority" and the "minority", the "Roma"

---

14   The Romani word *fajta* referred in Jolany to a vertically understood lineage, as opposed to the word *fameľija*, which refers more to the nuclear family and often included three generations of a single household. For a definition of the terms *fajta* and *fameľija* (also *familija*) as used by the Roma in Slovakia see Hübschmannová (1999: 27) and Kobes (2010).

and the "villagers", or the "Roma" and the "locals". The use of such dichotomies points to an asymmetry of relationships. It insinuates who possesses the inferior and who the superior status, who belongs to and who is excluded from the village community, and who enjoys local privilege and who must "adapt" as a new arrival. It is clear that such designations reinforce a non-Romani dominance and confirm the position of the Roma as "eternal outsiders" (Šotola et al. 2018). The ambiguity of such terms becomes clear if we take into account the position of the Roma themselves. On the one hand, such terminology ignores the fact that the Jolany Roma in part based their identity on being local and belonging to the local village community, and on the other it simultaneously reflects the Roma's own participation in the discourse centred around their exclusion and minority status. In Jolany it was the Roma who thought of themselves historically as newcomers and who emphasised the importance of possessing an ability to adapt to the local/*Gadžo* order.

I decided to disrupt the prevailing practice, and so in this book use the terms "local population", "locals", "villagers", and "residents of Jolany" as a collective designation of both Roma and non-Roma. I do so in order to interrogate discursively the implied distinction between "locals" and "Roma" and to emphasise the shared experience of all residents of Jolany, who under certain circumstances have defined themselves collectively in relation to the outside world. In this way I symbolically underscore the significance of belonging to the village community in the formulation of the identity of the Jolany Roma themselves. However, this attempt at a discursive reminder of the local sense of Romani belonging is not a fixed statement regarding their identity, nor is it an expression of any kind of belief in the omnipotence of the language used. On the contrary, in this book it represents a possible starting point for monitoring the dynamic of the negotiation of local relationships in which the Roma were not merely the passive products of dominant discourses, but rather active players who agilely used such discourses in different ways.

Finally, a focus on the dynamic negotiation of local relations reveals that it related not only to a specific place, but was necessarily situated in time. This book is not therefore a timeless and universal statement regarding the relationships between Roma and non-Roma in Jolany (and eastern Slovakia or Slovakia at large), but rather the record of a specific situation in which I participated as a researcher and which had its temporal level (Fabian 1983). So as to symbolically draw attention to the temporality of the research, I refer to specific statements, events and social interactions in the past tense.

Being local Roma

Silencing Gypsyness

So let us look now at some of the questions thrown up by what I have written so far. How was the idea historically formed of who belongs to Jolany and who does not, i.e. who belongs here more, and who less? How did such an idea relate to the categories Roma/Gypsy? How did individual actors deal with such categories, and how did they negotiate their meaning on a daily basis? Above all, how did those who identified and were identified as Roma approach these categories, and how did they negotiate them in their daily activities and their networks of socio-economic bonds? I will answer each of these questions in four ethnographically inflected chapters. Here I would like to offer a brief introduction to these chapters and to set them within a particular theoretical and comparative framework.

In Chapter One I define the position of the Roma within the social hierarchy of Jolany and Slovakia as a whole. I draw on the ideas of the psychiatrist and philosopher Frantz Fanon as set forth in his classic study *Black Skin, White Masks* (Fanon 2008). In this book Fanon discusses the experience of the "colored man in the white world" (Fanon 1955: 27), drawing not only on his own experience of a black man from Martinique who "had to meet the white man's eyes" (Fanon 2008: 83), but also on his psychiatric practice, when he deals with the impact of the colonial situation on the psychology of colonialised black people. Fanon argues that in the (post)-colonial situation black people are socialised within a society in which it is "normal" to be "white", and in which "[O]ne is white as one is rich, as one is beautiful, as one is intelligent" (ibid: 36). However, in an effort to attain "white" normality, black people find themselves caught in a double bind. In their attempt to put on "white masks" they end up copying the dominant logic of racialised relations and preserving the idea of the inferiority of black people. At the same time, they are doomed to failure upon forever encountering the prison of their own "black skin". Fanon concludes that the process of decolonisation does not break this double bind, but intensifies it, since in the end it was again the white coloniser who said: "Brother, there is no difference between us." (ibid: 172). Because if such a "difference" is concealed, it is preserved. The black person "*knows* that there is a difference" (ibid: 172), which, according to Fanon, is part of every interaction in the white world: "When people like me, they tell me it is in spite of my color. When they dislike me, they point out that it is not because of my color... Either way, I am locked into the infernal circle" (ibid: 88).

From the perspective of Fanon's analysis I shall show that, though the testimony of the inhabitants of Jolany regarding harmonious relationships might indeed have reflected their lived experience, such relationships cannot be understood via the multicultural concept of the coexistence of two mutually respecting cultures, but, on the contrary, as the shared acceptance of a social order in which the Roma, qua Gypsies, were subordinate to the non-Roma. I shall also show that in Jolany the category of Gypsy, the visible sign of which is skin colour, was present in every interaction involving a Romani person and their non-Romani surroundings. To paraphrase Fanon: the unspoken subtext of the narrative of harmonious relationships is that "harmonious relationships prevail in the village despite the fact that the Roma live in it". Without a shared idea of stigmatised Gypsyness, an important attribute of which is "problematic coexistence", the emphasis on harmonious relationships would make no sense.

For a more precise grasp of the position of individual actors in these sorts of relationships I turn to the anthropological studies by Kata Horváth and Cecília Kovai, which draw on similar ideas when talking about the status of the Roma in the post-socialist space, taking Hungary as their example (though they do not directly quote Fanon; see especially Horváth 2012, Kovai 2012).[15] Though the differentiation between "Hungarians" and "Gypsies"[16] was not publicly articulated in the village they wrote about, it was firmly embedded as a consequence of skin colour being deemed a distinctive feature ("everybody knew exactly who was a Gypsy and who was a Hungarian" [Horváth 2012: 117]), and in a key way structured social interactions, copying the asymmetrical relationship between patron and client (ibid: 118). The Hungarians had no reason to publicly name the Gypsies – as Fanon showed, the concealment of the existing distinction preserved what was for them a favourable, asymmetrical structure. However, the Gypsies also played their part in this concealment under the illusion that, by obscuring the characteristics of

---

15 I should add that in this book I will refer to the two texts published in the anthology *The Gypsy "Menace"* (Stewart 2012). The texts are closely related thematically, and though only one of the two anthropologists is cited as the author of each text, the essays are based on research they conducted jointly.

16 I am employing the distinction as used by Horváth and Kovai, albeit in the knowledge that there must be a reduction in the identities of the inhabitants of the village under examination: see my note on terminology as it applies to the terms Slovaks and Rusyns.

Gypsyness, they would rid themselves of their own inferiority and be ranked on the same level as the Hungarians (Horváth 2012).

Horváth and Kovai further elaborate on this basically Fanonian thesis when they argue that the publicly concealed category of Gypsyness was, on the contrary, constantly named and negotiated within the space of the Romani settlement, where it contributed significantly to the internal differentiation between the Roma themselves. Depending on the degree of (situational) adaptation to the world of the Hungarian villagers, entire families, but situationally speaking individuals too, could think of each other either as representatives of "exaggerated Gypsyness", or, conversely, as those who "pretend to be Hungarians" (Horváth 2012: 127). At the same time, according to Kovai, both designations stem from the fear of an intensification of the stigmatisation of the category Gypsyness. In the case of the first group this fear arose from concrete actions associated with Gypsyness, and in the case of the second group through the "concealment of Gypsyness" that acknowledges the dominant logic of stigmatisation and thus reinforces it (Kovai 2012: 288).

Fanon's analysis and its application within the context of research into the Roma residents of a Hungarian village tells us a lot about the situation in Jolany. Like Horváth and Kovai, we may conclude that, though the inhabitants of Jolany situationally scaled down or directly rejected the relevance of the local division into Roma/non-Roma, these categories were deeply rooted and played a key role in the structuring of social interactions in the village. While such distinctions were largely taken for granted during interactions between the Roma and the non-Roma, their articulation was manifest primarily in the negotiation of relations between the Roma themselves (cf. Horváth 2012: 125). As in the case of the colonised blacks who donned "white masks", and the Hungarian Gypsies who lived with the illusory promise that by silencing their Gypsyness they would become good Hungarians, so the Roma in Jolany accepted the normality of the non-Romani world and wished to "live like the *Gadže*" (*te dživel sar gadže*). However, though the Jolany Roma to varying degrees acquired the attributes of the non-Romani world, they were still identifiable as inferior Gypsies. Moreover, the Jolany Roma corrected this one-sided strategy when they situationally (or even more permanently) defined themselves in opposition to those who excessively "made themselves *Gadže*" (*kerenas pen gadženge*) or "reached out to Gadženess" (*cirdenas pen gadženge*). In Chapter One I show that, as in the case of the Roma of north-eastern Hungary, this is a mechanism of social control that kept solidarity networks alive within an environment of constant socio-economic uncertainty and marginalisation (Kovai 2012).

Within this dynamic of social relations a space was created in which the Jolany Roma could negotiate their belonging to the community and their own position in its social hierarchy through their handling of the attributes characterising Gadženess and Gypsyness. It is in such a space that the concrete research topics addressed in the chapters of this book will be situated. In Chapters Two, Three and Four I look at housing (the politics of space), language use, and economic strategies. I selected these areas of discussion for two main reasons. Firstly, they are topics that are often identified as pivotal in the formulation of state policies vis-à-vis the Roma and reveal how the state policy, or rather the policy of individual organs of the state apparatus, was negotiated in a specific place.[17] Secondly, they are topics that allow me to monitor not only the functioning of the category Gypsyness, but the creation and maintenance of ideas regarding who does and does not belong to the community.

Locals but not indigenous

In Chapter Two I again draw on the work carried out by Horváth and Kovai, one of the many important aspects of which resides in the fact that it captures the transformation in relationships over time. The writers argue that the silencing of Gypsyness in the community they were observing was related to Hungary's policy of assimilation under socialism, which regarded the rejection of "Gypsy origin" as a precondition of social equality. However, as a result of political, demographic and economic changes, at the start of the new millennium the Roma became increasingly present in the public sphere and even predominant in certain institutions. Socio-economic uncertainty also impacted local Hungarians, who, in an effort to regain full control of "their" territory, began openly to voice the category Gypsy and to label the Roma, including their Romani neighbours, as public enemies who were to blame for their precarity. In this situation the newly articulated Gypsyness retained all of what had previously been its implicitly negative content, the creation of which the Roma had themselves participated in through their strategy of

---

17　In this respect perhaps only education is missing from the main themes. However, this would require a significant expansion of research methodology (research in school classrooms, etc.).

"silencing". On the other hand, the category of Roma was foregrounded by means of bespoke "Romani" projects and enterprises, but also ethnically framed political mobilisation (Kovai 2012).

Like the Hungarian community described, Jolany, too, was situated in a socio-economically marginalised region experiencing major demographic change. At the time of my research the Roma were gradually assuming the role of a significant majority in respect of their non-Romani neighbours, though their presence in the public sphere of the community had not led to a similar articulation of the categories Roma/Gypsies. Unlike the Hungarian village, with its population of approximately 1,800 (Horváth 2012: 117), Jolany (pop. 150) represented a markedly de-anonymised environment. The non-Romani villagers knew the names and usually the nicknames of at least the adult members of individual Romani families, and many of them were aware of who was related to whom. To a certain extend, they excluded their Romani neighbours from the more general category of Gypsies and tended to think of them as "our Roma", with whom "there were no problems". Despite the differences between the communities, the emphasis on temporality in the work by Kovai and Horváth resonated strongly with the multidisciplinary element of my own methodology, in which I take into account the historical perspective of the locally negotiated relationships, the politics of memory of the local residents, and other relational transformations during the period of my stay.

And so in Chapter Two I focus on housing and the politics of space. I show that the spatial layout of the village, as it is understood by the locals, symbolises perfectly the ambivalent status of the Roma in the local community. Though Roma lived in close proximity to non-Romani villagers, the village as such was symbolically divided into two zones. The first, where the non-Roma lived, had no special name, because it was understood by the locals as the "village of Jolany", embodying all the normativity of the non-Romani way of life described above. In contrast, the Roma lived in substandard conditions in the zone known as the "Romani/Gypsy settlement", which, though it laid within the official borders of the village and was therefore viewed as a part thereof, was symbolically separated from it and associated in the minds of the Jolany population with the cultural "backwardness" of Gypsyness. This interpretation of the space of the village was accepted without question by everyone, including the Roma themselves. In line with the endeavour to "live like the *Gadže*", the Roma tried to find housing in the non-Romani part of the village "amongst the *Gadže*" (*maškar o gadže*). Using the example of the numerous Roma applications submitted for the allocation of building land in the non-Romani built-up area of the village, which could be traced back at least to the early 1960s, I show that the existing territorial boundary was very difficult to cross, because both the local non-Roma and targeted policies of the local authorities played an active part in consolidating it. Nevertheless, a few Romani families had managed to obtain housing under specific circumstances in the non-Romani part of the village. Since the movement of these families out of the Romani settlement was generally deemed a shift to a non-Romani way of life, the idea of the settlement as the space of Gypsyness was preserved and consolidated. Similarly, the construction of the low-grade council flats in the settlement served to underline the image of its inhabitants as passive recipients of handouts and confirmed an underlying internal differentiation between the local Roma according to their position in the spatial layout of the village (either they lived in the settlement or "amongst the *Gadže*") and the degree to which they displayed signs of Gypsyness.

Finally, monitoring the categorisation of Roma in relation to their position within the spatial layout of the village is related to the role of place in shaping their identity. The dream of relocating from the settlement to the non-Romani part of the village can be seen not only as an attempt to acquire the characteristics of a *Gadžo* way of life, but also as a determination to reinforce a person's sense of belonging to a particular place. This emphasis on the role of place in forming the identity of the Roma was formulated by the anthropologist Aspasia Theodosiou (2004, 2007), who observed that, when the Romani identity was being explained in anthropological studies, it was usually detached from place, either because of the alleged nomadism of the Roma or their creation of locally uprooted "imagined communities" (Anderson 1983). Theodosiou believes that, though modern ethnographers (she cites the classic studies by Michael Stewart on the Gypsies in Hungary [1997] and by Paloma Gay y Blasco on the Gitanos in Madrid [1999]) have rid themselves of the tendency to orientalise the Roma by focusing on their non-European origin, an emphasis on the performative concept of Romani identity withholds from them the possibility of a strong connection with a particular place:

> [B]oth authors [Stewart and Gay y Blasco] emphasise the centrality of interactions with the surrounding non-Gypsy populations they have been working with. But while space in these accounts functions as a central organising principle, it is analytically invisible. [...] For the Gypsies, we

are told, place is a matter of convention after all: it does not contribute anything to their understanding of themselves. Gypsies construct "imagined communities" in the here and now regardless/despite of where they are. (Theodosiou 2004: 52)

Theodosiou herself thinks of space not only as the backdrop to the interaction of the Roma with the non-Roma world, but as an integral part of their self-identification. She discusses the relationship between a specific place and identity using the example of the *Yifti* (Gypsies), who live in a village called Parakalamos on the Greek-Albanian border and find themselves in the ambivalent position of "being local but not indigenous" (Theodosiou 2004: 26). She demonstrates the ambiguity of *Yifti* belonging to a specific place by means of their identity as musicians. Although the Greeks (*Greki*) in Parakalamos view the musicianship of the *Yifti* as the manifestation of an essentialised Gypsyness, i.e. something that affirms their status as "not indigenous", the *Yifti* themselves view their proficiency in the sphere of traditional music (see Theodosiou 2007) as proof of their own embeddedness in local relationships and their belonging to place. Theodosiou also points out that, in the first half of the 20th century, the *Yifti* owned no land in Parakalamos and when performing music in the surrounding region lived in the village on only a seasonal basis. While the Greeks in Parakalamos viewed the *Yifti's* movement as a form of uprooted "Gypsy nomadism", the Yifti themselves related through precisely this movement to a specific region on the Greek-Albanian border. "Even for Gypsies who did move and did not have land, it does not necessarily mean that they did not have a loyalty to the area; movement does not negate 'attachment' in emotional terms," argues Theodosiou (2004: 42). From the *Yifti's* perspective, musicianship and mobility were not the attributes of a *people* (the Gypsies), but a *place*, and it was their sense of belonging to a place, and not a distinct culture, that formed their identity. And so when, after the Second World War, the *Yifti* purchased land in Parakalamos, converted to Christianity and changed their names as part of the process of Greek nationalism, they did not experience this as a disruption of their identity, but more as its confirmation through the continuity of their relationship to a specific place.

I should say right now that such a perspective is not new to the study of the Roma in eastern Slovakia. In this respect the work of the sociologist Tomáš Kobes, who views the inhabitants of the eastern Slovak countryside, categorised as "our Roma", as "inappropriate/d others" (Minh-ha 1998), is particularly interesting to a Czech reader. According to Kobes, these Roma, who according to the dominant logic displayed a high degree of integration, possessed an ambiguous status in the community defined on the one hand by kinship ("one family") and on the other, as in Jolany, by their way of life. Despite a relatively high level of inclusion in the local community that meant they avoided being categorised as "problematic Gypsies" by their non-Romani neighbours, they continued to possess characteristics that made them identifiable as Gypsies and, as such, were associated with a naturally different ("alien") way of life. In this study Kobes names other "diffractive patterns of difference", i.e. certain attributes (shared place, kinship, land ownership, a certain way of life), on the basis of which the inhabitants of the village where he conducted his research were excluded from or included in the local community. Within such a structure, "our Roma", like the *Yifti* of Parakalamos, were included in the local community asymmetrically. It was difficult for the local residents to concede a completely Slovak identity to the Roma (historically they had not owned land in the village, did not belong to the local "one family" and were associated with a different lifestyle), though at the same time they did not completely identify them as Gypsies (they had acquired certain attributes that set them apart). And therefore "our Roma" "became insiders in certain situations, and outsiders in others" (Kobes 2012: 27). In this way, Kobes in part adapts Theodosiou's perspective to the context of eastern Slovakia, the region I am concerned with in this book. However, Kobes's contribution is also important to my own work in that the category of "our Roma" is relatively widespread (cf. Grill 2015b) and historically embedded (cf. Hübschmannová 1998) in the region I conducted my research. Chapter One will show this to be true of Jolany itself.

The perspective that Theodosiou and Kobes share is to some extent also a position from which to question the conclusions of the anthropologist David Scheffel, who observed the Roma's belonging in another community of eastern Slovakia. Scheffel argues that the members of a certain group of Roma in the village of Veľký Šariš were deemed "autochthons". Like the *Yifti* of Parakalamos, the Roma of Veľký Šariš became part of the local community mainly as musicians (*lavutari*):

> [O]lder women and men who remember the time when all local celebrations involved and, indeed, required the participation of Romani musicians speak very highly of their skills and ability to play the right kind of tune at the right time precisely because of their status as *autochthons* whose lives were intertwined with those of the Slovaks. (Scheffel 2015: 143, emphasis added)

Scheffel recognises the subordinate position of the Roma in the hierarchy of socio-economic relationships, but does not interrogate further the status of the "autochthons" and settles for the right to remain in the municipality that the Roma were to be awarded (ibid: 141). With regard to place, he does not distinguish between the status of the Roma and the Slovaks, although it is possible in the text itself to infer a certain degree of "evictability" of the Roma (van Baar 2016): specifically this relates to an episode during the Second World War when the local authority had the Roma driven into a forest two kilometres away and into "inhuman" living conditions (ibid: 126–130, see also Lacková 1999: 102–104). However, even of this event Scheffel writes: "… unlike the Veľký Šariš Jews who perished in the Holocaust, the Roma managed to maintain a certain degree of legitimacy as *autochthons* who, for not always clearly articulated reasons, ought to be protected from outright annihilation." (Scheffel 2015: 128, emphasis in original) However, it is clear from the quote above regarding Romani musicians that the Roma in Veľký Šariš, like the *Yifti* in Parakalamos, were incorporated into the local community asymmetrically. As Romani musicians they were accorded a certain position in the hierarchy of socio-economic relations. I also believe that it would be true to say of the Roma in Veľký Šariš that though they might be deemed "locals", they would nonetheless not be considered "indigenous" (cf. Theodosiou 2004, see above).

These approaches bring us back to the ethical and methodological dilemma of this book in particular, and research among the Roma in general. When observing the relationship of the Roma to place, I believe we must break free from the dominant logic that ascribes to them the position of "eternal outsiders". On the contrary, we should attempt to view the Roma as an indigenous group (see also Olivera 2012). At the same time, we cannot ignore the mechanisms by which the Roma are excluded from a given place under certain circumstances. If I might return to Chapter Two for a moment, this ambiguous relationship of the Roma with place is visible in Jolany in the politics of space. Through their association with the settlement the Roma were on the one hand excluded from a given place as Gypsies. On the other hand it was the settlement that, through its unusually central positionality in the built-up area of the village, represented the strong historical continuity of the Roma's belonging to a given place. In this case, however, the Jolany Roma were not deemed local by virtue of the attributes of a non-Romani way of life, but in their capacity as Roma.

The robustness of Theodosiou's argument resides in the fact that she does not present Roma belonging to place as a general aspect of their identity, but tracks it through particular characteristics that make the place in question specific (historical, cultural, linguistic, etc.). Similarly, belonging to a specific place for the Jolany Roma is not only a response to the dominant discourse regarding the locally unanchored Gypsies, but the expression of a specific historical and cultural experience that is inextricably linked to the place in question (cf. Olivera 2012, also Olivera and Poueyto 2018). In Chapter Three, I shall examine in greater detail the embeddedness of the Roma in the "local system" (Olivera 2012: 32), as well as the ambiguous nature of their local belonging, through the topic of language and its use. It is the sociolinguistic situation of the village that demonstrates clearly the interconnectedness of the locally negotiated categories. Three basic languages (or their local varieties) are used on a daily basis in this small village: Slovak, Rusyn, and Romani. When the Roma reflected upon their belonging to the village (and thus to the region as a whole) by declaring "we are Rusyn Roma" (*amen sam rusňaka Roma*), a clear manifestation of this identity was their fluency not only in the officially required Slovak, but also their native Romani and the Rusyn specific to the area. As the entry in the village chronicle indicates (see above), a competence in Rusyn was part of the way of life in this region and the residents of Jolany were expected to have a working knowledge of it. The same could not be said of the Romani language. Moreover, the very act of switching from Romani to Rusyn could be a situational manifestation of the speaker's active participation in "silencing Gypsyness".

However, the fact that Romani was a fully functioning language code in Jolany shows that, even if to a certain extent the Roma wanted to "live like the *Gadže*", they were nevertheless in no rush to rid themselves of all the attributes that could see them labelled Gypsies. The dynamics of language strategies were complemented by the activation of a cryptic function of Romani that, surrounded by the dominance of the non-Roma, helped create a safe space for the Roma's own solidarity networks. However, the ambiguity of the Roma's links to place can be perceived even in the Romani language itself. Like their belonging to the Romani settlement, the association of the Roma with the Romani language was on the one hand something that distinguished them from the local way of life, and on the other hand was able to confirm their local affiliation (belonging), since their Romani possessed attributes specific to the region, and even to the village. The Jolany Roma recalled that they no longer used "original" or "true Romani" (*original romanes*), and pointed to the number of Rusyn loanwords as proof of their embeddedness in local relations. Moreover, they viewed their variety of Romani as specifically local, not only because of its Rusyn loanwords, but also because of specific lexical and phonological attributes that distinguished it from the dialects of the surrounding region. An inability to speak Rusyn and/or to speak a different Romani variety marked out certain Roma as not being local.

The Jolany Roma also drew attention to the way that a competence in Romani was divided down gender lines. Under a system of virilocal post-marital residence[18] it was mainly the men that had been born in Jolany, while most of the women had moved from surrounding villages into Jolany upon getting married. While I was living in Jolany there was only one woman who had been born in the village and remained there even after her wedding (to another native of Jolany). Otherwise, Romani girls born in Jolany tended to move out of the village and in with their husband. Local belonging therefore had a strongly gendered component, something that Theodosiou does not take into consideration in her analysis. I do not devote a specific chapter to gender in this book, though it is implicit in individual arguments and interpretations. At the very end of the book I shall return to this theme more systematically.

In the fourth and final chapter, I focus on economic strategies, which in many ways are crucial to the creation of local relations and conclude the section on the importance of place in the identification of the Jolany Roma. As in the case of the musicians of Parakalamos, these strategies involve economic practices by means of which the Roma would become part of the local community and yet through which they came to occupy an unequal status in it. The asymmetrical relationship between patron and client features in the narrative of the arrival of the first Rom in the village, supposedly invited to the village in the mid-19th century by the non-Romani residents to be their blacksmith. Indeed, the "harmonious coexistence" referred to in the newspaper report cited above meant in practice that the Roma worked for their non-Romani neighbours. However, the unequal status of the Roma was less the result of specific economic practices than entrenched ideas regarding "Gypsy attitudes to work". In a situation in which the relationship to work was accompanied

---

18 A situation in which a newly constituted couple set up their household in the man's place of residence. On the nature of kinship relations in the countryside of eastern Slovakia see Kobes (2009).

by a strong moral evaluation, the Roma were generally viewed as being workshy, and "Gypsy work" (*cigánska robota*) was the phrase used for poorly executed work. This prejudice, entrenched within society as a whole, was reflected in certain state labour policies, as well as in the practice of many employers, and led to the Roma finding themselves in a situation of precarity not only in Slovakia in general, but in Jolany in particular.

In Chapter Four I argue that the nature of the "Gypsy economy" (Brazzabeni et al. 2015) in Jolany was not characterised by a lax attitude on the part of the Roma to work or specific economic activity, but more by an ability to combine different economic practices within an environment of constant insecurity. Similarly to the combination of different language codes, economic practices did not involve the complete acceptance of the dominant demand for "adaptation" and a one-sided effort to adopt the characteristics of a *Gadžo* way of life. Instead, the concept of "adaptation" (*te prisposobinel pes*) was understood by the Jolany Roma as a kind of game in which they attempted to display an embeddedness in *Gadžo* social and economic networks, while leaving room for the subversion of the dominant logic of normative "whiteness". I shall show that strategies framed in this way were again firmly anchored in the given place, since they were effectuated in relation to specific non-Romani locals. Indeed, even migration, a frequent economic strategy with roots stretching back in time, both among the Roma and the non-Roma in the region, was also firmly anchored to place. Though able to escape temporarily the entrenched asymmetry of relations in their village, the Jolany Roma tended to enjoy the social and economic capital acquired through migration in their home village, which remained a safe and preferred place for them to live.

Facets of a harmony

Before moving on to support and develop more general theses with more concrete ethnographic content, I would like to return to my introductory statements regarding the harmonious relations pertaining in Jolany and briefly summarise what revealing them can show us. Right from the outset it should be made clear that the term "harmonious relations" covers various formulations that may differ in terms of semantic nuance, but correspond in respect of the basic differentiation of the inhabitants of Jolany into Roma and non-Roma and the way they coexisted side by side. In the media the village was spoken of in terms of "exemplary coexistence" and "crystal clear relationships", and during the course of my research individual residents were keen to assure me that "here we have none of the problems they have elsewhere" [i.e. in villages with strictly segregated Romani settlements], "here it makes no difference whether you are a Rom or a *Gadžo*", or whether you are "black or white", here, as the Roma were quick to point out, they are "one with the *Gadže*", etc.

When reading such statements one must, of course, take into account their context, i.e. who made them, to whom, and under what circumstances. Depending on this a host of different interpretations spring to mind. One might regard them as a reflection of lived experience, a way of emphasising the uniqueness of Jolany in comparison with other locations in the region, or as performative utterances that in and of themselves help create or maintain such relationships. In the case of the Roma one might read these statements as a declaration of their belonging in local relationships or a reminder of their prized ability to adapt. As regards the non-Roma such statements could represent a defence mechanism against accusations of racism, or a tendency to conceal and preserve their own superiority. It would be oversimplifying matters to reject such statements as merely products of non-Romani dominance. On the other hand, it is clear that even if we take such reflections upon local relationships seriously, it is impossible to ignore their asymmetrical character. As I have shown, the statements regarding harmonious coexistence are conditional upon a shared acceptance that the term Gypsy connotes "problematic". To be identified as a Gypsy does not mean "only" having to confront social stereotypes. It also involves the need to balance this category in every interaction with the non-Romani world. Given that it has been physically inscribed through skin colour, it is almost impossible to escape the category of Gypsyness. Nevertheless, it is possible to negotiate its significance. What the Jolany Roma have managed to do, and what is referred to in statements regarding harmonious relationships, is to overlay the category Gypsy with the category "local resident", reflecting their strong connection to a particular place and, to a certain extent, putting a distance between them and more general ideas of problematicity. Theirs is an ambiguous sense of belonging to the local community in a specific place that might be described as being "local but not indigenous". In this respect, however, Jolany is not simply a random place in which the interaction of Roma and non-Roma and the functioning of the category Gypsy can be studied. It is a place that is directly implicated in the form such interactions will take. In other words, this book is not only about how certain people experience Gypsyness, but above all about how they experience it in a specific place (the experience of Gypsyness is different in Jolany to what it is, for example, in a factory in the Czech Republic), and how they identify (as Jolanian Roma, Rusyn Roma, local residents, etc.) with a particular place.

Chapter One
"Our Roma" and "our Gadže"

When I informed Peter of my intention to live in the village, he immediately started coming up with ideas as to where I might stay. It seemed the most feasible option was to live with Kaleňák, a non-Romani villager in his fifties. Kaleňák lived in a house without any drinking water and several years previously had had his electricity supply disconnected. He had no siblings and his father had moved out shortly after he was born, and so Kaleňák had grown up in Jolany with just his mother and grandmother. He trained as a chef and travelled to Czechia to work. He ended up living there for some time. A major turning point in his life occurred when both his mother and grandmother died shortly after each other under tragic circumstances. Kaleňák continued to work as a chef in a pub in a neighbouring village, but lost his job due to problems with alcohol.

That evening Kaleňák popped into the pub, where I had been persuaded by the local men to join them in a juniper brandy. Despite an initial wariness, he was persuaded by the regulars to offer me temporary asylum in his house. He entrusted the keys to the house to Viktor, one of the non-Romani villagers, who, already well lubricated, helped carry my luggage to my new abode. As we were walking up the hill from the pub and away from what was known as the "Romani settlement", Viktor turned to me, pointed at the council flats that comprised the settlement, and with a heavy sigh declared that "it would be far better here without them [the Roma]". A crack opened up in the image of harmonious relations.

The next morning the conversation between Kaleňák and me naturally turned to life in the village. He admitted that the non-Romani villagers no longer wanted anything to do with him, and so his day-to-day social network comprised mainly local Roma. This was confirmed over the next few days. While staying with Kaleňák I rarely met any of the non-Roma who had sat at our table on the first night. On the other hand, several of the Roma spent entire days with me and

Kaleňák. I ended up crashing at Kaleňák's for ten days before arranging more permanent accommodation with Maroš and Katarína, one of the Romani families with their own accommodation outside the settlement.

Kaleňák was very plugged into the social network of the local Roma. However, although he shared many of the habits of the Roma, these were interpreted differently by the wider village community. The difference lay in the racialised category of Gypsyness. Even though Kaleňák displayed many of the socio-economic characteristics of this category, everyone in Jolany knew that he was not a Gypsy, not only because he did not have dark skin, but also because he had been born into a local non-Romani family. And this logic worked the other way around too. Regardless of the extent to which certain Roma embraced the attributes associated with a non-Romani way of life, they continued to be identified as Gypsies. In this chapter I shall look at how the residents of Jolany negotiated the category of Gypsyness, and how this participated in the structuring of local relations.

The Roma in Slovakia

Before homing in on the situation in Jolany, I would like to offer a brief overview of the historical development of the social position of the Roma in the territory of what is today Slovakia. I shall proceed in the same way in the following chapters, since it is important to keep in mind the fact that Jolany is not an island without any ties to broader (historically conditioned) social contexts. At the same time, I believe this relationship operates in both directions. The introduction of a more universal narrative will allow me to contextualise the situation as it pertained to Jolany, and conversely, by examining a particular village I will be better placed to verify and supplement this general narrative.

In the 1970s, the British sociologist Will Guy expressed his belief that the history of the Roma in Czechoslovakia represented invaluable material for study. The shifting sands of political boundaries and regimes saw diverse approaches to the Roma intersect. When they arrived in the Bohemian lands, harsh anti-Gypsy measures were enacted similar to those in western European countries, which forced the Roma to remain on the move. In contrast, in the region that now forms Slovakia the Roma settled very quickly in certain places, where their presence contributed to a lasting transformation of the local socio-economic structures (Guy 1998 [1975]: 16–17). However, this meant accepting a subordinate position in the newly formed racialised hierarchies (Hübschmannová 1998). These differences were reflected in the impact the Second World

War had on the Roma in these two historical regions. The Roma living in the Bohemian lands were for a long time systematically separated administratively from other citizens and designated "(wandering) Gypsies" (Baloun 2019). They were deemed a threat to public safety, the reason given for consigning virtually all of them to concentration camps. Only a few hundred survived this wartime persecution (Nečas 1999). In contrast, the 80,000 or so Roma who lived in Slovakia at the end of the 1930s faced various forms of persecution, but avoided the fate of their Czech brethren (Sadílková 2019a, 2020). Although many local authorities and individual villagers welcomed the existing anti-Gypsy measures and used them against their neighbours, in other cases the Roma confirmed their position in the socio-economic order, even being protected on occasion by their non-Romani neighbours (Hübschmannová 2005; Sadílková 2019a, 2020). This was basically the case in Jolany, where the devastation wreaked by the war was remembered as having impacted all of the local residents, i.e. both Roma and non-Roma.

With the arrival of state socialism, the Roma in Czechoslovakia, as in the Eastern bloc as a whole, were promised social equality, albeit at the cost of cultural assimilation and the abandonment of the "backward" (*zaostalý*) way of life said to spring from their "Gypsy origins" (*cikánský původ*; Guy 1998 [1975]). For many Roma, the period of socialism represented the possibility of socio-economic mobility, job opportunities, housing, and greater social participation overall. In Jolany, the period of socialism is associated with the golden age of the social life of the village, and the statements of the Jolany Roma regarding harmonious relations and a sense of belonging could be largely traced back to that time. However, anti-Gypsy prejudices on different levels of the state apparat and amongst the non-Romani population persisted in socialist Czechoslovakia and ensured the Roma remained socially segregated. Grill concludes that "while the socialist ideology in theory allowed for the exemplarily hard-working citizens of Gypsy backgrounds to merge into the (racially undifferentiated) proletariat, the Roma continued to experience racially tinged categorisations intersecting with their particular class positionalities." (Grill 2017: 5). Regarding the situation in neighbouring Hungary, Kovai argues that it was this illusion of equality that greatly reinforced the tendency to "silence Gypsyness" on the part of the Roma themselves, and ultimately contributed to a more permanent conservation of asymmetrical relations (Kovai 2012). As in socialist Czechoslovakia, the ever-increasing social mobility of the Roma was contrasted with their "Gypsy origins", thus reproducing the figure of the socially deviant and naturally "backward Gypsy" with which all Roma, regardless of their socioeconomic status, were confronted according to racial criteria.

The political, economic and social transformations following the events of 1989 injected a new dynamism into the development of the status of the Roma in individual municipalities. The privatisation of key enterprises, deindustrialisation and the corresponding drop in job opportunities in the marginalised region of eastern Slovakia impacted the Roma most of all and saw a rapid increase in unemployment. In addition, these processes were accompanied by a flare-up of what had until then only been latent anti-Roma attitudes through society as a whole, which led to racially motivated violence in many places (Donert 2017: 247–270, Guy 1998 [1975]). The introduction of (latent) anti-Roma policies went hand in hand with an increasingly neoliberal discourse and "securitisation" of the Roma (van Baar et al. 2019), who acquired the reputation of being scroungers, abusing the social security system in order to receive benefits (Grill 2018). These political and economic changes had a big impact on the situation in Jolany and other regions of eastern Slovakia. The privatisation and gradual closure of key corporations led to a deepening of the socioeconomic marginalisation of the entire region, which in turn led to increased migratory activity among its population. At the risk of generalising, one might cautiously argue that while the Roma were involved in mainly short-term migration and thus maintained the continuity of villages, the non-Romani population gradually aged, since young non-Roma often relocated permanently to work in Slovak cities and elsewhere. The ensuing changes to the demographic landscape contributed to a realignment of local relationships, and often to greater social segregation of the Roma.

At this point, however, it should be emphasised that the image of segregated Roma within the (itself marginalised) region of eastern Slovakia, which has long been the prevailing image in dominant social discourse and which to a certain extent includes the situation of the Roma in Jolany, is far from representing the experience of all the Roma in the region. Above all, it overlooks the experience of the less conspicuous Roma middle class, mainly in towns and cities, many of whose representatives were actively striving for the more active social and political participation of the Roma as a whole during the communist era. It is indicative of broader-based opinions of the Roma that most anthropological studies themselves focused on the marginalised environment of segregated settlements. In fact, later studies show that, despite the overall deterioration of the position of the Roma in Slovak society after 1989, the situation in the rural areas differed region by region, village by village, and even family by family. In some villages racial segregation took place against a backdrop of flagrant anti-Roma prejudice (Skupnik 2007, Scheffel 2005), while in other places the Roma achieved a high level of integration within the local community (Kobes 2012, Scheffel 2015) or completely rejected the legitimacy of dividing local populations into Roma and non-Roma (Vrbová and Šotola 2016). Moreover, in the villages, too, the Roma in general became more involved in public life, with some elected as local councillors or even mayors (Hrustič 2012, 2015b, 2020). At the beginning of the new millennium, what had until then been two somewhat marginal social phenomena also contributed to the greater transformation of local relations. These were migration to the West (especially Canada and Great Britain; Grill 2012, 2015a,b, 2017; Dobruská 2018; Ort and Dobruská 2018; Prokeš et al. 2016) and religious conversion (Podolinská and Hrustič 2011, Dobruská 2018), which challenged hitherto entrenched ideas regarding the socio-economically marginalised Roma and contributed to the dynamic transformation of local relations.

The Jolany Roma remained immune to both westward migration and religious conversion. They travelled to find work on a seasonal basis to the neighbouring Czech Republic, and as regards religion and culture declared a strong allegiance to and participation in the local way of life. Overall they were firmly embedded in the network of relationships linked to a particular place, and described these relationships as harmonious. In this chapter I will show that the category of Gypsyness, which was highly racialised and as such performed a pivotal role in the structuring of local relations, is crucial to understanding the narrative of harmonious relationships and the active creation thereof. I will focus on how those of the village residents who were associated with these categories and self-identified as Roma dealt with them. The first chapter thus lays the ground for the following chapters, in which I continue to track the functioning of the category of Gypsyness in selected spheres of the lives of the residents of Jolany.

Together but divided

During the course of my research I would hear many different variations on the theme of harmonious relationships from the Jolany Roma. Nevertheless, the basic message was encapsulated on my first evening by Peter: "Here [in Jolany] it's not like other villages in Slovakia, here the

Roma live alongside the *Gadže*"[19]. Such statements basically comprise two interlinked claims. Firstly, they differentiate the situation in Jolany from stereotypical ideas of "problematic coexistence" with the Gypsies, examples of which the Jolany Roma were able to pinpoint in other villages in the region. It should perhaps be noted that such statements attest far more to the way that relations are defined than to the specific status of the Roma in Jolany in relation to other Roma in Slovakia. Secondly, they remind us of the historically rooted embeddedness of the Jolany Roma in local (i.e. *Gadžo*) socio-economic networks.

According to the Jolany Roma, the much vaunted "communal life with the *Gadže*" had deep historical roots. They spoke, for instance, of their shared experiences during the Second World War. As one old Romani woman told me, after the war "everyone was in a bad way, not just us". They recalled with nostalgia life under communism, when joint cultural and social activities were overseen by individual socialist unions and the local inhabitants attended the same school, participated in the same leisure activities, and worked alongside one another in a sawmill in the neighbouring village. As an example of their social participation during the communist era they recalled how they themselves had led the local volunteer fire brigade or Union for Cooperation with the Army (*Zväz pre spoluprácu s armádou,* or *Zväzarm*). In Jolany there was even a local branch of the Union of Gypsies-Roma (*Zväz Cigánov-Rómov*), though it was abolished by central decree in 1973 after only one year of existence.[20] The Roma also recalled their own political participation. Beginning in the late 1980s they always had at least one representative on the local council.[21] They spoke of the shared characteristics of the local culture, the celebration of Christian festivals being a case in point. When I asked the Jolany Roma how they spent these public holidays, they were quick to dash my hopes of finding a distinct Romani culture by answering: "Just like the *Gadže*!" (*Kavka sar o gadže!*). On the contrary, their shared belonging to a specific place was reinforced by the fact that the entire region was predominantly Greek Catholic, unlike the rest of

---

19 Interview with Peter (b. 1953), conducted in Romani, 17 October 2014.

20 The founding of the union in 1969 represented the culmination of ongoing efforts on the part of the Roma in Czechoslovakia to create a socio-cultural organisation of their own (see Sadílková et al. 2018). It operated in parallel with the *Svaz Cikánů-Romů*, which was established in the same year in the Bohemian territory of what was the newly federalised country (Donert 2017: 180–2013).

21 Because of the smaller population, the municipal council elected in 2018 had only five members.

predominantly Roman Catholic Slovakia. Similarly, the Roma possessed no special style of clothing or appearance that would mark them out as belonging to a discrete culture of their own (cf. for instance Olivera 2012).

However, despite the historical roots of their communal life, both Roma and non-Roma recognised the transformation of relationships over time. They reflected upon the decline of the cultural and social life of the village, associated in their minds with the end of communism and the political and economic turbulence that ensued. They also conceded that a gulf was opening up between the worlds of the Romani and non-Romani villagers, with the gradual segregation of school attendance and the loss of permanent employment among the Roma. During the period of my research this image of separate worlds was manifest visibly. As well as segregated education, which had become an issue over the previous ten years (I began my fieldwork in 2014), the graves in the local cemetery were physically segregated into Romani and non-Romani, and the low-grade council flats that were unflatteringly referred to as the Romani settlement were both physically and symbolically separated from the non-Romani part of the village (see Chapter Two). The distinction between Roma and non-Roma was also framed by language. When speaking amongst themselves the Roma used Romani, a language that was largely incomprehensible to the rest of the villagers (see Chapter Three). Furthermore, these categories were crucial in terms of the selection of partners. Intermarriage was rare, not only in Jolany but across the entire region (with only one such couple in Jolany), and the marital affiliations of the Roma stretched across individual villages in the region.

During the time I spent in Jolany, perhaps the only reminder of the thriving social life of the past in which, by all accounts, the Roma had also participated was the way the men would meet in the local pub. Even so, this applied only to a few of the locals. Otherwise, my observations tallied with Kaleňák's initial description of everyday social interactions. Of the non-Roma he said they hardly ever set foot outside their homes, did not pay each other visits, and lived a very secluded life. The Roma, on the other hand, had maintained strong links, created their own solidarity networks and were forever popping in on each other.

In fact, the deep-rooted differentiation between Roma and non-Roma was very evident on those few occasions when all the residents gathered together. It was seven months into my stay before I saw all the villagers (or at least representatives of all the families) congregated in one place. In accordance with the local tradition, on Easter Sunday we went to church carrying a basket of food to be blessed. Later that same day, Stano, the twenty-odd-year-old son of my hosts Maroš and Katarína, asked me if I had noticed how the villagers had been positioned as they waited outside the church for the priest to arrive. The Roma all stood close together, side by side, to such an extent it was difficult to make out who belonged to which family. The non-Roma, on the other hand, were divided by individual household, each small group standing some two metres apart from the rest. This, according to Stano, reflected the cohesion of the Roma and the frostiness of the relationships between non-Roma. He did not mention the separation of the Roma and non-Roma worlds symbolised by this division: this was taken for granted. Two months later, the Greek Catholic priest Martin bade farewell after fifteen years in the village and organised a small celebration in the local House of Culture (a venue for social activities to be found all over countries of the former Eastern bloc) to which he invited all the villagers. No one present saw anything strange in the fact that Martin had photographs taken firstly with his non-Romani guests, and only then with his Romani guests. Something similar had taken place during the celebration of Children's Day, during which refreshments were distributed separately amongst the tables where the Roma and non-Roma sat.

Nevertheless, the situation overall in Jolany as I was able to observe it during my time there was not in complete contradiction with the claims of a shared social life and historical experience of Roma and non-Roma. However, what it did show was that the social interactions of the residents were strongly structured by the historically rooted distinction between the two categories. As in the Hungarian village where Kovai and Horváth conducted their research, in Jolany too "everyone knew" who was and was not a Rom/Gypsy (Horváth 2012). Roma and non-Roma together formed a single community in which they shared certain common characteristics and experiences. However, as I shall show, the Roma were at the same time set apart from this community.

Asymmetrical relations

As well as the regular meetings in the local pub, and more isolated, formal events involving the whole village, less obvious interactions took place between the Roma and non-Roma. Analysing these will help show that the relationships across the divide described above were very asymmetric. During the time I spent in Jolany, visits by Roma to their non-Romani neighbours took place almost exclusively within the context of the local informal economy, when the Roma went looking for an odd job (see Chapter Four). Such meetings were usually held in the garden or in a room set apart from the rest of the house. A similar type of interaction involved visits paid in order to borrow work tools or money, or to provide medication or other medical care. However, this latter type of visit was not sought after and only took place in cases of extreme emergency. The Roma explained that it was embarrassing for them to want something from the *Gadže*, which can be seen as an attempt not to confirm the entrenched idea of the Roma as beggars completely dependent on their non-Romani neighbours. During the period of my research the Roma would often avail themselves of my services for the purpose of such visits. When we went to play football, they would persuade me to ask one of the non-Romani villagers for a football pump. On other occasions they took me with them when they probably thought that my presence would increase the likelihood of their request being granted. I also used to visit the mayoress with the Roma when, for instance, they wanted to hire the local House of Culture for a dance party. A very specific type of visit that saw social distances broached was the Easter *Śmigus-dyngus* [*oblievačka*, a Catholic celebration held on Easter Monday]. On this occasion, adult Roma men roamed the village pouring water on women from a tankard the women had previously filled, and any thoughts of social distancing were soon dispelled under the influence of the copious amounts of brandy being consumed.

On the other hand, I was able to observe the typology of visits paid by non-Romani villagers to Roma residents from my vantage point in Maroš and Katarína's household, where I had moved after the ten days spent at Kaleňák's apartment. While visits to the Roma living in the settlement were rare and typically involved non-Roma from outside the village (the postman, rag-and-bone man, potato salespeople or personal loan providers), non-Roma visits to Maroš and Katarína, whose property abutted that of the non-Romani villagers, were quite frequent. Maroš himself liked to draw attention to such visits and claimed they revealed how good their relations were with the non-Roma. The occasions on which the non-Roma visited Maroš and Katarína were varied. From the very start of my visit, Lída, a girl of around twenty who lived in the vicinity with her parents and grandmother, was a regular visitor. She had almost no non-Romani peers in the village, and so often hung out with the Roma. She would sneak around to my hosts for a crafty smoke, and Katarína would roll her a cigarette using the tobacco shared by the entire household. Kaleňák was another visitor, usually when he needed to complete a form for the social security office, since, unlike the Roma in the council flats, Maroš and Katarína had an internet connection at home and Katarína was an expert in such paperwork. Some of the non-Roma would visit in order to get drunk, e.g. Viktor, a single man, who worked as a customs officer on the Ukrainian border and who enjoyed cleaning out his head with alcohol when staying in Jolany.

This last phenomenon I will look at in more detail via the example of Maroš's family interactions with Jarus, a non-Romani villager, since it demonstrates clearly the status of the Roma in the local community. Jarus enjoyed relatively high levels of social and economic capital in the village and Maroš himself often visited him looking for odd jobs or to borrow money. Jarus visited Maroš and Katarína right at the start of my stay in the village. He was lobbying Romani households to vote for his wife as mayoress in the forthcoming local elections. During this partic-ular visit, I could not but be aware of his air of entitlement, which was evident in the way he "pretended" to forbid Maroš's sons from smoking in their own home. During the course of my next stay, Maroš tended to invite Jarus over when he needed a favour, for example when Jarus delivered firewood from the forest by tractor. However, one incident really stands out in my mind. It was summer 2016 and I was visiting Jolany with my colleague Andrej Belák. As we were enjoying a drink with Maroš and Katarína on their veranda, suddenly Jarus, by now the husband of the lady mayoress, to whom I had that very day introduced Andrej, turned up. He had brought a bottle of pear brandy with him, and even though everyone clearly felt the convivial atmosphere had dis-persed somewhat with his arrival, nobody felt able so much as to hint to him that this might be the case. When Jarus had finally had enough fun for one evening and stood up to go home, I decided, perhaps for motives related to my research, to accompany him. However, Jarus emphatically refused the offer of my company, telling me conspiratorially that "no one must know that I have been here".

The asymmetry of reciprocal visits was such that, while the Roma saw in their non-Romani neighbours a source of economic capital and scarce commodities, the non-Roma viewed the Roma as a source of cheap labour, votes, entertainment, and the opportunity to escape albeit briefly from the confines of their own social bondage. For them, Maroš and Katarína's home was located in a strategic position, since it meant that they did not have to cross the stream to the council flats, thereby breaching the symbolic boundary separating the Romani settlement from the non-Romani part of the village.

A similar social role, in which the Roma represent a source of cheap labour and entertainment to their non-Roma surroundings, has been discussed by van de Port (1998) in the case of Serbia, and by Theodosiou (2007) in the case of the Greek-Albanian border region. However, this was not so much about the specific position of the Roma within non-Romani society, but was more a broader phenomenon associated with a hierarchy of relationships ensuing from a racial key. It is to be seen, for instance, in Fanon's classic analysis of the postcolonial situation, in which *Negroes* form "an insurance policy on humanness... When the whites feel that they have become too mechanised, they turn to the men of color and ask them for a little human sustenance" (2008: 98).

It was not only the visits by non-Romani villagers to Maroš's apartment that brought to mind such phenomena. The Roma were perceived to be naturally gifted musicians by the local community (cf. Grill 2017: 6), and in the past had been invited to play at municipal gatherings and the weddings and christenings of non-Romani villagers. During the period of my research, given the dearth of young people amongst the non-Romani population the only entertainment organised was purely Roma-based and the Roma no longer occupied the role of municipal musicians. However, when the weather was warm, young Romani boys would set up their sound systems outside the council flats over the weekend. The modern Roma songs they played, which could be heard all around the village, provoked on older non-Romani woman to tell me: "We would be sad here without them."

A shared understanding of Gypsyness

However, the comment made by the non-Romani woman does not point only to the racial logic of local relations, but also to the ongoing demographic changes taking place. With the vast majority of non-Roma seeking work in towns and cities, and the younger generation being represented in the village almost exclusively by the Roma, the old villager's comment was not necessarily a sigh of regret at the "mechanised whites" (to paragraph Fanon), but the nostalgia of an old woman simply glad that the Roma were maintaining some kind of life in the village. Factoring in demographic change highlights the dynamic and multi-layered nature of the relationships under examination, without undermining the key role of the category of Gypsyness in the structuring thereof. The distinction drawn between "them" and "us" cited above did not divide the older generation from the younger, but above all reflected the paternalistic attitudes of the non-Roma, who regarded themselves as being obviously local, to the Roma, who as Gypsies were allocated a certain social function and who found themselves in a subordinate position regardless of age. The non-Roma did not want any association with their Romani neighbours over and above the framework of these asymmetrical relationships. It was perhaps for this reason that Jarus was at pains to stress the brevity of his visits through his discreet, "invisible" return, not only home, but, by extension, to his prescribed position within the racialised hierarchy of local relationships.

In order to explain the racial basis of the category Gypsyness, I will return to the example of my sometime host Kaleňák, who, unlike Jarus, was unable to effect an "invisible" return to the prescribed positions. Though he had grown up in a respected local non-Romani family with its own smallholding and therefore occupied the status of an ordinary non-Romani villager, the other non-Roma gradually turned their back on him. When I look back on the analysis I carried out of my visits, I realise that Kaleňák was the only one of the non-Romani villagers that the Roma could visit without embarrassment. When I illustrated the asymmetry of local relationships I had observed in a conversation with my Romani friend Zoralo by pointing to the fact that I could not imagine a non-Romani villager performing odd jobs for the Roma, Zoralo promptly replied: "I recently asked Kaleňák to do some work, because there are snakes behind the apartment block, and I'm afraid of snakes. He took a scythe to the long grass and I gave him one euro and poured him a brandy."[22] Zoralo gave a hearty laugh when recounting this story, as did the other Roma in the room, no doubt relishing the absurdity of a situation in which he had inverted the traditionally defined roles and had even managed to include symbolically the features of an odd job, i.e. payment and refreshment (see Chapter Four).

Kaleňák lived without water and electricity and, along with some of the local Roma, he regularly bought a litre and a half of cheap wine (*čůčo*) for one euro. However, the local non-Romani villagers treated his drinking differently to that of the heavy drinkers among the Roma. When they spoke of Kaleňák's alcoholism, unemployment, and inability to pay

---

22   Interview with Zoralo (b. 1987), conducted in Romani, 27 September 2016.

his electricity bills, they concluded it was all the fault of his allegedly aggressive father, who had abandoned the family, and the tragic death of his mentally ill mother and grandmother. In their view Kaleňák was an exception, a victim of circumstance who had failed to live up to the status of non-Romani villager. However, in the case of the Roma, the very same characteristics were interpreted through the lens of Gypsyness, in which an inability to live an "orderly life" was encoded. According to this logic, the selfsame factors that demonstrated that Kaleňák had been dealt a poor hand in life were, in the case of his Roma drinking buddies, proof of their "Gypsy nature".

In order to understand how such a distinction structured local relationships, it is important that the racial perspective be largely shared by the Roma themselves. Like segregated Roma in other Slovak villages (cf. Belák et al. 2018, Grill 2017), the Jolany Roma situationally expressed their belief that the *Gadže* were simply naturally smarter, and unlike them "know how to manage their affairs" (*džanen te chulajinel*). As Zoralo once remarked, "it's simply in our [Roma] blood"[23]. In the context of the interview, he was referring to the Roma's supposed inability to live the well organised life of their non-Romani neighbours. I heard the same feeling expressed in different ways by other Roma, who went on to talk about how firmly rooted were several characteristics of Gypsyness. Although these and similar statements might have reflected internalised racism on a cultural and not necessarily biological level, it is important for an understanding of the structuring of local relations to realise that racial perceptions were shared amongst all the local residents.

The language of Gypsyness

The internalisation of a racial hierarchy could be observed amongst the Roma themselves on the level of language, in which ideas of the "backward" Romá and "civilised" *Gadže* were embedded. Whenever a Romani person wanted to say of another Rom that they enjoyed a good standard of living, they emphasised that "they live like a *Gadžo*" (*dživel sar gadžo*), and when highlighting the low status of certain non-Rom they would say "they live worse than the Roma" (*dživel mek horšeder sar o Roma*). As elsewhere in Slovakia, where "black" was the quality associated with

---

23 Interview with Zoralo (b. 1987) and Fabián (b. 1990), conducted in Romani, 14 June 2015.

the Roma (Grill 2017: 6–7), in Jolany there was a "clear hierarchy of beauty" in connection with skin colour (ibid: 7, see also Hübschmannnová 1999, Lacková 1999).[24] According to this logic, Romani girls with objectively lighter skin were "as beautiful as the *Gadži*" (*šukar sar gadži*), while boys were said to look "like non-Romani boys" (*sar raklo*), usually just after they had shaved or put on smart clothes. A lighter skin colour was especially appreciated in a newborn baby, who would be described as "a non-Romani little girl/boy" (*sar rakľori/rakľoro*). Sometimes skin colour was explicitly referred to, for instance when a Rom was described as being "as white as a *Gadžo*" (*parno sar gadžo*), or when the Romani villager Churdo was boasting of his grandson, who at that time was living in the Czech Republic with his father: "He is so white that a *Gadžo* is nothing in comparison".[25]

A very similar situation is described in *Black Skin, White Masks*, the book by Fanon already referred to. Fanon demonstrates convincingly that black people are socialised into an inferior position in the "white world", and in an effort to attain "white normality" they find themselves imprisoned by a physically inscribed stigma – their own "black skin" (Fanon 2008). As in Jolany and among the black people of Martinique, the racialised situation was nested in the language used, in which "one is white as one is rich, as one is beautiful, as one is intelligent" (ibid: xiii 36). However, the parallels in respect of references to skin colour go further. As in Martinique, so in Jolany, skin colour was the theme of several jokes, humorous stories and banter that released the tension from bodily inscribed stigma (cf. Fanon 1955). In Martinique someone said of a particular family that "...on nights when there was a power failure the children had to laugh so that their parents would know that they were there" (Fanon 2008: 126). In Jolany not a day went past without someone saying "Put the light on, you can't be seen!" (*Labar, bo na dičhol tut!*), or when the light was switched on asking ironically "When did you arrive?" (*Kana avľal?*). Teenage Roma would often compete to see who could come up with the funniest ending to "You're as black as..." (*Sal kalo sar...*; a favourite was "a porn video"). The warning "Don't stand in the sun, you're going black" was popular (*Ma terďuv pro kham, bo kaľoha*), as was the teasing contained in the question "Where's that white t-shirt

24 For example, Elena Lacková, who was born into a Roma family in an eastern Slovak village, describes in her biography her mother's desperate attempt to scrub her daughter's skin, to wash away the dark skin and remove the physically inscribed stigma (1999: 17).

25 Interview with Churdo (b. 1960), conducted in Romani and Slovak, 17 April 2015.

heading?" (*Kaj džal o parno tričkos*) when one of the younger Roma was seen walking around the village in the evening wearing light clothing.

The ingrained association of "black" with the Roma and "white" with the non-Roma led to a situation in which the categorisation of lighter-skinned Roma was open to question on both the Roma and non-Roma side. Specifically this involved several lighter-skinned Roma from the neighbouring village of Maslovce, who had close family ties to the Jolany Roma and paid them frequent visits. Speculation was rife that their father had been non-Romani. Skin colour prompted questions around the identification with Roma/Gypsies and a partial disruption of the distinction in the racialised hierarchy of relations. Although lighter skin allowed these Roma greater room for manoeuvre during interactions in the non-Romani world, within the local context they were still easily identifiable as Gypsies on the basis of other characteristics, e.g. name, family affiliation, language, place of residence, etc. (cf. Grill 2017: 8).

Silencing Gypsyness

The comments of the Romani residents of Jolany regarding relations with their non-Romani neighbours can also be interpreted from the perspective of the generally accepted racial logic of social hierarchy. The proud declaration of some Roma – "I'm one with the *Gadže*" (*Me som le gadženca jekh vast*) – was intended to indicate higher social status and create an association with non-Romani sources and prestige (Piasere writes in a similar context of "capital *gagikano*" [1985]; see also Manrique 2015: 236, Olivera 2015: 152, Solimene 2015: 114–115). The entire narrative of harmonious relationships can be viewed in the same way. Although the Jolany Roma identified with the general category of Roma, as specifically "Jolanian Roma" they defined themselves in contrast to the Roma living in surrounding villages, who were unable to get along with their non-Romani neighbours, thus confirming entrenched ideas of "problematic Gypsies". Nevertheless, these claims were not simply a discursive game, i.e. declarations of relatively higher status in relation to other Roma in the region. The narrative of harmonious relations was also the articulation of an experience in which the Roma regarded themselves as an integral part of a specific community tied to a particular place. Similar identifications could reach different levels of local belonging. Situationally the Jolany Roma identified more broadly with the Roma in the Svidník District and set themselves apart from the somewhat unspecified "problematic"

Roma in other parts of Slovakia and/or those whose image was created by the media. However, it was not enough merely to talk of harmonious relationships. If important non-Romani contacts were to be maintained, these relationships had to be nurtured and baked into everyday practice and social interactions.

The anthropologist David Scheffel believes that the non-conflictual relationships that are a feature of the village Veľký Šariš (about seventy kilometres from Jolany) result from the fact that the "Roma and the Slovaks of Veľký Šariš have learned to curb ethnocentrism and to avoid excess in their interactions not out of allegiance to the ideals of egalitarian multiculturalism, but because of a pragmatic inhibition against open conflict" (Scheffel 2015: 144). Rather than a bipartite suppression of ethnocentrism, the situation in Jolany indicated an acceptance of the concept and a shared consensus as to who embodied the unquestioned normality of "whiteness" and who was expected to "adapt". In specific strategies for maintaining non-conflictual relationships, it was clear the Roma made every effort not to give cause for the activation of the category of Gypsyness with all its negative associations. As I have shown above, their musical skills provided the Roma with an entrée into the public sphere without fear of conflict (perhaps in line with the belief that the *Gadže* rated them highly in this sphere). However, on other occasions they opted for a strategy of self-abnegation. Tomáš, the thirty-odd-year-old son of Maroš and Katarína, drew my attention to such a strategy when he recounted matter-of-factly how he would stand at the back of the queue when they were practising artificial respiration on a dummy when learning first aid at driving school, "so that the *Gadže* [other participants] weren't repelled by having to use the dummy after me".

I was able to observe such strategies firsthand. When Martin the priest organised his farewell celebration in the House of Culture, he laid on lashings of food, including goulash, and invited all the villagers. The Roma were very fond of Martin, who had won their affection by remembering not only their names, but even their nicknames. He would never refuse an invitation to the reception following baptisms, weddings or funerals, and above all he did not "flinch" from the Roma (*na odcirdelas pes*), but ate with them in their homes. However, when Martin's farewell banquet was about to begin, not a single Rom was to be found in the hall. This surprised not only me, but Martin too, and he sent the Roma children hanging about in front of the building to tell their parents that everyone was welcome without exception. Maroš later explained to me that the reason the Roma did not turn up was so that the "*Gadže* could not claim that they [the Roma] simply wanted to eat for free". This situation is not unrelated to the ethics of reciprocity, with the Roma characterised as those who want something for nothing. Not wishing to arouse such suspicions, the Roma were painfully aware that it might be a good idea to arrive at the celebration with a gift, and those who eventually turned up brought at least a box of chocolates. However, many Roma could not afford so much as a box of chocolates, and preferred to stay home.

The formulation "so the *Gadže* don't say that..." (*kaj o gadže te na phenen*) was to be heard quite often among the Jolany Roma. Sometimes it involved the suggestion that they deploy an intelligible and transparent, i.e. non-Romani, language code ("so the *Gadže* don't say that we are bad-mouthing them", see Chapter Three). On other occasions, e.g. the priest's farewell party, it was manifest in a strategy of self-exclusion from the social life of the village. However, this strategy was not without its ambiguities, as Maroš pointed out in reference to their (non-)participation in a local celebration of the Easter holidays:

> Everything is nicely laid out in the basket, and in the morning we go [to church] to have it blessed. If we didn't go, you know what? The *Gadže* would be like: "He wasn't here because he's skint." In the city nobody knows you. But when you live in a village, yeah, you see immediately what the *Gadže* would say.[26]

In an effort not to conform to stereotypical ideas of the Gypsies who "came simply because there was free food", or who "didn't come because they have no money", the Jolany Roma perform a delicate balancing act between a performative demonstration of their social participation and a strategy of preventative isolation.

This is very reminiscent of a phenomenon Horváth and Kovai observed in Hungarian villages, to which they gave the name "silencing Gypsyness" (Horváth 2012, Kovai 2012). Both these researchers argue that the Roma lived under the terms of an illusory promise that they would be welcomed as true Hungarian villagers if only they successfully concealed the attributes of the category Gypsyness that were inextricably associated with subordinate status. In interactions with their Hungarian neighbours the Roma lived in constant dread of their Gypsyness inadvertently rising to the surface by means of some giveaway mannerism (Horváth 2012: 129).

---

26 Interview with Maroš (b. 1967), conducted in Romani, 17 March 2015.

They found themselves in a very similar position to the Roma in Jolany, who were trying to be perceived not as Gypsies, but as local residents.

"Our Roma"

In the village described by Horváth and Kovai, the local non-Roma ("Hungarians" – Horváth 2012, Kovai 2012) had no interest in articulating the category of Gypsy, since from their perspective silencing the existing distinction maintained its asymmetrical character and was to their advantage. The non-Roma of Jolany took a similar approach to the structure of harmonious relationships. However, throwaway comments betrayed their sense of superiority to their Roma neighbours. Whenever the non-Roma insisted they made no distinction between "black" and "white" (which would have reproduced the distinction thus understood), I had the impression that they were preventatively defending themselves against possible accusations of anti-Gypsy bias from me in my capacity as a Romani speaking researcher. Similarly, the mayoress, whom the Roma called Hrickaninka, reiterated her belief that "a decent person does not make such distinctions" (between Roma and non-Roma), a claim she based on a comparison with other village outsiders: "I mean, we have a Polish family here and when you look at their backyard, it's more of a mess than the Roma's. And they say that they're 'white'..."[27]

Leaving aside the fact that the comment "those whites are even worse than the Roma" merely serves to consolidate entrenched stereotypical views of the Roma on the level of language, it also indicates a reluctance to express explicitly anti-Gypsy attitudes. In conversation with me, non-Romani villagers were often reluctant to formulate opinions regarding their immediate Romani neighbours in Jolany, all the while shamelessly reproducing folk sayings and jokes featuring the highly racialised figure of the Gypsy, or recounting the stories of anonymous third parties and their allegedly negative experiences with the Roma. This affected disingenuousness allowed them to deny claims that they were saying anything inflammatory even while expressing their own superiority vis-à-vis the Roma in general and their immediate neighbours in particular.

Typical in this respect was a comment made by Janka, a non-Romani village woman, who told me that "*our Roma* are a bit more cultured [than

---

27   Interview with Hrickaninka (b. 1955), conducted in Czech and Slovak, 8 August 2016.

others]". As the sociologist Kobes observes (2012), and as Grill (2015b) remarks of an eastern Slovak village, the historically based designation "our Roma/Gypsies" acknowledges that the Roma belonged to the local community (thanks to the modifier "our"), while attributing a particular, inferior status to them as Gypsies (confirmed by the highly patronising possessive mode of speech). It should be noted that within the context of eastern Slovakia such a categorisation method had concrete impacts on the fate of the Roma in individual villages. The historically entrenched division between "our" and "alien Gypsies" determined who was allowed to settle in the village and who was expelled (Hübschmannová 1998). During the Second World War, inclusion in the category "our" served as protection against centrally organised persecution, such as the eviction of settlements or internment in labour camps or the concentration camp (Hübschmannová 2005).

Association with the category "our Roma" guaranteed the Jolany Roma asymmetric inclusion in the community of a particular place. By definition, however, this association possessed an exclusively local legitimacy. Kobes observes that, beyond the border of the village, the Roma thus described reverted to being "simple Gypsies, and people behaved to them accordingly" (Kobes 2012: 24). Kobes's observation resonates strongly with the experience of the Jolany Roma, who spoke of being subject to overt discrimination beyond the borders of the village when dealing with the authorities, at the doctor's, when looking for work, etc.

"Our Gadže"

The experience of the Roma in their own locally defined community gave rise to a specific category that they reserved for their immediate non-Romani neighbours on those occasions when they excluded them from the general class of anti-Gypsy oriented *Gadže*. Peter, a Romani villager, illustrated this well.

> One time we were all round at Jarus's. I was sawing wood with his chainsaw and the lads were splitting the logs, when Jarus called us inside for some food. He set the brandy on the table, but there was no more bread. He told us: "Stay here, I'll nip round to my mother-in-law's." So he left, and then suddenly his brothers arrived by car from Michalovce and entered the building. Immediately they wanted to know where Jarus was. I told them he had popped round to his mother-in-law's for bread. When

Jarus returned, they asked him: "You're not afraid to leave them alone in your house like that?" Jarus said: "Not at all, I trust them. They're more honest than me! I mean, they even know where I keep the money, but I'm sure no one will go looking for it." And his brothers were like: "They must be different to the Roma in Michalovce. There, if you let a Rom into your house, you're left wondering what you had in it to begin with."[28]

Peter's comments replicate the dominant understanding of the category of "problematic Gypsies". His own explanation for the non-conflictual local relationships was that, unlike other Roma, those who lived in Jolany were "honest". Jarus, who married into Jolany himself, understood that there was no danger from these Roma, and thus became a "local *Gadžo*". However, looked at from the perspective of Peter's story, his brothers remained in the more general category of *Gadže*, who were unaware of the specific nature of local relationships.

Notwithstanding the fact that the Jolany Roma excluded themselves from the category of "problematic Gypsies", they nevertheless recognised its existence and applied it to other Roma in the region, whom they described in Romani as "filthy Roma" (*degeša Roma*).[29] It was due to the behaviour of such "filthy Roma" that the Jolany Roma had a degree of understanding for the discriminatory practices of certain non-Roma. For example, they viewed the operation of racially segregated pubs in the district town of Svidník as a legitimate defence against these "genuinely problematic Gypsies". It was Zoralo who drew my attention to classified ads that brazenly specified "no Roma". Although this underscored just how difficult it was for someone in Zoralo's position to break into the labour market, when I myself expressed outrage he excused the employers in question, saying that they "had probably had bad experiences with the Roma". The Jolany Roma backed this argument up with stories of "problematic" individuals or entire communities from the surrounding

---

28 Interview with Peter (b. 1953), conducted in Romani, 22 December 2014.
29 The Roma of Tarkovce in Slovakia used the term *degeša* (plural) or *degešis / degeškiňa* (masculine singular / feminine singular) in a similar context (Grill 2017: 7). The concept of *degeša* was associated by the Jolany Roma with destitution, i.e. with a certain type of conduct linked with the loss of shame (*ladž*, cf. Hübschmannová 1999). In addition to the more commonly used general category of the "backward Gypsies", the term *degeša* (in its forms) often possessed a situational character. I was once called by this label when, in the presence of some of the older women, I failed to appreciate fully the vulgar connotations of certain expressions in Romani. A woman who was unable to look after the home, or a man who shamelessly tramped from home to home asking for a little tobacco, could also be called *degešis / degeškiňa*.

villages, or of the Roma from highly segregated settlements who featured on the daily news reports.

In light of the above it is clear that the relationship between Roma and non-Roma in Jolany was conditional upon belonging to a specific place made up of "our *Gadže*" and "our Roma". This shared sense of belonging to a specific place enjoyed by the residents of Jolany was manifest, for instance, in attitudes towards the Polish family referred to by the mayoress. The family had moved to the village shortly before I began my research, and while I was in Jolany several residents, both Roma and non-Roma, came out strongly against what they called their way of life. They pointed to the messy garden, the filthy interior, and the rudeness of the young boy to his Romani peers. Although the way of life of this Polish family was described in terms that inadvertently disclosed the subordinate status of the Roma (the mayoress claimed "they're worse than the Roma"), within these contexts the Poles were viewed as "alien" compared to the "local" ("our") Roma. The interconnection of these categories again demonstrates that Jolany did not simply operate as a backdrop to the relationships under observation, but through the sense of local belonging and local identification participated in creating the form within which said relationships were instantiated.

Still just a Gypsy

No matter how local the Roma might be relative to the newly arrived Polish family, the quality of their belonging continued to have its limits. As in the Hungarian village, so in Jolany, the idea that a complete sense of belonging to place could be achieved by masking the characteristics of Gypsyness was illusory. On the contrary, such a strategy served merely to reinforce the stigmatisation of the category of Gypsy.

At this point I would like to focus on Ľuba, a Romani woman aged around thirty-five living in Jolany. Her example shows clearly that the negotiation of social status is not simply a question of the degree to which a person displays the characteristics associated with a non-Romani way of life. During the period of my research, Ľuba married into Jolany from the neighbouring village of Maslovce. What made Ľuba's story exceptional was that her husband, Juraňák, belonged to a non-Romani family. His father had run the pub for a long time in Jolany, and while I was staying in the village a significant number of the non-Romani population were Juraňák's relatives. Members of his immediate family – specifically his mother, his unmarried brother and two teenage children – lived with him in a large house surrounded by a garden. Juraňák's first wife and the mother of the two teenagers had abandoned the family and moved to the Czech Republic, allegedly because of his problems with alcohol. Ľuba was Juraňák's second wife.

During one of our conversations Ľuba confided in me that she had not expected to get married. She had very bad eyesight and shunned the company of others. She said that when she and Juraňák began their relationship both her parents and his found it difficult to come to terms with. She spoke of the pressure she had been under since she and Juraňák had moved in together. But she also spoke of a dream she had: that her son, who was at this point in time in his first year at primary school, "achieve something", unlike his mother, whose "bad eyesight had made it impossible"[30]. I would sometimes see Ľuba in the local pub where Juraňák worked. She would sit to one side until the pub closed, but otherwise was not much involved in the social life of the village. She rarely visited Romani households and was thus more aligned with the non-Roma, whose social life tended to remain within the four walls of their own home. Though the Roma did not openly declare their distance from Ľuba, it was clear that this was not how they envisaged fulfilling the dream of "living like a *Gadžo*". By marrying Juraňák, rather than achieving higher social status, Ľuba had merely confirmed her own status as outsider.

When Peter wanted to illustrate the harmonious relationships of the local Roma and non-Roma during our very first conversation in the pub, he told me that the village even included a mixed marriage. In fact, however, the example of Ľuba and Juraňák, like the story of Kaleňák and his relationships with the local Roma, served far more to reproduce the racialised character of local relationships. Several local Roma agreed and pointed out that even though Ľuba basically stood Juraňák back on his own two feet and took care of the children from his first marriage, amongst the non-Romani villagers she continued to be viewed as "simply a Gypsy". This was confirmed to me by several non-Roma, who claimed that Juraňák had "ruined his life" by marrying a Gypsy.

30   Interview with Ľuba (b. 1979), conducted in Romani and Slovak, 1 June 2015.

Experience of the subordinate position

The Jolany Roma were well aware that they occupied a naturally subordinate position within the local community. Though situationally they spoke of harmonious relationships, they were at the same time fully capable of enumerating the inequalities on which such relationships were based. This applied to the Roma who observed that Ľuba was still "just a Gypsy", and was expressed more explicitly by my host Maroš:

> Compare Kaleňák with the Roma. Who is better? Except that he's a *Gadžo*... He may be filthy and shameless [*degešis*], but he's a *Gadžo*. And so he will fit in more with the *Gadže* than some rich Roma ever would.[31]

Zoralo's older brother Robo eventually shifted considerations of the embeddedness of racialised relationships to the level of his own lived experience:

> For example, this [non-Romani] lad I worked with. We used to pop in on each other. He let me roam his house. I used to visit him and they'd give me food. It was just as though I was visiting my brother [Zoralo]. He's never told me I'm a Rom or that I'm different from them [the *Gadže*]. He's still seeing me. Do you understand? But it's always understood that you're a *Gadžo*, I'm a Rom. You see what I'm saying? You act like "wait, I'm at a *Gadže*'s house, so [I'd better act] a bit different". I can say what I like to this lad, I can tell him to fuck off, even in front of his wife. I'm telling you, just like with him [Zoralo], but you visit his house and you behave a little differently because he is a *Gadžo*.[32]

Robo here demonstrates how embedded the subordinate status is that forms part of the everyday lived experience of the Roma and their interaction in the non-Romani world, notwithstanding the much vaunted equality of relations.[33] According to Robo, such an awareness of difference and inferiority was impossible to overcome. As he said later on, "there is always a part of you that you can't change".

---

31 Interview with Maroš (b. 1967), conducted in Romani, 6 March 2015.
32 Interview with Robo (b. 1974), conducted in Romani, 24 September 2016.
33 Not to mention the fact that Robo's words contain the same emphasis on a visit to the *Gadže*'s as Peter's comments, the aim of which is to highlight the equality of relationships being described despite the improbability of such an outcome.

Virtuous Roma and amoral *Gadže*

Since Robo and the other Jolany Roma were well aware of their fixed racial status within local relations, a strategy of "adaptation" to the non-Romani world did not comprise the absolute determinant of their social practice. On the contrary, they left room for the formulation of ideologies accentuating their own moral superiority. Rather than dwelling on the stigmatising category Gypsy, they focused on the category of Roma, which they then filled with positive content, contrasting themselves with the amoral *Gadže*.

The ambivalence of attitudes towards the *Gadžo* world in which, according to the Roma, prestige and economic possibilities run in parallel with a selfish individualism and the absence of moral values, is well illustrated by a discussion the Romani villager Churdo had with Maroš and Katarína. During one of Churdo's regular visits to the home of my hosts, they talked about the phenomenon of loan sharks in the Romani settlements in Slovakia (there were no loan sharks in Jolany). They used this example to illustrate the unequal status of the Roma in the non-Romani world.

> *Churdo:* That's what we learned from the *Gadže*, to lend money with interest. The Roma had never done this. Just like they learned to play [musical instruments] from us, so we learned from them, but only bullshit. They're better at stealing than us.
> *Katarína:* But why do the *Gadže* steal so much? [rhetorical question]
> *Maroš:* Because they know how to.
> *Katarína:* Because they're smart! The Roma are stupid!
> *Churdo:* I guess so. Gypsies don't steal millions. Don't take this personally [addressed to me]. You can, because you have access to it. The state is robbed only by someone with some brains in their bonce, not a Gypsy. A Gypsy doesn't have it in him. A Gypsy steals iron, a *Gadžo* steals millions. That's the way it is, isn't it Jan?[34]

In the scenario played out above, scheming *Gadže* who have access to resources but engage in amoral actions are in antithesis to the Roma, who are naturally stupid and have no resources, but are untainted, naturally gifted musicians. Possessed of such a disposition, even if they adopt some

---

34 Interview with Maroš (b. 1967), Katarína (b. 1967) and Churdo (b. 1960), conducted in Romani and Slovak, 20 January 2015.

of the less salubrious practices of the *Gadže*, the Roma cannot match them in terms of degree. According to my Romani friends, the *Gadže* steal on a much larger scale while remaining far less visible and not being caught.

Similar attitudes lay behind the opinion the Roma had of those of their non-Roma neighbours who took themselves too seriously and guarded their property jealously. The Roma I spoke to cited a former resident of the village who had moved to the city in search of work and placed security cameras around her house in Jolany. Zoralo says the local non-Roma are "forever saving for their retirement without even knowing if they'll live to see it", and "accumulating property for no good reason except to pass it on to future generations". The Roma contrast these stories with their own hospitality, functional solidarity networks and the ability to make do on very little. It should be noted that the ambivalence of their own status is something the non-Romani villagers may be aware of. They contrasted the Roma's community spirit with their own lack thereof, and in a conversation with me an older non-Romani village woman called Balagáňa wondered with some embarrassment whether the Roma, by virtue of their modest needs, were not fulfilling "the will of God" better than she herself, who, though she attended church every week, nevertheless enjoyed considerable material security.

Although an ideology of moral superiority existed among the Jolany Roma, I do not believe that it played as central role as, for instance, Stewart observed among the Roma of one Hungarian town who, drawing on said ideology, were able "to relocate themselves from the margins of society to the center of humanity" (1997: 232). In Jolany this ideology did not completely define the Roma's relationships with the *Gadžo* world, but coexisted alongside other aspects of the local Romani identity, such as belonging to a specific place and community and an ability to adapt to the non-Romani world. This was far more reminiscent of the strategy deployed in another eastern Slovakian village, where the Tarkovce Roma adopted certain elements of the "*Gadžo* social order", while retaining the space for the formulation of their own distinctive cultural identity (Grill 2015a,b).

Balancing the *Gadžo* way of life

The image of the subaltern but nonetheless virtuous Roma versus the successful but amoral *Gadže* sat alongside the Roma's unilateral efforts to assimilate into the *Gadžo* world. In addition to the endeavour to "live like the *Gadže*", there was a social imperative among the Jolany Roma to "stop trying to make out you're a *Gadžo*" (*te na kerel pestar gadžes*), or rather, "don't reach out to Gadženess" (*te na cirdel pes gadžeske*). A Romani person might find themselves situationally "trying to make out they were a *Gadžo*" by using a non-Romani language code for no good reason (see Chapter Three). However, it was common knowledge that certain Roma were more prone to manifestations of *Gadže* behaviour, and such designations stuck to them more permanently. This was so in the case of Katarína's sister Majka, who lived with her husband in their own house in neighbouring Maslovce. It amazed the Roma that the couple had only one child (during the period of my research three-child families were already commonplace), with whom they spoke Czech following a long trip to that country and over whose upbringing they hovered nervously like helicopter parents, i.e. in a typically *Gadže* fashion.

However, such designations did not attach themselves only to specific individuals, but also to groups of Roma categorised according to their belonging to a particular village. And so while the Jolany Roma jeered at the backwardness of the Roma in certain neighbouring villages, the Roma in other villages were characterized as being "too attached to the *Gadže*". This was a common accusation levelled against the Roma living in villages where there had been a significant language shift from Romani to non-Romani language codes (Slovak and/or Rusyn). Elsewhere such designations were used to put a distance between oneself and Romani relatives now permanently resident in the Czech Republic. Finally, however, these designations served to support more deep rooted distinctions between the Roma who continued to live in Jolany. These were largely dependent on the position a person occupied in the spatial layout of the village. According to the residents of the council flats in the local Romani settlement, it was the Roma who had managed to buy their own apartments in the village who were prone to "doing a *Gadžo*", whereas the council flat dwellers were situationally referred to as *degeša*, or backward, who were unable to look after themselves. As I shall show in the next chapter, the Roma who lived "amongst the *Gadže*" also derived their relatively higher status among the Roma in Jolany from belonging to a different *fajta* (lineage), specifically one that they defined mainly on the basis of their roots in another village in the region. Looked at from this angle, the Roma negotiated the category of Gypsyness in connection with local and kinship identification.

This dynamic of relationships also corresponds to Kovai and Horváth's findings in Hungary. They observed that, although the category of Gypsyness in the village where they conducted their research was deliberately silenced in interactions with non-Romani inhabitants, among the Roma themselves it was a constant feature and contributed to the shaping of an internal differentiation, especially on the basis of belonging to a certain *fajta* (Horváth 2012: 125). As in Jolany, entire families and, situationally, individuals were described either as representatives of "exaggerated Gypsyness", or conversely as "pretending to be Hungarians". Kovai argues that both designations were motivated by fears that the stigmatism associated with the category Gypsyness would intensify. While those accused of "exaggerated Gypsyness" confirmed the entrenched stereotype of the "backward Gypsy" by virtue of the way they behaved (their economic practices and the way they dressed), those "pretending to be Hungarians" also reinforced it by seeking to conceal any trace of their Gypsyness, so defining themselves in relation to a stereotype whose existence they thus acknowledged, together with the dominant racial logic from which it arose (Kovai 2012: 288).

Similarly, according to the Jolany Roma it was the "filthy Roma" (*degeša Roma*) who were the cause of the anti-Gypsy attitudes of non-Romani villagers or non-Romani society in general. On the other hand, when one of the Roma bought a new car, took out a large loan or attempted to buy a house, the rest of the Romani community would mock them. Their usual explanation for such intra-community behaviour was that "the Roma are a very envious people" (*o Roma hine igen zavistliva*). For a greater understanding of the envy referred to, we again turn to Kovai, who states that the mockery of those who had attained socio-economic mobility and were "pretending to be Hungarians" was related not only to a fear of intensifying the stigmatisation of the category of Gypsyness, but above all to the fact that the socio-economic mobility of such Roma represented a potential weakening of the solidarity networks between the Roma themselves. These networks, within which mutual assistance and the circulation of different items or foodstuffs took place, were crucial under conditions of social marginalisation and constant economic uncertainty. This applied not only to the Roma in the Hungarian village (Kovai 2012: 287–289), but also the Roma in Jolany.

If, along with Kovai and Horváth, we keep in mind that a negotiation of the category of Gypsyness participates in the structuring of relationships between the Roma themselves, we notice that the locution referred to above – "so the *Gadže* don't say..." – also existed in the variant: "What would the Roma think of me/us". Thinking back to the non-participation of the Roma at the farewell party in honour of the priest (for fear of conforming to an entrenched idea of Gypsyness), we observe also that the Jolany Roma often refrained from participating in the celebrations of other Roma, simply because they could not afford a suitable (i.e. sufficiently costly) gift. The fear was similar, but was now transferred onto relations between the Roma themselves – "so the Roma don't say that we are *degeša*". At the same time, working for other Roma in the village was perceived differently to performing odd jobs for the *Gadže*. While the work provided on an occasional basis for non-Romani, informal employers was to be properly remunerated, work for other Roma was carried out in a spirit of mutual neighbourly assistance and only the basic hospitality was expected. The possibility of financial remuneration for work carried out for other Roma, and even more so for relatives, was rejected by the Jolany Roma. The upshot was that anyone who wanted to enjoy a good reputation amongst the Jolany Roma had both to exhibit the characteristics of a *Gadžo* way of life and prove they belonged to the local Romani community. Cutting oneself off from Romani solidarity networks would necessitate surviving on one's own in the non-Romani world where, as we have seen, the Roma were always identified simply as Gypsies, regardless of the degree to which they displayed *Gadže* characteristics.

The narrative of social mobility

However, the Jolany Roma did not only make comparisons with each other, with other Roma in the region, and with entrenched ideas of the Gypsies of Slovakia. In their narratives they also measured themselves against how the Roma had lived "back in the day" (*darekana*). They did this in a similar fashion to the Roma in Tarkovce, eastern Slovakia, who declared that they had been able to break free of their dependence on the *Gadže* (mainly due to migration to England), and pointed to how some Roma continued to live as their ancestors had lived "back in the day" (Grill 2015a,b). When, at the very start of my fieldwork, I ventured to ask my host Maroš somewhat naively about specifically "Romani customs", he bristled at the question and explained that, while older generations of Roma must be respected, it was necessary to rid oneself of some of their "customs" and move forward. He concluded with the words: "Just because my father lived the life of a *degeš* doesn't mean that I have to too!"[35] Maroš's feelings were made clearer by something his friend Berti

---

35 Interview with Maroš (b. 1967), conducted in Romani, 3 November 2014.

said, namely that the concept "back in the day" in this context referred above all to begging (*phirnas po žobraní* – "they used to go begging"):

> I bought a car [and upon collecting it], a *Gadži* walked out of the doctor's and nearly started crying. "The Roma used to live in poverty, in destitution," she said. And so it was, because the Roma used to go begging. They went from village to village asking for potatoes. The *Gadže* would give them things. They thought the Roma would live like that forever. But step by step the Roma were digging themselves out of that situation.[36]

This story, which Berti reckoned took place in the late 1970s/early 1980s, brought to mind the period of communism in Czechoslovakia, which the Roma recalled with nostalgia as a time of plentiful economic opportunities and their own material security. On the one hand, Berti emphasised the fact that the Jolany Roma ceased to be completely dependent on their non-Romani neighbours during the communist era, while on the other, he underscored the agency of the Roma and expressed his opposition to any notion of a deep-rooted Gypsy stagnation. Maroš's concern that "the *Gadže* would say we came here to eat for free" can be seen within the context of the life of the Roma "back in the day". The Jolany Roma sought not only to avoid being lumped in with the general category of Gypsies, but also to put a distance between themselves and their Romani ancestors, who had been obliged to beg from the *Gadže*. Such a connection to the past reveals two important things about the Jolany Roma. On the one hand, their experience of the status of the Roma in the non-Romani world was deeply embedded on a local level (the Romani way of life "back in the day" referred to life in Jolany), and on the other, the Roma thought of themselves as active agents who were gradually managing to conform to the material standard of the local way of life and extricate themselves from full economic dependency on their immediate neighbours.

The narrative of resistance

However, this type of thinking, in which the Roma move ever closer to the non-Romani world, continued to affirm the dominant narrative, according to which the locally harmonious relationships were mainly due

---

36 Interview with Berti (b. 1964), conducted in Romani, 27 December 2014.

to the Roma being more "civilised" than their counterparts elsewhere. In addition to the Roma highlighting their own agency and subverting dominant notions of the "stagnating Gypsies", they added a counter-narrative according to which they were actively fighting for a more dignified status in local relations. Such narratives were best represented by the shared belief that "a Rom will never allow himself to be humbled" (*O Rom pes ňigda na kamel te del te podceňinel*), which I heard articulated in various forms during the time I spent in Jolany.

For although the Roma thought of their neighbours as "our *Gadže*" and to a certain extent excluded them from the generally anti-Gypsy non-Romani society, they were nevertheless able to detect in them manifestations of superiority. In this context, the narrative based around active resistance to the arrogance of non-Romani villagers was a feature of the everyday interactions of the Jolany Roma and attributed to them greater agency in the negotiation of local relationships. The level of support for such narratives in practice depended on the status of the parties to the interactions concerned, be they Roma or non-Roma. Maroš enjoyed a great deal of respect from the non-Romani residents of Jolany and was extremely sensitive to any obvious manifestations of paternalism displayed towards him or his family. He regularly made this clear to certain non-Roma. Peter on the other hand, who had a reputation as an alcoholic, found it difficult to counter the patronising attitudes of several of the non-Romani villagers, such as when Jarus greeted him upon his arrival at the pub with the words "How's it going, Gypsy?" (*Ta što, Cigán?*), only the next moment to have a shot sent to his table. (I have already shown how even Maroš had difficulty defending himself when Jarus chose to be patronising, though Jarus would certainly not have got off lightly had he called Maroš a Gypsy to his face.) However, as I showed earlier, the non-Romani villagers were also far from being a homogenous bunch. The kind of patronising behaviour a complacent Jarus could afford to indulge in would not have been possible for, say, Kaleňák.

The determination to confront the dominant status of the non-Roma was expressed in concrete terms by Katarína one time when she was denouncing the systemic racism present in Slovakia. I asked her where the situation in Jolany stood in relation to the country at large, and she replied:

A *Gadžo* won't look a Rom in the eye and express it like that, because he knows he'd be in for it. He might say it to another *Gadžo*, but if he spoke like that to a Roma, he'd have his ear bitten off. The *Gadže* here are all like that. I'm telling you, the Slovaks are a bunch of wankers.[37]

In addition to Katarína praising the Jolany Roma for standing up to those who would patronise them, she also demonstrates that unspoken attitudes can be difficult to dislodge. Her comments are strikingly reminiscent of Fanon's analysis of illusory equality, where it was again the "white man" who said:

> "Brother, there is no difference between us." And yet the Negro knows that there is a difference. He wants it. He wants the white man to turn on him and shout: "Damn nigger." Then he would have that unique chance – to "show them…" (Fanon 2008: 172).

This aspect concludes the complexity of the scheme of harmonious relationships as it was possible to observe in Jolany. The comments made about such relationships might have reflected the lived experience of specific relationships with particular non-Romani villagers. They might also have been reflections on the part of the Roma on their own status within the community of a particular village and a way of measuring themselves against other Roma. However, the pattern of harmonious relations was also indicative of a certain social practice. A strategy of maintaining harmonious relations could be seen as an attempt on the part of the Roma to attain a certain socio-economic capital within a predominantly non-Romani world. As such, however, it prevented any social change that would disrupt the logic of the racialised hierarchy of relationships. As Katarína implied, the non-Romani villagers might themselves be aware of this, and their active adherence to non-conflict could be a preventative measure against the potential disruption of their own unthreatened superiority.

Conclusion

In this chapter I showed that the narrative of harmonious relations and the active maintenance thereof arose in Jolany from a shared understanding of a strongly racialised hierarchy in which "black" Roma were in

---

37   Interview with Katarína (b. 1967), conducted in Romani, 6 March 2015.

a naturally subordinate position to "white" non-Roma. I drew on Fanon's theory of internalised racism in order to analyse these relationships. Fanon's arguments also resonate powerfully with the concept of symbolic violence formulated far later by Bourdieu (Bourdieu 2000; 2004), which was used for a similar analysis by Grill (2017). Symbolic violence is defined here as "violence which is exercised upon a social agent with his or her complicity" (Bourdieu and Wacquant 1992: 167). In this respect I gave preference to Fanon's analysis for its psychological elements, and for the striking similarities between his description of the situation of black Antilleans and what I observed for myself among the Jolany Roma. For the latter group the category of Gypsyness underpins every interaction with the non-Romani world, even in situations in which it was not articulated as relevant. Just as black people wore "white masks" in Martinique, the Jolany Roma tried to conceal the tell-tale signs of their Gypsyness during the process of their own socialisation into a position of inferiority, and released the tension from this physically inscribed stigma by means of humour centred around the topic of skin colour. As regards Fanon's psychiatric practice it is no mere coincidence that Stewart claims in the introduction to the anthology *The Gypsy "Menace"* that the texts by Horváth and Kovai (Horváth 2012, Kovai 2012), which are devoted to "silencing Gypsyness" (cf. Fanon's "white masks"), demonstrate clearly what it means when "anthropologists act as psychoanalysts" (Stewart 2012: xxv).

As Grill points out, the very concept of "race" is neglected in Czech and Slovak academic discussions (see also Herza 2020), and its analytical significance has to an extent been taken over by the far more frequently deployed concept of ethnicity, which in academic circles sometimes means "possessing essentialised qualities transmitted across time and space" (Grill 2017: 4). I use the concept of race in order to understand the category of Gypsyness precisely since, unlike ethnicity, it makes it easier to follow the negotiation of "blackness" as its defining characteristic. The concept of race allowed me to show that Gypsyness in Jolany was not simply a question of certain social stereotypes, but played a key role in the structuring of locally negotiated, socio-economic relationships. This was clear from the story of Kaleňák, who "lived worse than the Roma despite being a non-Rom", and also the story of Ľuba, who "remained a mere Gypsy" even though she helped Juraňák, her non-Romani husband, "to stand on his own two feet once again". It was also clear in comments made about the way of life of the Polish family, who were said to "live worse than the Roma" despite being "white". The very narrative of harmonious relationships was based on the racialised category of

Gypsyness, since if the entrenched idea of "problematic coexistence with the Roma/Gypsies" did not exist, it would make no sense.

In the text by Grill cited the author expresses a wish to balance up the academic debate on the racialisation of the Roma in Europe,[38] which, he claims, has focused mainly on "how Roma are constructed and racialised", yet remains "relatively (ethnographically) 'thin' when it comes to discussing the complexity of Roma responses, socially and regionally embedded particularities" (2017: 3).[39] In the case of both my work and Grill's, the broader regional context was the racially homogenised environment of Slovakia (and by extension the whole of eastern Europe), in which the designation "black" was associated almost exclusively with the Roma in their capacity as the only visible minority, historically speaking (ibid: 6). A comparison with Grill's study, which examines the transformation of the racialisation of the Roma within the context of their migration to western Europe, as well as with studies that describe strong racial segregation (e.g. Scheffel 2005), reveals the diversity of the negotiation of racialised hierarchies within the region of eastern Slovakia. As regards the situation in Jolany, I have shown that the local population had established an exception to the otherwise country-wide conflictual "coexistence" of the Roma and non-Roma on the basis of a common belonging to a specific place. In relation to Jolany the non-Roma would speak of "our (more cultured) Roma", and the Roma of "our *Gadže*", i.e. the people who understood that "their Roma" were not like the other Gypsies. However, I am not interested in emphasising the uniqueness of Jolany in relation to other places in Slovakia, but in the way the category of place is included in the negotiation of the form and implementation of the racial hierarchy.

When thinking about Grill's challenge to seek out the "complexity of Roma responses" to their own racialisation (Grill 2017: 3, for a similar emphasis see, for instance, Brazzabeni et al. 2015, and in the Slovak context Guy 1998 [1975], Sadílková 2017, 2020), one must not forget that the social practice of the Jolany Roma was not determined only by an unconditional attempt to rid themselves of those characteristics that

---

38 Grill refers to the work of Sigon and Trehan (2011), Hepworth (2012), Fassin et al. (2014) and van Baar (2014a,b).

39 When speaking of the concept of "migrating racialisation" Grill is specifically referring to the transformation of the racialisation of the Roma and the understanding they have of their own status in non-Romani society within the framework of their migration from Slovakia to Great Britain.

could lead to their identification as Gypsies. The Jolany Roma sought not only recognition from the non-Roma environment, but the maintenance of their position in their own solidarity-based socioeconomic networks. As in the Hungarian village (see Horváth 2012, Kovai 2012), so in Jolany, the ambivalent concept of Gypsyness contributed mainly to the structuring of relations between the Roma themselves. This was not only about defining relationships in the present, be this within Jolany or beyond its borders, but also the method of relating to Roma in the past, i.e. to the life of the Roma "back in the day", and understanding their own position as the outcome of complex processes and their own status as actors over time.

However, this reminder of temporality also possesses a firm historical anchorage in the network of socio-economic relationships embedded and evolving in a specific place. In the next chapter I shall examine temporality and territorialisation in the context of the development of the position of the Roma in Jolany. I will try to show how the individual actors in Jolany participated in the continuity of territorialisation not only of the Roma, but of the very category of Gypsyness. I will focus more on the stories of specific Romani families and show how their changing position in the spatial layout of the village contributed to a more permanent differentiation between the Roma of Jolany themselves.

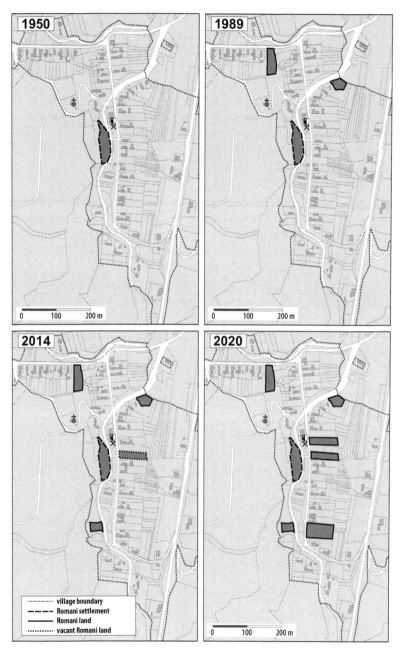

The development of Romani settlement in Jolany from the end of the Second World War

Chapter Two
Housing and the Politics of Space[40]

It was almost three years after the end of my initial stay in Jolany that I made the acquaintance of Štefan and Marika, a married couple who had lived for a long time with their children in the village, Štefan's birthplace, but had moved away in the late 1980s. Both admitted that they had strong emotional ties to Jolany and had not wanted to move. However, living in a wooden cabin in the settlement with two daughters became intolerable, and since, as Štefan claimed, the local authority was in no hurry to resolve the housing situation of the Jolany Roma, they decided to move. They had their cabin demolished and with the money they received as part of the communist policy known as "liquidation of the Gypsy shantytowns", they moved into an apartment in Svidník. At the turn of the millennium they managed to obtain land in Marika's hometown Buková, where they built a two-storey detached house.

Born in the early 1950s, Štefan and Marika were among the oldest of the original Jolany Roma, and so I used my interview with them mainly to clarify certain events that had taken place during the post-war development of the village, with an emphasis on the housing situation of the Roma. Štefan and Marika no longer maintained close relationships with the village, and recounted the story of the Romani settlement dispassionately. They said the Jolany Roma lacked initiative. They insisted on remaining in the village, and were only encouraged to live in decent housing through the construction of council flats initiated by the mayoress at that time. However, Štefan and Marika spoke of a joint letter sent by the Roma to the president of the republic in the 1970s, something none of the Jolany Roma

---

40 This chapter is based on an article published in Czech entitled "Roma as Locals? Local Belonging, Gypsyness, and the Politics of Space in an Eastern Slovak Village" (Ort 2021).

had mentioned over the previous four years of my research during our frequent conversations. I eventually tracked down the letter in an archive:

Dear Comrade (Comrades),
We are writing to you from the municipality of Jolany in the Dukla Pass on behalf of the Gypsy Settlement. We lived in shacks for 30 years until 18 July 1974. We visited the municipal authorities in Svidník and requested that they provide us with land. Neither the Svidník authorities nor the local committee in Jolany heeded our request. Since 18 July 1974 there has been flooding in the Svidník district, which has damaged our shacks to the extent we can no longer inhabit them. Several of them were swept away. We have been provided with a two-room apartment in which forty-eight people live. From here the children go to school and the rest of us are employed. Dear Comrades, we hope that you will heed our request. Thanking you in advance for your kindness.
Peace to the world,
The Jolany Gypsy Settlement[41]

Leaving aside the very existence of the letter, the way it is formulated is remarkable. The purpose of the request remains implicit. Instead, the representatives of the "Gypsy settlement" devote a lot of space to defending the claimants' position. By recalling the strenuous efforts they had made to acquire building land, and referring pointedly to their regular jobs and school attendance, they targeted precisely those areas in which, according to the dominant discourse, "the backwardness of the Gypsies" and their resistance to assimilation into socialist society was manifest. It was this image the letter writers were trying to escape from.

At the same time the letter illustrates the efforts made by the Roma from the end of the Second World War onwards to obtain their own housing "amongst the Gadže", and thus to confirm symbolically their belonging in addition to their material advancement. However, the territorial boundary between the Gypsy settlement and the rest of the village was too deeply rooted. The settlement was still in existence when I was living in Jolany, i.e. forty years after the letter was written, though its appearance had changed considerably over time. In addition, the idea of the cultural "backwardness" of its inhabitants had persisted amongst both the non-Romani villagers and those Romani families that by now had their own accommodation in the village. To a certain extent the idea had been internalised by the residents of the settlement themselves.

---

41 ŠA, Svidník, f. Odbor soc. zabezp. ONV Svidník, „Sťažnosť", 10 September 1974.

The category of Gypsyness was associated in Jolany with a specific place that was both part of the village and yet detached from it. By this logic, the question of who sought housing outside the settlement and how often was not important in terms of the structuring of local relationships. All this remained forgotten, as did the letter to the president that I only found out about at the very end of my research thanks to a throwaway comment by Štefan. What was of overriding importance was who had actually received their own housing in the village and who remained imprisoned in the cultural stagnation of the Romani settlement.

In this chapter I will focus on the politics of place. I will show how the Roma insisted on belonging to a particular place, how the category of Gypsyness was territorialised, and how positionality in a particular place was in part responsible for forming not only the relations pertaining between Roma and non-Roma, but the ongoing differentiation between the Roma themselves.

The territorialisation of the Roma in Slovakia

However, in this chapter, too, I shall first focus on the broader context of the historical development of the negotiation of the territorialisation of the Roma in what is today Slovakia. Historically speaking, this region was dominated by rural communities (Hojsík 2012: 262), and it was in this kind of environment that individual Romani settlements began to emerge in the early 17th century, if not before (Hübschmannová 1998: 233). Attitudes towards the Roma on the part of non-Romani villagers were based on a differentiation made between "our Gypsies", who were allowed to settle and practice a craft, and "other Gypsies" that the local authorities attempted to keep from entering the municipality (ibid: 234; see Chapter One). At any given time, the local authorities might fall back on the implementation of specific regulations issued by the central authorities in their approach to "their own Gypsies". During the Second World War this referred mainly to a decree enacted in 1941 and revived in 1943, under which the Roma were to be relocated to "outlying places" situated at a sufficient distance from municipalities and state and regional highways (Jurová 2002). The utilisation of such decrees to forcibly expel the Roma from municipalities (for specific examples see Hübschmannová 2005: 87–197, and Scheffel 2015) in many places caused not only a spatial segregation that persisted for decades to come (see, for instance, Jurová 2003), but also a traumatic breach of the trust the Roma had in their non-Romani neighbours (Sadílková 2017, 2020).

In Jolany things were somewhat different. During the Second World War the entire village, including the Romani settlement, was razed to the ground. After the war, the Roma took it upon themselves to build wooden shacks on the site of the previous settlement, which were separated from the centre of the village by just a stream.

After the war, large-scale construction projects were undertaken in Slovakia. The aim was to react to the devastating impacts of the Second World War and to meet the demands of ongoing urbanisation (Hojsík 2012). This construction work was in stark contrast to the situation of the Romani settlements, the highest concentration of which were in the socio-economically marginalised region of eastern Slovakia. Plans to "liquidate" (*likvidovat*) the settlements under health and safety regulations were drawn up in centralised documents from the start of the 1950s. Failure to implement these measures saw a decree issued in 1965 on the "controlled dispersal of the Gypsies" and their "transfer" to cities in partnered districts in the Bohemian region of the country. This large-scale operation, in which a large number of eastern Slovak settlements were to be liquidated between 1966 and 1970 and thousands of Gypsies relocated, was terminated with the repeal of the regulation in 1968 (Donert 2017: 159–168). One reason the project failed (from the perspective of the central state authorities) was the reluctance shown by the local authorities to accept newly arriving Gypsies and to integrate them into "non-Romani" built-up areas (Guy 1977: 249–342). Though such attitudes remained unspoken in Jolany, the policy led to the territorialisation of the Roma being maintained.

After the change of political regime in 1989, housing policy was redirected towards the construction of social housing and, in the case of the Roma, the construction of "low-grade council flats" (*obecné byty nižšieho štandardu*) in "Romani settlements" (*rómske osídlenie*; Hojsík 2008). Though these policies were ostensibly about improving the lives of the Roma and enacting desegregation, the construction of council flats met these objectives only in part. In later amendments to the decree, the minimum standard of accommodation was reduced, the explanation being that the "Roma would destroy the new apartments" (ibid.). Moreover, in the vast majority of cases, including Jolany itself, these new developments merely ensured the continuity of segregation, since the new apartments were erected on the site of the original segregated settlements, or in some cases even further from the village (Hojsík 2008, 2012).[42]

The outcome of the historically negotiated housing policy of the Roma was a situation in which, according to the Atlas of Romani Communities (*Atlas romských komunit*) of 2019 (Mušinka et al. 2019), around 415,000 Roma lived in Slovakia, of which 80,000 lived an "integrated" life in villages, while the rest lived in ethnically homogenous "concentrations" situated in municipalities (128,000), on the outskirts of municipalities (150,000), or completely beyond the borders of a municipality (57,000). As regards Jolany, the Atlas records several dozen Roma living in "concentrations" and none in the "integrated" category. This was not a particularly accurate reflection of the situation in the village, since when I was conducting my research there several Roma families lived outside the settlement and "amongst the *Gadže*" (*maškar o gadže*). On the other hand, it does serve to illustrate the fact that such families had managed to escape not only the official category of Roma as used by the authors of the Atlas, but to certain extent even the stigma of the "backward Gypsy" way of life associated with the settlement on the local level.

In this chapter I shall focus on the historical development of the territorialisation of the Roma in Jolany. By *territorialisation* I mean a kind of social practice that led to the maintenance of the territorial boundary between the Romani settlement and the rest of the village and to the preservation of a non-Romani territorial hegemony. These practices not only prevented specific Roma from relocating from the settlement to the village "amongst the *Gadže*", but also maintained the "territorial stigmatisation" of a certain place (Wacquant 2007) through its association with the category of Gypsyness. The chapter comprises two interconnected parts. In the first part I examine the (post-war) historical development of the territorialisation of the Roma in Jolany. I draw mainly on an analysis of archive materials and oral history. In the second part I focus on how an interconnection was maintained between the category of Gypsyness and the Romani settlement in the latter's capacity as a specific place in Jolany. When considering these politics of place I will therefore be interested in how the place itself contributed to the structuring of local relationships, both between the Roma and non-Roma and among the Roma themselves. I will also look at the impact of related social practices on the structure of harmonious relations we have been tracking.

---

42 Regarding segregation policies on a local level see, for example, Škobla and Filčák (2016).

The asymmetry of post-war construction

According to both Romani and non-Romani villagers the "first of the Roma" in Jolany was a blacksmith, who arrived from a nearby village at the invitation of the non-Romani villagers sometime in the latter half of the 19th century. Though there is scant information on the subsequent fate of the Roma in the village, in respect of the questions I have set myself it is telling that, during the period of my research, all the residents of Jolany continued to view with equanimity the "natural" division between the village (the non-Romani space) and the settlement (territorially and symbolically designated for the Roma/Gypsies). However, this perspective had been preceded by a somewhat unexpected historical development.

As in many surrounding villages, so in Jolany, both the village and the settlement had been razed to the ground during the fighting that took place at the end of the Second World War. The inventory of war damages drawn up in 1945 in Jolany demonstrates clearly the differences in property values and the unequal approach to the reimbursement of war damages. While the "Gypsies" were awarded damages only in the categories of foodstuffs and agricultural tools, the rest of the population was awarded significantly higher compensation not only in these categories, but also for residential buildings, farm buildings and livestock.[43] Another document from this period is a list of citizens who were to be granted a second financial advance as compensation for war damages. The entire population was to receive at least some form of compensation, with the exception of those labelled in the regulation as Gypsy labourer (*cig[ánsky] robotník*). In the case of the latter a note was appended in place of the amount to be awarded, which read as follows: "...has already received enough".[44]

These documents indicate that the differences in post-war compensation paid out did not only reflect inequalities in pre-war property ownership, but a discriminatory approach to the process of compensation in which the assessment of residential buildings was carried out on the basis of their owner (i.e. non-Rom) and location (i.e. in the "non-Romani" part of the village). In discussions I had with the former mayoress of Jolany

---

43 ŠA, Svidník, f. MNV v [Jolanech], "Vojnové škody", 1945. [without further specification of the date]

44 ŠA, Svidník, f. MNV v [Jolanech], "II. preddavok. Soznam poškodených obce [Jolany], okres Svidník, ktorým sa poskytuje II. preddavok na náhradu vojnových škôd", 1946. [without further specification of the date]

(Pištáňa as she was known to the Roma), she inclined towards this inter-pretation of the post-war construction work. According to her, during the period of new builds, non-Romani villagers could select one of three types of brick buildings, to which they could add a stable. The Roma, on the other hand, were completely excluded from these organised construc-tion works and built wooden shacks on their own initiative.[45]

Politics of the Gypsy settlement

The asymmetric development of the post-war housing situation was remarked upon in 1960 by the local committee (*Místní národní výbor* – MNV) in Jolany, which reported that a total of fifty-eight Roma lived in "unsuitable conditions" in the settlement.[46] However, concrete plans for the construction of new housing for the Roma, set to commence in 1961[47] and then rescheduled for 1962,[48] remained unrealised for reasons that remain unknown. In contrast, in proposals drawn up for the centralised policy of "dispersal", the MNV repeatedly prioritised the "relocation" of the Jolany Roma to the Bohemian part of the country.[49] Representatives of the "Gypsy commission" of the district committee (*Okresní národní výbor* – ONV) in Bardejov, later responsible for the "dispersal decree" of 1965, scheduled "liquidation" (*likvidácia*) of the Jolany settlement for the early 1960s.[50] The first mention of the proposal for a specific "liq-uidation" method on the part of the ONV is to be found in archived

---

45 Interview with Pištáňa (b. 1953), conducted in Czech and Slovak, 3 July 2015.

46 ŠA, Svidník, f. MNV v [Jolanech], "Bytových otázok občanov ciganského pôvodu", 21 Novem-ber 1960.

47 ŠA, Svidník, f. MNV v [Jolanech], "Poradovník pre určenie žiadateľov bytových otazok občan-ov ciganského pôvodu", 21 November 1960.

48 ŠA, Bardejov, f. Odbor výstavby ONV Bardejov, "[Jolany] MNV – vyvlastnenie parcely č. 9, 10 pre obč. cig. Pôvodu", 25 September 1962.

49 It proposed the transfer of four of eight families at the end of 1962, and originally intended to provide accommodation to those remaining in the form of individual or corporate building works in the surrounding region. In 1963, 1966 and 1968, i.e. when the government approved Decree No. 502/1965 on "dispersal" was already in force, the MNV consistently proposed the relocation of all families from the Jolany settlement to the Bohemian lands. See ŠA, Svidník, f. MNV v [Jolanech], "Rozhodnutie likvidácie cig. osád. – tunajšej obci", 24. September 1962; ŠA, Svidník, f. MNV v [Jolanech], "Likvidácia osád cigánského pôvodu [sic!]", 19 May 1963; ŠA, Svidník, MNV v [Jolanech], "Situačna správa o rešenie otázok cig. obyvatelstva v obci [Jolany]", 2 August 1966; ŠA, Svidník, f. MNV v [Jolanech], "Správa o plnění uznesenia Vlády číslo 502/1965 o riešení otázok občanov cigánského pôvodu", 16 December 1968.

50 After a temporary restructuring of the districts, Jolany became part of the district of Bardejov. At the end of the 1960s, the status of county town was returned to Svidník.

materials dating back to 1968. While the MNV in Jolany was still propos-
ing the relocation of all families from the settlements, representatives of
the ONV were planning to "liquidate" the settlement through the construction of "semi-detached houses" for families in the village of Jolany
itself.[51] However, neither the plans for relocation nor the construction
project were realised.

Unlike some Roma from other villages in the district, who availed
themselves of the policy of "dispersal" in order to relocate permanently
to the Bohemian part of the country where they had previously been
employed (Ort 2022), the Jolany Roma made every effort to remain in
their home village, a claim borne out by numerous archived documents.
Contemporary witnesses explained that this was very often because they
had work waiting for them at the sawmill in neighbouring Drevany.
Beginning in the early 1960s, the ONV regularly considered applications
for the allocation of planning permission in the village and appealed
for a positive outcome in letters addressed to the MNV in Jolany.[52] The
intensity of Roma efforts to acquire building land is evidenced by other
individual applications sent directly to the Jolany MNV.[53]

At the start of the 1970s, the Jolany Roma attempted to resolve the
stagnating housing situation in cooperation with the district branch of
the short-lived Union of Gypsies-Roma (*Zväz Cigánov-Rómov*). Though
the Union looked out for their interests, in the words of its chairwoman
it was limited in what it could actually achieve. Shortly after the government terminated the Union's activities in 1973, the situation deteriorated
significantly. In the summer of 1974, a flood swept through the village,
mainly affecting the wooden shacks in the settlement, which were situated right by the river.[54] According to the MNV report, the floodwater

---

51 ŠA, Svidník, f. MNV v [Jolanech], "Výstavba rod. domkov pre občanov cig. pôvodu", 17
October 1968.
52 The first such letter of May 1961 contained a request by one Jozef L and in February 1966 by
Lajoš G. A larger number of requests arrived at the ONV in October 1961, and from four more
Romani families in 1968, i.e. during the period the "dispersal policy" was being enacted. See
ŠA, Svidník, f. MNV v [Jolanech], "[Jozef L], [Jolany], veľmi zlé obytné podmienky – vyriešе-
nie", 24 May 1961.; ŠA, Svidník, f. MNV v [Jolanech], "Vybavenie žiadosti o vyvlastnenie rodinného domku v obci [Jolany]", 14 February 1966; ŠA, Svidník, f. MNV v [Jolanech], "Súpis
voľných staveb. pozemkov v obci – prevedenie", 20 October 1961.
53 ŠA, Svidník, f. MNV v [Jolanech], "Vec: Pridelenie stavebného pozemku – žiadosť", 17 July
1963.; ŠA, Svidník, MNV v [Jolanech], "Žiadosť o pridelenie stavebného pozemku pre výstavbu rod. domku pre [P. S.]", 16 June 1967.; ŠA, Svidník, MNV v [Jolanech], "Žiadosť o pridelenie stavebného pozemku na výstavbu rodinného domku", 16 August 1968.
54 The disproportionate amount of flood damage to non-Romani and Romani dwellings is perhaps no coincidence. In addition to spatial segregation, the Roma of Slovakia often faced

"completely destroyed" five of the eight shacks, while three remained "seriously damaged".[55] The MNV provided emergency accommodation for thirty-nine Roma[56] in a two-room woodland cabin.[57] This was assessed as being highly unsuitable housing not only by the District Hygiene Station (*Okresní hygienická stanice*) in Svidník,[58] but also in a letter to the Office of the President of the Republic (*Kancelář prezidenta republiky* – KPR, see the opening remarks to this chapter) from the Roma living there. The KPR forwarded the letter to the ONV in Svidník, which issued a statement to Romani applicants (with a copy for the MNV in Jolany) to the effect that four Romani families had already been found alternative housing in the surrounding villages. However, all but one of these families allegedly refused to move out of Jolany. The other families were told to return their wooden shacks in the settlement to their original state with the aid of a grant from the state insurance company.[59] In the years following the flood, Romani witnesses say the construction of apartment blocks was planned and prepared for all Roma from the Jolany settlement, but that they rejected the offer, allegedly because the ground on which the flats were to be built had been undermined by the flooding.

By this time all the Romani families forced to move out of their homes because of the flooding had returned to the settlement, including those for whom housing had been sought in the surrounding villages. This included Alojz and Margita, the parents of Peter, my drinking partner going back to the first afternoon I spent in Jolany (see Introduction). They had been the only ones to avail themselves of the offer of alternative accommodation, since as employees of the sawmill they had received a company flat in an apartment block in neighbouring Drevany. However, as Peter recalled, his parents were too "used to life in Jolany" (*sikhade te dživel Jolaňate*), where in spring 1975 they began to build a house in

what was known as "environmental discrimination", in which they were placed in locations of increased environmental risk within the residential structure of the municipality (Filčák 2012).

55 ŠA, Svidník, f. MNV v [Jolanech], "Záznam napísaný dňa 19. VII. 1974 na MNV v [Jolanech] vo vecí zistenie škôd u cigánskych spoluobčanov nasledkom živelnej pohromy – povodne", 19 July 1974.

56 This data on the number of people is based on the District Hygiene Commission Report (17 September 1974). At the beginning of August the local committee (MNV) put the number of people in Jolany at thirty-eight (1 August 1974) and the signatories to the letter to the Office of the President of the Republic cited a figure of forty-eight (10 September 1974).

57 ŠA, Svidník, f. MNV v [Jolanech], "Preveriť hygienu v cigánskej osade", 1 August 1974.

58 ŠA, Svidník f. MNV v [Jolanech], "Ubytovanie občanov ciganského pôvodu v obci [Jolany] – odpoveď", 17 September 1974.

59 ŠA, Svidník, f. MNV v [Jolanech], "Sťažnosť ohľadom prídelenia bytu – odpoved", 3 October 1974.

the settlement using wooden beams. The absence of planning permission and questions hanging over ownership of the land saw construction work halted several times on the initiative of the MNV. However, when, at a specially convened meeting, representatives of both the ONV and the MNV failed in their attempt to come up with another suitable building plot,[60] Alojz and Margita simply completed the construction of their new home back in the settlement.

Failure to resolve the issue of who owned the land on which the settlement stood might explain why the grounds of the settlement were left out of the post-war modernisation of the entire village. In the non-Romani part of the village the post-war construction of brick houses was accompanied by electrification and the introduction of a water supply network. However, the settlement had to wait until the start of the new millennium for electricity to be introduced, even then on a temporary, illegal basis, while the only source of water for all residents was a single well. The Roma sought to reverse the historically entrenched asymmetry of land ownership in further applications for the allocation of building plots. In 1988, four applicants expressed their desire to remain in Jolany using identical words: "I would like to build a detached family house in [Jolany], since I have favourable working conditions nearby."[61] However, these too were rejected by the Jolany MNV, the end result being that the housing situation of most of the Roma in Jolany did not change significantly between the period of post-war construction and the end of the communist regime. Only two Romani families succeeded in acquiring housing in the non-Romani part of the village, and I shall return to their case later.

Actors of territorialisation

In short, although the stagnating situation of housing in the settlement might have supported the idea that Roma territorialisation was a natural state of affairs, the development that preceded it demonstrated instead that it was the unpredictable outcome of the actions of diverse actors that were in conflict within the social space of Jolany. However, it is clear that individual actors were endowed with different levels of decision-making

---

60 ŠA, Svidník, f. MNV v [Jolanech], "Záznam napisaný v kancelárii MNV v [Jolanech] dňa 17. apríla 1975 vo veci riešenia výstavby rod. domkov pre občianov cig. pôvodu", 17 April 1975.
61 ŠA, Svidník, f. MNV v [Jolanech], "Žiadosť o pridelenie pozemku na výstavbu rodinného domu", 7 October 1988; 12 October 1988.

authority. The Roma themselves represented one group of actors, and their interest in the construction of the detached houses in the village is clear from the numerous applications they submitted for building plots from the early 1960s to the end of the 1980s. Their readiness to prosecute their interests is clear from the way they approached bodies on various levels of the state apparat. They addressed individual applications to the local and district committees (MNV and ONV), and joint requests to the district organisation of the Union of Gypsies-Roma. After the floods they even wrote to the Office of the President of the Republic. These attempts at obtaining accommodation on the part of the Roma were predicated on a desire to remain in their home village.

Basically, from the start of the 1960s the district committee (ONV) in Svidník (and for a short time in Bardejov) had similar interests. When communicating with the local committee (MNV) in Jolany it appealed for a positive resolution of the applications. It pointed out that the allocation of land in the village was fully in accordance with the orders received from above for the "liquidation of Gypsy settlements". However, the Jolany MNV continued to reject these applications. Communications regarding the allocation of building plots belonging to the Jolany Roma have been examined by several authors, who concluded that in its long-term attempt at the "liquidation of the settlements" the socialist policy might to some extent have coincided with the interests of the Roma as the inhabitants of said settlements (Sadílková 2017), and that failure to implement this policy was due to the reluctance of local authorities to deterritorialise the settlements in question (Guy 1998 [1975]). In the case of the MNV in Jolany, such motives cannot be automatically assumed, given that, when rejecting the applications, the local authority stated that it had no land at its disposal, and that the "municipality is not a catchment area" and as such had limited opportunities for new construction. However, other documents would seem to indicate that the MNV was dragging its feet. According to a report dated 1963 for the Regional National Committee (*Krajský národní výbor* – KNV) in Košice, which in the same year unveiled the regional concept of the "liquidation of Gypsy settlements", the Jolany MNV arrived at an "incorrect decision [...] on the allocation of building plots to the detriment of the Gypsy inhabitants."[62] The Roma themselves submitted a complaint regarding the

---

62 *Zpráva z previerky /prieskumu/ z riešenia cigánskej problematiky vo Východoslovenskom kraji, prevedenej v dňoch 3. – 11. VI. 1963* (Jurová 2008: 946–951).

approach taken by the MNV not only in the letter referred to addressed to the KPR, but two years later at the plenary session of the district organisation of the Union of Gypsies-Roma, where their representative stated that "citizens in the settlement have submitted applications for apartments or building land. The MNV has sat on these applications for three years and has still not replied."[63] It is worth noting that even in the case of concrete proposals for the resolution of the Roma's housing situation, the MNV assumed they would be resettled completely outside the cadastral territory of the municipality, whether this involve their relocation to the Bohemian lands in the 1960s or a search for housing in neighbouring municipalities after the flooding. The maintenance or intensification of their segregation was also a feature of unrealised plans for the construction of new detached houses. In the early 1960s, what had formerly been Jewish land was earmarked for the construction of "family houses" for the Roma, which were separated from the village by the main road to Poland. The apartments designed in the 1970s were to be located a few dozen metres behind the last non-Romani building.

As Guy argues when writing of other east Slovak villages, the situation can be summarised thus: though central planning entailed genuine restrictions on new construction projects for "non-central" municipalities, in specific cases it could also be an effective tool for maintaining non-Romani territorial hegemony (ibid.). We see this in some of the "central municipalities" in the region I monitored. Despite the greater opportunities for new construction work, a strong territorial boundary was constantly enforced between the non-Romani municipality and the Romani settlement. In this sense, I believe that references to administrative restrictions on construction work must be seen within the context of the definition of the category of Gypsyness, which to an extent excluded part of the population from the category "local". In the case of these individuals, who did not own any land in the village, belonging to the village was subject to constant verification, and was something they were obliged to actively negotiate and renegotiate. On the other hand, the MNV in Jolany managed to maintain the territorial hegemony of the "non-Romani" village (though quite how deliberately is open to question) through argumentation and practice in which the category of Gypsyness was present only implicitly. In this way the MNV both

---

63 ŠA, Svidník, f. Zväz CIgánov-Rómov, Svidník, "Zápisnica napísaná pléna OV-ZCR rozšírenom o predsedov a tajomníkov MO-ZCR", 28 February 1972.

pre-empted accusations of discrimination from higher authorities while contributing to a perception of the territorialisation of the Roma as a natural state of affairs based on the "cultural backwardness" of the Roma themselves.[64]

The story of Jozef: a Gypsy in the village

As I mentioned above, only two families managed to receive housing in the non-Roma part of the village. The case of the first, Jozef and Haňa, is illustrative not only of communication with the local authorities, but also of the attitudes of the non-Romani villagers, who have thus far only appeared by implication in this text through their local representatives at the MNV.

Jozef was the father of my host Maroš, and had already died by the time of my research. He was born into a family that lived in nearby Sľivany prior to the Second World War. His father Vasiľ was the local blacksmith, and his family, as the only Roma in the village, enjoyed the respect of the non-Roma, according to my Jolany-based witnesses. After the war, however, none of the Roma remained in Sľivany. Jozef's parents died and his siblings moved away, some to surrounding villages and some to the Bohemian part of the country. Jozef himself moved to the Jolany settlement, where he lived with Haňa, a native of Jolany. Starting in the early 1960s, he was the most active applicant for the allocation of a building plot in the village according to the documents in local archives. His application was considered in 1961 by the Construction Department (*Odbor výstavby*) of the ONV,[65] which asked the Jolany MNV to resolve the matter by acceding to the request in accordance with the established policy of "liquidation", either by allocating state land or arranging for the sale of private land. In its reply, the MNV emphasised that there were no state-owned building plots in the village. It also pointed out that the applicant was living "illicitly" (i.e. out of wedlock) with Haňa H, "a citizen of Gypsy origin", and advised him "to apply for land in Sľivany,

---

64   Having said that, I am aware that this argument would be considerably more robust were it supported by the circumstances of the construction of the detached houses belonging to the Jolany non-Roma. Leaving aside post-war building activities, during the communist period only two such houses were built (in the 1980s), though I was unable to track down any documentation pertaining to their construction.

65   ŠA, Svidník, f. MNV v [Jolanech], "[Jozef L], [Jolany], veľmi zlé obytné podmienky – vyriešenie", 24 May 1961.

since that is his place of birth", especially given that in Jolany "he does not enjoy a good reputation, either amongst the *citizens of Gypsy origin* or the *local population*".[66] It is worth noting that, when defending their rejection of the application, the representatives of the MNV in Jolany make a distinction between local and outsider. According to this line of argument, Jozef, as an outsider, has less of a right to the allocation of land in the village. Jozef's status as "outsider" was underscored by the council of the MNV, which argued that he was not bound to the village by place of birth, wedlock or any embeddedness in local relationships (i.e. he stood out in respect of both kinship and way of life, see Kobes 2012). Significantly, Jozef's position in local relations is illustrated by means of his "bad reputation" not only among the "local population", but also "citizens of Gypsy origin". According to this logic, the latter, though included in the local community (as "our Roma": see Chapter One), nevertheless do not attain the status of "locals".

Despite the situation being distorted in this way, Jozef and Haňa found new housing relatively quickly. In the spring of 1962, they bought a small wooden house from a non-Romani villager, in the heart of the village. According to contemporary witnesses and archive materials, however, Jozef and Haňa found themselves in sharp conflict with their new neighbours. An example of just how sharp is to be found in a report on misdemeanour proceedings in which Haňa admits to striking her non-Romani neighbour with a cane, but claims she only did so after said neighbour threatened to burn down their newly purchased wooden house.[67] Moreover, the new house could not meet the housing requirements of a family of eight, and so in 1963 Jozef submitted another application for the allocation of a building plot in order to build a detached house. The application was again rejected by the MNV.[68]

Jozef finally bought the much sought after building plot four years later from a local teacher. The circumstances surrounding the acquisition were lodged in the memory of the local villagers. During the period of my research both the Romani and non-Romani villagers agreed that Jozef and Haňa's future neighbours could not reconcile themselves to the presence of a Gypsy in the village, and attempted to prevent the

66 ŠA, Svidník, f. MNV v [Jolanech], "[Jozef L], [Jolany], veľmi zlé obytné podmienky – vyrie-šenie", 2 June 1961.
67 ŠA, Svidník, f. MNV v [Jolanech], "Protokol o přestupku", 27 July 1962.
68 ŠA, Svidník, f. MNV v [Jolanech], "Vec: Pridelenie stavebného pozemku – žiadosť", 17 July 1963.

construction of a house on the purchased land. They repeatedly back-filled the foundations that Jozef had dug with the help of the local Roma, forcing Jozef to invite some non-Romani villagers from his native Sľivany, with whose assistance he completed the building.

This conflict has echoes of similar anti-Gypsy attitudes in other villages in eastern Slovakia (see Guy 1977, Lacková 1999,[69] Scheffel 2005), as well as references in the region's archived material. In the 1960s, the ONV in Bardejov, which included Jolany, stated that a key obstacle to implementing the policy of "dispersal" was the fact that non-Romani landowners were refusing to sell their land to the national committees "upon learning that it was for Gypsies".[70]

Within the conflict thus framed, Jozef was regarded by the Jolany Roma as having resisted the deeply rooted territorialisation of the Roma and having gradually won the respect of the non-Roma. However, though the Jolany Roma spoke of how he had "outsmarted the *Gadže*" through sheer doggedness, overall what they appreciated about his actions was how they reflected a *Gadžo* way of life. In order to explain Jozef's relatively high social status, the Jolany Roma and non-Roma cited his origins in nearby Sľivany, thanks to which he was "used to living amongst the *Gadže*" (unlike the rest of the Roma in Jolany) and possessed, according to some of the Roma, a special "*Gadžo* sense" (*gadžikano citos*).

In the end, Jozef's example points to a certain dynamic by which the categories local and Gypsy are negotiated. His first application for land was rejected because Jozef was one of the "other Gypsies". Later, however, he was able to break through the entrenched territorial boundary separating the Gypsies from the "local population" in Jolany with the aid of "his *Gadže*" (cf. Chapter One) from Sľivany. In the eyes of the Jolany Roma it was the fact that he did not belong among the "local Roma", but was used to living "amongst the *Gadže*" in Sľivany, which ultimately confirmed the validity of his relatively higher status within the Jolany community. The story of Jozef thus bears out the notion that the historically based belonging of the Jolany Roma to a specific community was won at the cost of an equally entrenched idea of their inferior status as

---

69 Lacková, who herself grew up in one of the eastern Slovak settlements, refers to a similarly bitter conflict in her autobiography in the chapter entitled "We don't want a Gypsy in our village" (1999: 183–184).

70 ŠA, Bardejov, f. Komisie pre riešenie cigánskych otázok, "Zpráva o realizácii koncepcie pre riešenie otázok občanov cigánskeho pôvodu do roku 1970 a návrh opatrení, vyplývajúcich z uznesenia vlády č. 502 z 13. 10. 1965" [without date].

Gypsies. As I show below, public identification with a place other than Jolany became, paradoxically, the condition for the possibility of moving from this asymmetric belonging towards a more egalitarian anchorage within non-Romani socio-economic structures.

Maintaining the settlement's size

However, the story of the spatial (im)mobility of the Jolany Roma does not end with the large number of rejected planning applications, the stagnation of the construction of housing and infrastructure in the settlement, and the story of Jozef building his new house. Firstly, there were the Romani women who, in accordance with the prevailing virilocal post-marital residency customs, left Jolany for the birthplace of their partners. In this respect the concept of who was local (i.e. who belonged to the category "our Roma" or "Jolanian Roma") was patrilineal. Women did not feature as applicants for land and their situation was ignored even when their partners' applications were being dealt with. This is clear from the example of Jozef, who married into Jolany himself, while the origins of his partner Haňa in Jolany were not taken into account in either his application or the response from the local committee (MNV). The topic of migration, too, has hitherto remained to one side. I shall examine this topic in more detail in Chapter Four. Here I will limit myself to stating that from the post-war period right up to the time I spent in Jolany, many Roma families moved in search of work to the Bohemian lands (later the Czech Republic). Though most returned to Jolany after a short time, some remained there for good.

During the latter half of the 1980s, there was a great deal of movement on the part of the Jolany Roma within the region. Firstly, corporate apartments were built in nearby Drevany, into which some of the Jolany Roma and their families moved as employees of the sawmill. Around the same time, three families availed themselves of a state grant to demolish their "shacks" (*chatrč*). This grant was part of the ongoing "liquidation" campaign. Given that right up to 1974 at least the Romani settlement comprised eight households (according to the report on the flooding), the departure of such a large number of mainly young families must have represented a significant reduction in the number of Roma in Jolany. It is worth noting that the families who moved out were not associated with specific sociological characteristics (i.e. kinship or social status) that would distinguish them from other Roma in Jolany. Their departure was more down to their own individual initiative and the offer of new housing. The only exception was Štefan, to whom I referred in the introduction to this chapter, and his two brothers, who availed themselves of the "liquidation of shacks" campaign to move out of Jolany, each to a different village in the region. Their extended family remained separate from the kinship networks of the other Jolany Roma, and none of the brothers maintained closer contact with the Jolany Roma after leaving the village.

However, as regards the context within which the position of the Roma in Jolany's residential structure was negotiated, the story of Miro and Pavlína and their family is worth looking at in greater detail. They also had their shack in the settlement "liquidated" and bought a house in the village with the grant money they received, thereby becoming the second Romani family after Jozef and Haňa to live "amongst the *Gadže*". According to witnesses, Miro's father Lajoš bought the house for his son from the daughter of a deceased non-Romani villager in 1986. This daughter had long been married and living in a different village, and had no interest in maintaining the property she had inherited. It would appear that Lajoš's established position within the social networks of local non-Roma played a part in the purchase of the house. In addition to having submitted two individual applications for the allocation of a building plot back in the 1960s, in 1973 Lajoš was chosen by the MNV to be the Roma's representative on the newly founded regional Assembly of Gypsy Residents (*Aktiv cigánskych obyvateľov*) of the ONV in Svidník, the task of which was to organise educational activities amongst the "Gypsy citizens" of the district following the dissolution of the Union of Gypsies-Roma.

I shall return later to how their position in the spatial layout of the village affected relations between the Jolany Roma. For the moment, however, we might summarise the situation thus: by the end of the 1980s, the outcome of the movements we have been tracking was such that not only the material conditions of accommodation in Jolany settlement had stagnated, but the number of residents had not increased on the post-war period despite a natural demographic increase (in 1960 the settlement was home to fifty-eight people, while in 2006 the ground plan of the council flats for the Roma from the settlement reckoned on a figure of forty people). Though the centralised socialist policy had failed to "liquidate" the Romani settlement in Jolany, in the long run it had managed to prevent its expansion.

Council flats for the Roma

Following the Velvet Revolution of 1989, it seemed as though all the elements were in place for a new housing development on the site of the original settlement in Jolany. During the 1990s, there was to be a partial legal settlement of land ownership, though the central share in the construction work was assigned to Pištána, mayoress of Jolany from 2002 to 2014. To begin with the area was connected up to the electricity mains and water supply. In 2004, as part of a government programme for the construction of "low-grade council flats" in "Romani settlements", Pištáňa submitted a proposal for the construction of eight apartments in two single-storey apartment blocks for a total of forty people. The state would pay the bulk of the cost, with the future residents taking a twenty-percent stake. In practice this outlay was covered by the participation of the planned tenants in the construction work. The project included modifications to the adjoining area, including the construction of a bridge over the stream and an access road. In spring 2006, the Roma moved out of the settlement and into two temporary military tents on the edge of the village. Every day they went to work on the building site where the flats were being built. They moved in at the end of the same year. The monthly rent included instalments for the total price of the apartments, which were to be transferred into the full ownership of the tenants thirty years after building approval (i.e. in 2036).

It was following the completion of the council flats that the newspaper report was published that spoke of the harmonious "coexistence" of the local residents (see the Introduction). Pištáňa the mayoress was the public face of the project and was awarded the Gypsy Spirit prize in Slovakia[71] for her "work with the Romani community" and the "maintenance of non-conflictual relations in the municipality". The central position ascribed to Pištána and the stereotypical portrayal of the Roma was reinforced by the accompanying text, according to which there was "no theft, truancy or social security scrounging" in the village "thanks to her authority". Pištáňa herself was more than happy to highlight the importance of her own involvement in the project. In an interview with me she described it as a politically unpopular step that she nevertheless

---

71 The Gypsy Spirit prize (since 2014 the Roma Spirit) has been awarded in Slovakia since 2008. The award was set up in order to promote the "dissemination of positive examples that support and reward active efforts of individuals and organisations to improve the living conditions and integrate the Romani minority fully and with dignity" (Roma Spirit 2020).

forced through in the face of strong opposition from the non-Roma. She claimed that the non-Romani villagers were forever "throwing spanners in the works" and protesting that "the state was giving the Roma something for nothing". Whatever the case, the narrative according to which mayoress Pišťáňa took it upon herself to push through the construction of the council flats, thus raising the living standards of the local Roma, was generally accepted in Jolany, even amongst those villagers who had been critical of the construction project.

Both in the text accompanying her award and in Jolany itself, the emphasis placed on the mayoress's agency to a large extent confirmed entrenched ideas of the inability of the Roma living in the settlement to "manage their own affairs". This narrative completely ignored historical developments to date, not only the ongoing efforts made by the Roma to acquire their own housing in the village, but also the resistance of the local committee and the territorial boundary itself. This conviction that the Roma lacked will, responsibility and ambition was clear even from the highly patronising narrative spun by Pišťána herself, who, for instance, claimed that "the Roma need to be spoken to, sometimes praised, sometimes shouted at".[72]

Continuity of territorial stigmatisation

In Jolany the required housing standards were met, something that cannot be said of the construction of council flats in other villages (cf. Hojsík 2008). The new standards were appreciated by the new tenants, especially with regard to the hot water supply. Even so, one would still from time to time encounter nostalgia for the good old days in the "wooden houses". For instance, the council flat residents were convinced that they had been healthier and more resilient in their previous habitations. They also observed a decline in solidarity between individual families, who, they claimed, had begun to compare how these pristine apartments were being treated.

Moreover, the new tenants continued to view life in a "Romani environment" as a barrier to their own socio-economic mobility, and spoke in particular of its negative impact on the education and upbringing of their children. They were convinced that, even if their children were

---

72 Interview with Pišťáňa (b. 1953), conducted in Czech and Slovak, 3 July 2015.

intelligent and received good grades at school, they would in the end be dragged down to the level of the rest of the Romani children. Monika, a resident of one of the council flats, told me you wouldn't even raise a dog in such an environment, and Zoralo felt similarly:

> If I was a member of parliament I'd abolish these settlements. Did they actually improve anything by building these apartment blocks? We're still in one place, still in the settlement. I would have put one building here, one there, even if there were only to be two buildings... If the Roma were to be dispersed in this way, I believe it would be better for everyone.[73]

Zoralo's criticism is similar to a way of thinking that views the construction of council flats in many Slovak municipalities as the confirmation, not to say intensification of racial segregation (ibid.). However, although his reasoning was highly reminiscent of the plans of the socialist state for an organised "dispersal", the question remains as to whether Zoralo and the rest of the residents of the council flats would genuinely wish to be "scattered" in this way (let us not forget that after the flooding of 1974, individual Romani families in Jolany apparently turned down the offer of independent housing in surrounding villages). Zoralo's feelings are more a reflection of the hopelessness of his own situation: he had attempted to obtain accommodation in the village, but, in the face of repeated failure, called instead for a systematic intervention from outside. I am of the opinion that the situationally nostalgic recollection of life in the "wooden houses" can also be seen as an expression of dissatisfaction with the state of affairs at the time of my research, in which the tenants of the council flats faced ongoing precarity.

The question therefore arises as to how the construction of the council flats corresponded to the previously formulated interests of individual actors during the communist period. In the text explaining why the mayoress received her award, we read that she was responsible for the "liquidation of the settlement", a formulation that in itself creates a continuity with earlier socialist policies. However, the aim was not only to oversee the material "liquidation of the Gypsy shacks" (*likvidácia cigánskych chatrčí*), but also the "liquidation of Gypsy concentrations" (*likvidácia cigánskych koncentrácií*) in their capacity as places characterised by a "backward" way of life. The construction of council flats had the effect

---

73 Interview with Zoralo (b. 1987), conducted in Romani, 11 May 2015.

of preserving such "concentrations" and was thus in its way a continuation of the policies of the local committee (MNV), which under socialism had sought to preserve non-Romani territorial hegemony.

As well as the construction of the council flats ensuring the continuity of the territorialisation of the Roma, the location in question retained its association with a certain "backward" way of life despite its makeover. This continuity of the stigmatisation of place was symbolically implied in the designation "settlement" (*vatra*), which the local residents, both Roma and non-Roma alike, used to describe the area where the council flats were located. Zoralo had put his finger on things: the Roma remained "still in one place, still in the settlement". I take this "territorial stigmatisation" (Wacquant 2007), in which a certain segment of the population is categorised and stigmatised on the basis of its place of residence, to be a dynamic process that reflects both the centralised policy of the state and that of the regional authorities, especially the municipality of Jolany. At the same time the particular social practice of the residents of Jolany, including the Roma themselves (both those inside and those outside the settlement), entered into the process.

Covert discrimination

I have already shown that the material progress represented by the construction of low-grade council flats only partially satisfied the long-held desire of the Roma to build housing on their own land, and that the Roma themselves considered the settlement to be a "bad address" (cf. Wacquant 2007). The task now is to show how their specific social practices entered the context of these sentiments.

During the period of my research, as previously in history, the Roma attempted to quit the settlement and find alternative housing. These attempts were prompted by the symbolic stigmatisation of the settlement and the desire to "to manage their own affairs" (*korkoro peske te chulajinel*), though they were also a reaction to the gradual overcrowding taking place of the council flats. Three-room flats, each with a total floor area of 64 m², were soon insufficient for growing families, and the plans some of the Roma had to built wooden extensions were quashed by the local authorities. As well as conserving the existence of the settlement, the construction of the council flats basically set a limit on the number of residents and led to strict controls on any expansion. With the continuing unavailability of housing in the non-Romani part of Jolany, many young Romani families were obliged to relocate to the surrounding villages, usually into its "Romani" quarter. This applied not only to young Romani women born in Jolany, who in accordance with tradition moved in with their husbands, but also to many Romani men who would otherwise be expected to remain with their families in their home village. This situation was again basically in line with what had earlier been the interests of the MNV, which had sought to prevent the expansion of the settlement and had at different times and in different contexts proposed displacing its residents outside the village.

Martin and Fabián were young brothers, each of whom had a wife and three children, who lived in a three-room apartment with their parents. With twelve people living under the one roof, the brothers took matters into their own hands. During the course of my research, they both managed to secure a large bank loan in order to buy a house. They were aware that they would not find a property in Jolany. However, they had their eye on a long abandoned two-storey brick house with garden in a village a few kilometres away. Together we went to view the house and ask the local mayor about the possibility of buying it.[74]

Like the writers of the letter to the president from the 1970s, in talks with the non-Romani side Martin and Fabián made every effort to evince their credibility in specific ways. With the mayor they made frequent mention of the fact that their maternal grandfather hailed from this village, where he had enjoyed good relations with his non-Romani villagers. In a similar spirit they pointed out that they themselves were from Jolany, pinning their hopes on the good reputation of the Jolany Roma amongst the non-Roma in the region. In both cases, in order to establish their credibility, they emphasised their (historical) embeddedness in the socio-economic networks of place.

The local mayor heard them out. He then proceeded to explain in a friendly enough fashion that the purchase of the house would not be possible, that ownership of the land on which the building stood was shared amongst a number of different people and the agreement of all of them would be difficult to reach. The two brothers nodded understandingly and bade farewell. On the way back to Jolany in the car they parsed the entire conversation thus: "It's obvious he doesn't want to sell [the house] to the Roma".

---

74 Martin and Fabián told no one of their plans. They feared that other Jolany Roma would be envious and on our departure would "spit at us", so as to bring us misfortune when negotiating the sale (cf. the fear of weakened solidarity networks in Chapter One).

This ascription of an anti-Gypsy motive explaining the brothers' failure was embedded in the historically entrenched experience the Roma shared of the difficulties involved in accessing housing in a "non-Romani" part of a village. The Roma themselves believed the causes lay in a non-Romani dominance that was manifest in both the economic marginalisation of the Roma in an already economically marginalised region, and the basic unwillingness of non-Romani neighbours to "allow the Roma to mix freely with them". Many Roma had experienced blatant discrimination on the part of non-Romani villagers, who simply refused point-blank to sell vacant plots to Gypsies. However, everything about the conversation with the mayor points to yet another aspect of non-Roma dominance. The automatic agreement on the part of the brothers that the mayor was discriminating against the Roma was in sharp contrast to the friendly atmosphere of the conversation itself, during which Martin and Fabián appeared sympathetic to the mayor's explanation. Neither brother based their claims of anti-Gypsy discrimination on a specific comment, but instead drew on shared historical experience. Similarly, in the documents that have been preserved, it is impossible to point to an unambiguously anti-Gypsy feeling on the part of the MNV from the seemingly rational arguments deployed in their rejection of applications for building plots submitted by the Roma. As I stated in Chapter One, in non-conflictual situations, anti-Gypsy attitudes remained concealed, making it difficult to name, blame and confront them directly.

Territorialisation: the *Gadže's* perspective

Nevertheless, in interviews with me, several of the non-Roma conceded the existence of anti-Gypsy motives within the context of the housing situation. Čirčáňa, a retired native of Jolany who lived in a house situated close to the Romani settlement, confided that she owned some empty land between two other non-Romani houses. She had already been approached by interested parties from the ranks of the Roma, but she did not want to sell to them. She assured me that she had nothing against the Roma, but that "in such a small village" she did not want to put at threat her relationships with other non-Romani villagers. Speaking of anti-Gypsy feelings she cited the example of land on which a detached house stood that had been for sale in the village at the turn of the millennium. It was rumoured that the owners had entered into talks with a Romani family. At this point a non-Romani family whose building abutted the land became involved. This family did not want Gypsies as neighbours and so bought the land itself. Such attitudes can be seen as part of a wider phenomenon in which non-Romani, especially in geographically marginalised regions, harboured fears that the value of a house or land would drop precipitously were it to find itself next to a Romani family (Filčák 2012: 171).

Čirčáňa's disclosures not only confirmed the fear prevalent among the Roma regarding efforts to keep them out of non-Romani areas, but also revealed a strategy that involved avoiding the formulation of specific anti-Gypsy attitudes. Čirčáňa claimed she herself had nothing against the Roma, though implied that the same could not be said of some of the other non-Romani villagers. Nevertheless, her sympathy for such attitudes was revealed later on in our conversation as she spoke of the ingrained inability of the Roma to "manage their finances" and keep their homes tidy. Her husband backed her up, adding a standard formulation that was clearly aimed also at the Jolany Roma: "One Rom buys a place and then the entire family moves in and suddenly the whole place is a settlement."[75]

I also had a conversation with mayoress Pišťáňa on the topic of the Roma and land in the village. She claimed the problem lay not in discrimination against the Roma but more in the unavailability of suitable land (in words highly reminiscent of the MNV). She added that vacant land tended to be divided amongst multiple owners, making any definitive settlement highly problematic, and that this was a contributory factor in the territorialisation of the Roma. She said the idea that there were buildings lying empty in the village was delusional. Though part of a building might be unoccupied, its owners had no intention of selling and had plans for it (e.g. to leave the property to their survivors, to spend their retirement in Jolany, etc.)[76]. Nevertheless, even within such a curated narrative Pišťáňa admitted the presence of anti-Gypsy attitudes, though claimed that these only began to appear in the village with the arrival of new non-Romani residents who had disrupted the harmony of local relations. In effect, she re-emphasised the distinction between "locals" and "outsiders", within which the Roma functioned as part of the local community and the "outsiders" were non-Romani newcomers who did not understand the locally

---

75 Interview with Čirčáňa (b. 1950) and her husband (b. 1948), conducted in Czech and Slovak, 12 June 2015.

76 Interview with Pišťáňa (b. 1953), conducted in Czech and Slovak, 3 July 2015.

formed concept of harmonious relations and thus sundered the accepted relationship between "our Roma" and "our *Gadže*".

However, as I have shown, all the non-Romani residents came together in the belief that the continued existence of a space symbolically separated from the village was primarily the result of entrenched differences (i.e. "backwardness") of the people living there and identifying as Roma/Gypsies. After Čirčáňa and her husband had spoken of the "natural" tendency of the Roma to cluster together and create settlements, Pišťáňa introduced another aspect of collective difference. In her patronising statement cited above, she attributed to the Roma a "historical negligence", the outcome of which was supposedly the lack of perseverance in achieving mobility outside the settlement. Hrickaninka, Pišťáňa's predecessor and successor in the post of mayoress, felt the problem was more a lack of funds. However, she too offered an idiosyncratic take: she acknowledged that, in a region with few job opportunities, where work was gained mainly through contacts, the Roma were in a marginalised position. Nevertheless, she felt they themselves were to blame, because "even when they find work, they stick it out for a couple of months and then beat it".[77]

Placing Gypsyness

However, the narrative of the Gypsies as passive recipients of outside aid, scroungers whose entrenched ideas prevent them from resolving their acute housing crisis, was far more often voiced by the Roma who now lived in their own homes in the village "amongst the *Gadže*" than by non-Romani villagers. This was so not only in interviews with me, but situationally in conversations with their non-Romani neighbours. Like the Roma in the Hungarian village referred to above, these Roma were involved in an ongoing attempt to persuade their non-Romani surroundings that they were not "'that kind of Gypsy', in the sense of 'a Gypsy who behaves like a Gypsy'" (Horváth 2012: 125).

It should be noted that at the time the council flats were being built, there were already three Romani families living in their own homes "amongst the *Gadže*". As we know, the first was the family of Maroš and Katarína, who inherited a house from Maroš's father Jozef (who built it on land he purchased in 1967, see above). The second was the family of

---

77   Interview with Hrickaninka (b. 1955), conducted in Czech and Slovak, 8 August 2016.

Miro and Pavlína (who were bought their house by Miro's father Lajoš in 1986, see above). That left one family, that of Maroš's cousin Churdo and his wife Linda, who moved into Jolany in 2004 from neighbouring Drevany. Churdo and Linda had already lived briefly in Jolany at the end of the 1980s, when Churdo, an employee of the State Forestry Administration, lived with his family in a house reserved for forestry workers situated at the edge of the village.[78] This building was privatised at the turn of the millennium and Churdo, as the current tenant, availed himself of the right to buy.

Inasmuch as the non-Romani villagers viewed the territorialisation of the Roma in the settlement as natural and attributed it to the entrenched mentality of its inhabitants, the Roma who lived "amongst the *Gadže*" played a significant role in the creation of this image and derived higher status for themselves from it. It was these Roma who were fond of pointing out that, had it not been for mayoress Pišťáňa, the "laziness" of the Roma in the settlement would have prevented them from ever acquiring new decent housing. When I presented the results of the research I had conducted in archives to my host Maroš, and drew his attention to the numerous applications submitted by the Jolany Roma for the allocation of building plots in the village, he was sceptical. He declared that the Roma in the settlement were "loafers" who "would in any case not have built anything"[79].

The Roma living "amongst the *Gadže*" used the interpretation of the council flats referred to above as a way of confirming their own superior status and setting themselves apart from the Roma of the settlement. It is clear that this distinction arose from the dominant logic of Gypsyness. In this respect it resembled the internal differentiation of the Roma in the little town of Tercov in southern Bohemia, where certain of the Roma accuse others of Gypsyness based on their belonging to a particular location in the town, specifically a different block of flats (Abu Ghosh 2008: 14–62).[80] In Jolany, too, there was an internal distinction made between those able to "live like the *Gadže*" and those who, through their Gypsyness, were stuck in the cultural backwaters of the stigmatised settlement.

What is interesting is that, leaving aside their position in the spatial layout of the village, there were no other "objective" differences between

---

78 This was the same building that offered temporary asylum to Roma affected by the floods of 1974.

79 Interview with Maroš (b. 1967), conducted in Romani, 15 August 2018.

80 For similar dynamics of differentiation of the Roma in individual villages in Slovakia see, for example, Grill (2015b) and Hrustič (2011, 2015a).

these families. Neither in Tercov nor in Jolany did these families differ in terms of wealth (all the Romani families were in debt regardless of where they lived). And although the Roma living "amongst the *Gadže*" sometimes remarked that the Roma in the council flats were crammed in "like Indians", the surface area of their respective abodes was in reality quite similar, and only in the case of two of the eight apartments was the number of people per household higher than in the highly populated households of Churdo and Maroš. Even the existing kinship ties intersected the spatial layout of the village, a fact admitted even by the Roma living "amongst the *Gadže*". Maroš and Churdo had a first cousin Peter in the settlement, while Katarína, who herself came originally from neighbouring Maslovce, had three sisters living there.

This distinction was not even reflected in the degree to which attempts were made to acquire better housing. When families living "amongst the *Gadže*" pointed out that the Roma in the settlement had "received free flats from the state", whereas they themselves had had to build their own, they wilfully ignored not only the participation of the Roma on the physical construction of the council flats, but also the circumstances by which they themselves came by their home. For instance, it seemed not to matter that Maroš simply inherited his house from his father, that Miro and Pavlína were able to buy their home thanks to state support for "liquidation of the Gypsy shacks", and that Churdo availed himself of his extremely advantageous position as existing tenant just as a right-to-buy policy was initiated as part of the fire sale of state assets. As in Tercov, in Jolany the relationship between "established" and "outsiders" (Elias 1994) did not depend on objective socio-economic factors, but on the ability of one Romani fraction to impose an image of Gypsyness on the Roma living in council flats. In the case of Jolany, the decisive factor was the shared, historically entrenched association of Gypsyness with the place that continued to be called the "settlement".

"Jolanian Roma": local, but stuck in a place

However, the category of place featured in the differentiation of the Jolany Roma in yet another way. Specifically it involved negotiating the very category of "Jolanian Roma" (*Jolaňakere Roma*). As I have already shown, this designation was to a certain extent associated with the ability of those so designated to adapt to a non-Romani way of life and to maintain good relations with the non-Romani villagers. The brothers

Martin and Fabián deployed the category in this way when applying to buy a house in a different village, and several Roma identified with it who no longer lived in Jolany. For instance, Robo and his brother Zoralo lived with their parents in one of the council flats in the settlement. Both with growing children, Robo decided to add an extension using wooden beams. However, the authorities in Jolany put a halt to construction work, and so Robo, his wife Stáňa and their two young children moved to neighbouring Maslovce. The Roma from Maslovce fell collectively into the category of "problematic Gypsies". In order to put a distance between himself and these Roma, Robo would occasionally add: "But I'm still at heart a Jolanian" (*Ale me som furt Jolaňakero!*).[81]

This logic, by which Robo lived in Maslovce but reminded listeners that "he is not from here" in order to demonstrate higher status, was at work in Jolany itself. The category of "Jolanian Roma" was ambivalent, as was the ambiguous belonging to the village of the residents thus designated. Though the "Jolanian Roma" enjoyed good relations with their non-Romani neighbours, their historically embedded belonging to the village and nestedness in the network of socio-economic relations was limited to a specific social position and a specific location within the geographical layout of the village. In this respect they found themselves naturally ranked within the subordinate positions of the racialised hierarchy.

In order to reinforce their relatively higher social status and demonstrate a more meaningful belonging to the village, even those Roma who lived "amongst the *Gadže*" would paradoxically remind their listeners that "they were not from here" and situationally exclude themselves from the category of "Jolanian Roma". In this respect belonging to a particular place was linked to an emphasis on aspects of kinship. In these circumstances the cousins Churdo and Maroš identified with the lineage (*fajta*) of the Slivany blacksmith Vasiľ (see the story of his son Jozef above), grandfather of both (the father of their fathers), when they proclaimed themselves "Slivanian Roma" (*sliveňakere Roma*). The third family that managed to acquire housing "amongst the *Gadže*" was that of Miro and

81 It is worth adding that in Maslovce itself the differentiation of Roma took place on the basis of their location in the geographical layout of the village. There were two places in which the Roma lived. The first was among non-Romani villagers and was called the "housing estate" (*sídlisko*), where higher status Roma lived, including the family of Robo and Stáňa. The second was known as the "dump" (*smetisko*) and was around five hundred meters from the village. The inhabitants of this location were deemed "problematic" and "backward Gypsies".

Pavlína. In a conversation with me Pavlína recalled that, when she married into Jolany, the Roma were crammed into the settlement "like sardines in a tin", and that she herself, who had grown up in a brick house, had, she claimed, persuaded her husband (already deceased during the period of my research) to move out of the settlement[82].

And so although these Roma often identified with the category "Jolanian Roma", their situational identification with categories anchored in other places demonstrated how remaining in a particular place was associated with a certain cultural and socio-economic stagnation and that upward social mobility was linked to spatial mobility (cf. Grill 2012). Although a relatively higher status was asserted within the social space of Jolany, it could in certain respects be demonstrated via links to places outside. As Grill shows and as I shall demonstrate in Chapter Four, this was not only about drawing attention to belonging to another place in the region where Roma were supposedly used to living more "like the *Gadže* / amongst the *Gadže*", but to the entire phenomenon of migration (ibid.).

One might summarise the internal differentiation of the Jolany Roma thus: the Roma living "amongst the *Gadže*", though they disrupted the existing territorial boundary, did not disrupt the positionality of Gypsyness associated with a particular place, given that their mobility was framed by a recognised shift to a non-Romani way of life (which itself could be explained by means of a connection to a place outside Jolany).

In the end, even Jozef's story (see above), often recalled by the locals, was not that of the seismic disruption of non-Romani dominance that would open the way for other Roma from the settlement, but, on the contrary, the story of an individual who by all accounts stood out from other Roma by virtue of his activities, contacts with other non-Roma in the area (from Slivany), and more generally his "*Gadžo* customs", and after whose incursion into the village the territorial boundary was reclosed for a long time. At the end of the 1960s, this was to a certain extent visible in the actions of representatives of the local committee (MNV), when in their list of "citizens of Gypsy origin" who could be counted upon to move to the Bohemian part of the country, Jozef's family, by that time already living in the village, was the only one missing, i.e. already not considered "proper Gypsies" (cf. Sokolová 2008). Similarly, when I was living in Jolany it was not true that the Roma all without exception lived in the settlement. However, the idea was maintained that Gypsyness was

82   Interview with Pavlína (b. 1958), conducted in Romani, 1 June 2015.

situated in the settlement. This logic was even reproduced by the authors of the Atlas of Romani Communities, who focused mainly on Roma living in "concentrations" and did not record the Romani families living in Jolany outside the settlement.[83]

"Amongst the *Gadže*": confirming Gypsyness

Although these Roma could escape the registration of Roma in Slovakia carried out for the needs of the state thanks to their positionality outside the settlement, in Jolany itself they were easily identifiable as Roma and therefore as Gypsies. And though they enjoyed a higher status than the Roma in the settlement, they too came face to face with non-Romani dominance, which was reflected, as we have seen, in the housing sector. The ever-increasing number of people living in these Romani households was in sharp contrast with non-Romani households, from which young families tended to migrate to towns and cities on a permanent basis. Even newly established families of young Roma living with their parents outside the settlement faced the challenge of finding new housing and to a large extent encountered the same obstacles as young Romani families (or any other Romani families) from the council flats.

Unlike the space of the settlement, where the occupant capacity was basically preserved, ownership of the land in the village allowed for extensions to the original brick houses. Vašo, son of Miro and Pavlína, who lived "amongst the *Gadže*", built a home from breeze blocks for his family on the same plot of land right next to his parents' house. His house remained without any facade for the duration of my stay in Jolany. In the courtyard of the home owned by Maroš and Katarína, i.e. on land originally purchased by Maroš's father Jozef, no fewer than three wooden buildings were built over time. The first was put up by Jozef at the end of the 1980s for the family of his youngest son Maroš. When both of Maroš's parents died at the end of the 1990s, Maroš and Katarína moved into the original brick house and gradually moved the family of one of their three sons into the wooden building. Maroš then added an annex to the same building in which his older brother lived to the end of his life and where I lived while conducting my research. When Stano, the

---

83 The problems of this data collection methodology were referred to by the authors of the Atlas (Mušinka 2019).

youngest son, followed in the footsteps of his older brothers Vlado and Tomáš and started a family, Maroš decided to build yet another wooden building in the courtyard, which he completed at the end of 2018.

As one might expect, such developments only served to confirm the non-Romani villagers in their belief that "when one Rom buys a place, suddenly the whole place is a settlement". The result was that, on the one hand the Roma living "amongst the *Gadže*" confirmed the territorial stigmatisation of the settlement by defining themselves in opposition to the people living in it, while on the other, through their own practice, they provided empirical proof of the argument that the creation of the settlements had been an inherent part of Gypsyness, an argument deployed by the non-Romani villagers to justify efforts to keep the Roma outside the non-Romani part of the village.

Indeed, the story of these families was a signal not only for the non-Romani villagers, but for the Roma living in the settlement too, who eventually conceded that the efforts on the part of the non-Roma to keep the Roma out of the non-Romani part of the village were justified. When Zoralo and Jana went to ask about the possibility of buying a specific building plot in the village (they were at that time living in a council flat in the settlement), the owner refused to sell. Jana said that the reason given was the way of life of those Roma who were already living in the non-Romani part of the village. What is remarkable is that Zoralo and Jana did not blame the non-Romani villager for their failure to acquire a building plot, but rather the Romani families living in the village. When Zoralo was trying to persuade me why this was so, he cited the example of a Romani family that had moved out of Jolany in the 1980s to a neighbouring village, where at the time of my research they were the only Romani family:

> What pigs! You know how they should live there? Among so many *Gadže*? The odd jobs there are there to be done. How much they could earn. They would always have money. A garden, everything… They could raise animals, grow vegetables… They're useless, all they know his how to play the slot machines and booze! And now tell me, is that the fault of the *Gadže* or the Roma? Surely of the Roma![84]

Similarly, the way that the brothers Fabián and Martin accepted that the mayor of a nearby village did not want to sell a building to the Roma does

---

84   Interview with Zoralo (b. 1987), conducted in Romani, 11 May 2015.

not have to be interpreted as an accusation of racism, but as a resigned shrug of the shoulders in response to his (unexpressed) acceptable attitude. Non-conflictual ("harmonious") relationships that at the same time, as I have shown above, helped to preserve non-Romani dominance, were maintained not only because concrete manifestations of anti-Gypsy prejudice were difficult to pin down, but also because the Roma themselves had a certain understanding, even sympathy, for these very prejudices.

Creating a safe space

It remains to describe what dilemmas the Roma living "amongst the *Gadže*" spoke of when resolving their housing needs in light of these developments. Maroš and Katarína began to look into the possibility of new accommodation for their sons at the start of 2015, when Stano, their youngest, became a father. During one discussion Katarína indirectly drew attention to the threat of social stigmatisation: "They can't all remain in one yard. The children will grow up and it will be like a new settlement here!" Maroš saw things differently: "So what? At least we won't be depressed. As soon as they can, they'll leave. If not, they'll stay. Are you suggesting I throw them out?"[85] It is clear from what has been said above, that Maroš and Katarína, faced with the decision of whether to create a safe space for their family at the risk of attracting the stigma of "yet another settlement", decided unequivocally in favour, and less than four years later another wooden house (by now the third) stood in their yard. The number of people living in the yard rose to nineteen (two of Maroš's sons had four children, and the third had three). Katarína's fears were to an extent realised and people in the village started to mutter that a "second settlement" had grown up "at Maroš's". Unlike Churdo, who lived in his own house "amongst the *Gadže*" and who by his own admission had thrown his sons out when they started looking for the materials to build their own homes on his land, Maroš did not mind the presence of all of his sons and grandchildren in the same grounds.

Maroš did not support his sons' endeavours to find their own accommodation and repeated that he was happy to have the family together. Both he and Katarína recalled how, when they were living alone with the children in a brick house, they would pay long visits to what were still at

---

85 Interview with Maroš (b. 1967) and Katarína (b. 1967), conducted in Romani, 27 January 2015.

that time the wooden shacks in the settlement, because life "amongst the *Gadže*" could be boring. Furthermore, the presence of the entire family in the "one yard" had economic advantages in addition to the social security it offered. The family budget, which was largely shared, allowed for flexibility in financial management, and the presence of four adult men in a single place represented a sought-after work unit that Maroš, with his natural authority, was able to mobilise swiftly for odd jobs provided to the non-Roma living nearby. In this respect, Maroš was less concerned by the stigma of a "second settlement" than by how the "yard" would operate without his authority after he died. Looked at from this angle, the creation of a common space for an expanding family did not necessarily have to be a sign of helplessness in the face of non-Romani territorial domination, but can be seen as an active strategy reacting to existing socio-economic relations, and more specifically neighbourly or family relations.

The settlement: discontinuity of material conditions

However, Maroš's middle son Tomáš and his wife Helena took a somewhat different view of the situation in the yard. This created a certain tension, with different visions and strategies predominating across different generations. Tomáš respected his father, but as he confided in me several times, he wanted to "strike out on his own". He and Helena had to an extent managed this by splitting the budget. However, what they desired was complete independence, and while I was living in Jolany were forever on the lookout for new housing.

During a conversation we had in summer of 2018, Helena confided to me that after several unsuccessful attempts to buy a building plot or a new house, she and Tomáš had applied for one of the council flats in the Jolany settlement. She explained that several families in the flats were in arrears with their rent and that there was a real threat of eviction. When I asked cautiously how this fitted into the overall scheme to escape the settlement for good, she replied that there were already too many people in one space where they were living with Tomáš's parents and his brother's families and that it was becoming difficult taking turns with only one bathroom, which was in the original brick house. In the council flats they would have their own bathroom and WC[86].

---

86 Interview with Helena (b. 1985), conducted in Romani, 13 August 2018.

The surprise I felt was indicative of the extent to which I had become overly focused on following the mobility of Roma outside the settlement and how I had allowed the stories of the residents of the council flats, who were displaying no signs of moving in this direction, to take a back seat. For the same reason I had initially overlooked the story of Kalo. At the time of my research, Kalo was living in a council flat (i.e. in the settlement) with his wife, three children and sick mother. In addition, however, he owned a brick house with a garden located in close proximity to the properties of the non-Roma directly opposite the settlement. Kalo inherited the house from Moldas, the brother of his mother who, though born in Jolany, had spent most of his life in the Bohemian lands. At the start of the new millennium, Moldas decided he would like to retire to his native Jolany, and in 2012 he bought a house and garden from a non-Romani villager who had some time previously moved to Svidník. However, Moldas died suddenly in the very same year without having moved into his new house. His daughters, who had lived their entire lives in the Czech Republic, had no interest in the house whatsoever, and so it became Kalo's. Interestingly, when I began my research in 2014, Kalo was not planning to move into his own house. He used only the garage for his car and the shed for firewood, and even spoke of selling the property. The problem was the house needed refurbishing from top to bottom, and Kalo lacked the wherewithal. A relatively small council flat in the settlement represented more pleasant accommodation than a house with a garden that was a completely unfurnished husk.

These stories show that, despite the ongoing territorial stigmatisation associated with the council flats in Jolany, they were in many cases the most acceptable form of accommodation for local Roma. In the case of the families of Kalo and Tomáš this choice was not necessarily linked with the social security of the Romani settlement (cf. Skupnik 2007), but paradoxically with its material side. I say paradoxically, because for a long time it was the original settlement that was associated with unhygienic, poor quality accommodation, as evidenced by the many applications submitted by the Roma for building plots in the village. However, the construction of the council flats lifted this association and offered better material security in comparison with living "amongst the *Gadže*", something Kalo and Tomáš could both have done if they wanted. For Tomáš and Helena, a council flat represented the fulfilment of their dream to have full control over their own household.

In the end the stories of these families were to change course significantly. Given the unavailability of other housing, Tomáš returned to the space that, more than fifty years earlier at the end of the 1960s, his grandfather Jozef had famously left. Tomáš and Helena were finally successful in acquiring a council flat, thanks to Kalo. In 2018, he had found a long-term job and managed to save up enough to refurbish the brick house completely, meaning the next year he was able to move in. Tomáš and Helena moved into the council flat Kalo had left vacant in June of 2020. They were full of praise for their new habitation and told me "they had everything they needed" in their council flat.

Beyond territorial stigmatisation

While Maroš's indifference to the stigma that might be caused by the increased concentration of residents in one backyard could be seen as reflecting his relatively strong ties to the non-Roma in the area, the "return" of his son Tomáš and family to the space of the settlement raised the question of to what extent the residents of Jolany genuinely shared the principle of territorial stigmatisation. In the case of the Roma living in the settlement it is clear that a certain acceptance of territorial stigmatisation at the time of my research did not necessarily lead to a denial of belonging to the place thus stigmatised, as Wacquant assumes (2007, cf. Jensen and Christensen 2012).

Sixty-year-old Peter, who lived in one of the council flats, presented a counter-narrative to the dominant logic of the territorialisation of the Roma in the settlement when recounting the history of the place:

> Look, the thing is the Roma are and always have been grifters. They didn't want one to be here and another one there. They wanted to be together, together forever. [...] So the apartment blocks suit them down to the ground. Everything is within reach. The House of Culture, the shop, pub, everything is within spitting distance. We live in the middle of the village and that's all there is to it. [...] [Under socialism] [t]hey wanted the Roma to build for themselves. And bear in mind that everyone had a job, everyone went to work. And so it wasn't a problem to take out a loan and build a house. But the Roma were crafty. Nobody took out a loan and yet we still have homes. The Roma run rings around the *Gadže*.[87]

87　Interview with Peter (b. 1953), conducted in Romani, 2 June 2015.

What Peter omitted to say was that in 1988 he himself was one of the unsuccessful applicants for a building plot in the village. He also kept quiet about the fact that his son Zoralo, who lived in the same household, was one of the Jolany Roma who had actively attempted to find accommodation outside the settlement, and that Robo, his other son, had had to move with his family to nearby Maslovce due to lack of space and the unavailability of alternative accommodation. In contrast, Peter accepted the prevailing idea of the tendency of the Roma to form concentrated settlements. However, he reworked the implicit category of "Jolanian Roma" into a currency, using which the Roma retained a central position in the residential structure of the village and even "run rings around the *Gadže*" by acquiring homes "without having to take out a loan".

Though Peter's narratives were not backed up by the statements of the other Jolany Roma, they did make some interesting points that introduced an element of doubt into the logic of territorial stigmatisation. Firstly, Peter drew attention to the preservation of the central position of the settlement in the layout of the village, which was very unusual compared to other segregated Romani settlements in eastern Slovakia. As Peter himself implied, the maintenance of such a position for the settlement could be seen as a sign of Romani resistance to sporadic proposals for their wholesale displacement to the Bohemian lands (in the 1960s), attempts to relocate individual families to surrounding villages (e.g. after the flooding of the 1970s), and repeated proposals for the construction of detached houses for the Roma on the outskirts of the village. (Under a plan dating back to the beginning of the 1960s, for instance, the Roma would have remained separated from the village by the main road from Svidník to Poland.) Looked at from this angle, although the "Jolanian Roma" (as Peter described them) remained associated with the local settlement, they could boast of an ongoing continuity of belonging to the village by virtue of having lived in it and retained their position in the geographical layout.

Another point raised by Peter concerned the construction of the council flats. We should not forget that despite confirmation of the stigmatisation of the settlement and the substandard quality of the flats, the very fact that they were built represented undeniable progress that many of their residents spoke highly of in conversation with me. Furthermore, it was the newly built council flats that gave rise to the media image of "harmonious coexistence" in the village and thus the "civilised character" of the local Roma. The newspaper report already cited claimed the area around the flats was "beautifully clean and tidy" and that "there were even northern white cedar trees growing in front of the flats". It is perfectly clear that the contours of such a narrative again arose from shared prejudices regarding the Gypsies, who supposedly lived in squalor and who would immediately destroy any apartments provided them by the state.[88] However, it again shows that the "civilised character" of the local Roma, and thus their embeddedness in the local (non-Romani) way of life, could be viewed from the dominant perspective not as being in direct contradiction with life in the settlement, but as the embodiment of its concrete form (i.e. its cleanliness, the northern white cedar trees etc.).

Finally, in the light of Peter's claims and the stories of the families of Kalo and Tomáš, it is time to examine the diverse attitudes of the council flat residents to the settlement, without necessarily contradicting its stigmatisation (cf. Pattillo 2009). I must admit that in the past I, too, through my focus on the efforts made by the Roma to move out of the settlement (cf. Ort 2017), failed to analyse the attitudes of those Roma who believe, in Tomáš's words, that "they have everything they need" in the council flats and who have not formulated a negative relationship to place (cf. Jensen and Christensen 2012). The materials held in archives must also be taken with a pinch of salt. Though they document the ongoing efforts of the Jolany Roma to be allocated a building plot in the village, in the vast majority of cases (leaving aside the collective letter to the Office of the President of the Republic) these were individual applicants who were active to varying degrees in this regard. We do not know the opinions of representatives of those families who did not submit applications (and according to the regular lists of "Gypsy residents" such families existed), just as we know little of how the women felt who came to Jolany from other villages, often from a different economic and social background.

These reflections should clearly not lead to a complete relativisation of the stigmatisation of the Jolany settlement. Rather, they are a reminder of the importance of monitoring the degree of stigmatisation, the specific contexts in which stigmatisation is negotiated, and the diversity of attitudes and social practice of individual actors.

---

88 This was also the argument for lowering the standard of apartments during their planned construction in the Romani settlements in Slovakia (see Hojsík 2008).

Conclusion

When examining the relationship between place and identity of the Roma, the anthropologist Theodosiou observes that the concept of place in ethnographic studies is often an "invisible category of analysis" side-stepped by authors in an attempt to avoid an essentialising understanding of the unity of place, culture and identity (Gupta and Ferguson 1992), i.e. in an effort to leave behind ideas of the "origin of the Roma" or to avoid the necessity to deal with their supposed nomadism (Theodosiou 2004). In fact, the research she conducted in a Greek village called Parakalamos on the border with Albania showed that it was precisely belonging to a particular place and not the distinctive features of a self-contained culture (cf. Stewart 1997, Gay y Blasco 1999) that was key to identifying the local Roma (*Yifti*). Neither the fact that they had settled permanently in Parakalamos nor the change of name and religious conversion associated with the broader process of Greek nationalism represented an interruption of the continuity of their own identity, but rather its confirmation through their remaining in a particular place (ibid.).

Several authors think about place in a similar way within Slovakia. In research conducted in Brzotín in south-eastern Slovakia, Sadílková showed that the local Roma, who had been historically territorialised in a Romani settlement (that was repeatedly relocated by the local authority), underline their belonging to the village, and that this is reflected in their attempts to move toward the physical centre of the village (Sadílková 2017). With regard to Veľký Šariš, another village in eastern Slovakia, Scheffel shows how the Roma managed to acquire the status of "autochthons", which historically guaranteed them the right to remain in the village (Scheffel 2015). By tracking the historical development of the position of the Roma within the geographical layout of specific villages, these studies demonstrate what Theodosiou discusses from another perspective, namely that Romani belonging to place is not a simple given, but has to be negotiated by individual actors in a particular way.

By examining a similar historical negotiation I have shown how the Jolany Roma, similar to those of Brzotín and Veľký Šariš, displayed a firm determination to remain in the village and in many cases were resistant to proposals for their displacement beyond its boundaries or to its outskirts. However, their attempts at confirming their local belonging and material progress in respect of housing by means of mobility outside the settlement came up against the historically embedded territorial boundary that divided the settlement from that part of the village naturally perceived to be "non-Romani". Similarly to Sadílková, I argue that in this respect the interests of the Roma might coincide with the central policy of "liquidation of the Gypsy settlements" (Sadílková 2017), in that they come face to face with non-Romani territorial hegemony and the reluctance of the local authorities to deterritorialise the Romani settlement (Guy 1998 [1975]).

Although some Romani families managed to cross the territorial boundary between the Romani settlement and the non-Romani part of the village, their mobility was viewed as representing a shift towards a *Gadžo* way of life and continued to reinforce the logic of Gypsyness and its association with a specific space in the village. The category of Gypsyness thus territorialised led to an ongoing internal differentiation between the Roma themselves. Though this distinction between "established" and "outsiders" was formulated as representing a fundamental difference in the "quality of humanity", leaving aside a person's position in the geographical layout of the village there were no other socio-economic indicators that might have distinguished families along these lines (cf. Elias 1994, Abu Ghosh 2008). Although families living "amongst the *Gadže*" claimed that their status had been won through the logic of meritocracy, their success in acquiring their own housing was less to do with perseverance and individual effort than a certain social capital and a measure of serendipity.

The interpretation of the existence of the settlement through the category Gypsyness was largely shared even by its inhabitants. Even in their case, the culturalist explanation largely overlapped with the aspect of non-Romani (territorial) dominance. This was partly because its concrete manifestations remained hidden, both in the communications put out by the authorities, and in the statements of non-Romani villagers. In light of the practice of "not naming Gypsyness" that I described in Chapter One, it was difficult for the Roma living in the settlement to confront such manifestations. Moreover, even when they were able to put a name to specific anti-Gypsy attitudes, they exhibited a great deal of understanding for them, not only referring to "problematic Gypsies" in the area (or featured in television news stories), but also to the way of life of those Romani families living in Jolany "amongst the *Gadže*". The culturalist explanation of the existence of the settlement in the end led its inhabitants themselves to what Belák calls a "Romani ideology of self-exclusion", according to which the Roma are "simply unable to live like the *Gadže*" (Belák et al. 2018). And it was this self-blame that

Wacquant describes as part of the principle of territorial stigmatisation (Wacquant 2007).

By deploying Wacquant's concept of "territorial stigmatisation" I was able to show in this chapter how the category of Gypsyness was territorialised in Jolany, as well as how the place thus stigmatised participated in the structuring of local relationships. Wacquant himself pointed out that when reflecting upon not only territorial stigmatisation but more broadly upon racialised relationships, it is essential to take into account the specific social context in which these phenomena are instantiated (e.g. Wacquant 1993). The dynamic of territorial stigmatisation is understandably different in the more anonymous urban environments[89] researched by Wacquant from that in the highly de-anonymised environment of a small village, where everyone knows exactly who is and is not Rom (Horváth 2012) and who lives where.

Therefore, in order not to view the Roma as a homogenous racialised object, we should note that although relationships in Jolany were partially based on the logic of the stigmatisation of the settlement given its association with the category of Gypsyness, this category did not necessarily represent the sole determinant of the related social practice. In the context of eastern Slovakia, home to a large number of highly segregated Romani settlements (Mušinka et al. 2019, cf. Scheffel 2005), one can view the maintenance of the central position of the settlement in Jolany not only as a manifestation of non-Romani dominance, but also as a manifestation of the resistance of the Roma themselves and the outcome of their ongoing efforts to maintain a certain position in the village.

Finally, in this chapter I took seriously the appeal to respect the diversity of responses to the territorial stigmatisation amongst individual residents that Pattillo (2009) makes in her polemic with Wacquant. Drawing on the life trajectory of specific families and individuals I was able to show that, under certain circumstances, accommodation in the settlement was in fact the preferred option. This was largely (but not only) due to the fact that the construction of the council flats, notwithstanding their inferior quality, removed the historically entrenched association of the grounds of the settlement with material and hygienic deprivation.

When Theodosiou included the category of place in her analysis of the formation of the identity of the Roma, she did not regard it as an abstract element but as a category with definite contours. Similarly, we

---

89 Wacquant conducted his research in Chicago, the USA, and Paris, France.

must not view the Roma in Jolany as "newcomers" attempting to put down roots, but as an inherent feature of both the place and the "local system" (cf. Olivera 2012). In the next chapter, therefore, I will shift the focus of my attention away from the Roma's belonging to place and look instead at what specific form this place took. I shall do this by means of an analysis of its socio-linguistic situation.

Chapter Three
Language of the "Rusyn Roma"

During the first few months of my research I established a close relationship with Zoralo, who was around three years older than me (he was 26 at the start of my research) and lived with his wife Jana, son Samík, and parents Peter and Šuki in one of the council flats. Zoralo and Jana were among those who had actively sought housing outside the settlement. They were the only council flat tenants who adapted their language policy to the goal of attaining socio-economic mobility (in its dominant logic). They had therefore decided that Samík their son and the two daughters Jana gave birth to over the next few years would not have Romani as their first language, as was customary among the Jolany Roma, but Slovak. They did this so as to ensure their children were best placed in the education system and in a predominantly Slovak language society. They felt sure that their children would pick up Romani from their Romani peers. However, in addition their children were to learn Rusyn, the primary language of their non-Romani neighbours.

Zoralo and Jana, along with certain other Roma in Jolany, associated the Romani language with restricted domains of language use, specifically with inter-Roma communication. They were all the more surprised, therefore, when at the end of summer 2018 lady mayoress Hrickaninka proposed adding another sign to the official Slovak sign that hung on the building of the local authorities, this one in Romani. The mayoress went ahead with this plan despite the confusion of the local Roma. However, both the Roma and non-Roma viewed this move as a cheap political gesture before the upcoming municipal elections.

On election day itself, another text in Romani appeared on the notice board of the local authorities headed Information for Voters (Informaciji pedal o voličos). *The text was part of a wider campaign initiated by the Office of the Government to encourage the Roma to vote. On election day Zoralo took a photo of the text and sent it to me via Facebook. From a linguistic point of view there had clearly been an effort made to replace easily recognisable Slovak idioms with Romani neologisms. This in itself could be seen as the outcome of centrally managed Romani language planning (an attempt at purification being one of its manifestations). In his commentary on the text Zoralo took aim at precisely this aspect:*

> *Given that the* Gadže *are always saying that the Roma should adapt, then why is this allowed? In my opinion this will divide us. After all, I understand the Slovak version more easily than I do the Romani. Why didn't they write it in the kind of Romani we speak here [in Jolany]? And why didn't they write it in Rusyn? I mean, there are plenty of Rusyns here, aren't there?[90]*

In response to the question as to why they had not written the notice in Rusyn, I sent Zoralo the mayoress's explanation, which she had offered me in answer to a similar question regarding the Romani sign above the municipal office. According to her the number of Rusyns recorded in the most recent census had not reached the required percentage of the overall population that would ensure the language appeared on the notice board (which according to the information available from the census was not true). Zoralo was not impressed: "Ok, so if there is a Romani community in the village, how come she doesn't speak Romani with us when we visit her office?"[91]

These comments, as well as the confusion of the other Jolany Roma, demonstrate how centrally planned initiatives aimed at supporting the Romani language find themselves in conflict with its locally contextualised use. The Jolany Roma were not used to associating Romani with the discourse of officialdom, and its appearance grated on them.

Looked at from a broader perspective, however, Zoralo's reaction highlighted another point, namely, that the use of certain languages was strongly linked to the social hierarchy of the multilingual community of a given place, and that through a competence in individual languages, it was possible to negotiate ideas linked to certain types of categorisation of the inhabitants of Jolany. Slovak was the language of education and associated by the residents of Jolany with a certain prestige and socio-economic mobility on a society-wide level. This was another reason Zoralo and Jana decided it would be their children's first language. In contrast, Rusyn symbolised the specific culture of a particular place, which explains why Zoralo was surprised that the signs were not written in Rusyn, but

---

90   Internet chat with Zoralo (b. 1987), in Romani, 10 November 2018.
91   Ibid.

in Romani. Romani itself was strongly associated with the category of Roma/
Gypsies. However, as Zoralo indicated in his observation regarding the compre-
hensibility of the text on the notice board of the municipal office, Romani too had
its local form.

This brief excursion into the languages spoken locally is the starting point for
this chapter, in which we move from an identification of the Roma with a specific
place to the specific characteristics of said place.

The Romani language in Slovakia

Looking at the broader historical context of language policies in relation
to the Roma in the territory of what is today Slovakia, it is clear that
the question of language has received almost no attention whatsoever
in comparison to that of housing (and "undesirable Gypsy concentrations"). The communist regime deemed the "Gypsy language" to be one
of the features of a "Gypsy way of life", and its use was therefore not to
be supported within the logic of the policy of assimilation. The ideolog-
ical commission of the Communist Party of Czechoslovakia considered
it desirable to offer a grounding in the basics of the Gypsy language as
a tool for those who came into contact with Gypsies at work, e.g. police-
men and teachers. Nevertheless, however this was achieved (e.g. through
written grammar lists of textbooks) it was not to lead to the "erroneous"
idea that Romani was an independent language and potential stepping
stone to other cultural rights (Donert 2017: 149–151).

After the Velvet Revolution of 1989, Romani nationality was officially
recognised in Czechoslovakia and the Romani language acquired the
official status of a minority language. There was already a substructure
on which to base specific activities aimed at promoting Romani, especially the work of the language commission of the Gypsy-Roma Union
(active from 1969 to 1973, see Závodská 2021), which was responsible
for the first standardisation of Romani in the former Czechoslovakia
(Červenka 2014, Hübschmannová 2000a) and the introduction of the
language into literature (Hübschmannová 2000a, Závodská 2021). As far
back as 1992–1994, the Ministry of Education had approved a Romani
language and literature curriculum, which made it possible to teach it
in schools in Slovakia (Gažovičová 2015: 20). In practice, however, this
only took place on a local level thanks to the activities of individuals and
particular groups with a significant representation of Romani speakers
(see, for example, Sadílková 2019a).

The spread of Romani into new language domains was subsequently supported by a bespoke legal framework, namely the enactment of the National Minorities Languages Act in 1999 (Sloboda et al. 2018) and ratification of the European Charter for Regional or Minority Languages in 2001 (see Halwachs 2020: 447–450, Halwachs et al. 2013). Since the adoption of the European Charter, other activities have taken place in the sphere of Romani language planning in Slovakia, including the experimental teaching of Romani at some secondary schools. The activities of Romani intellectuals in this sphere culminated in a second, more systematic standardisation of Romani in Slovakia in 2008 (Červenka 2014).

Although a centralised pressure to abandon one's native language in favour of the dominant language was associated primarily with the assimilation policy of socialist Czechoslovakia (Hübschmannová 2000a), in everyday use Romani continued to be seen partly as an inadequate and stigmatised language, even in the new political climate that followed the events of 1989. For example, Gažovičová described the ongoing status of Romani as a stigmatised language code to be a key obstacle to the introduction of Romani as an educational language in Slovakia (2015).[92] As the introductory vignette to this chapter shows, some of the activities related to the expansion of Romani into new language domains even caused embarrassment among the Roma in Jolany (as well as their non-Romani neighbours). Of course, one cannot pass sweeping judgement on the form of language planning in respect of the Romani language in Slovakia on the basis of two somewhat marginal examples from Jolany. In addition, as I indicated above, many of the activities aimed at supporting the use of Romani were not top-down policies formulated by a centre wholly ignorant of the peripheral context, but often originated in bottom-up local initiatives. For example, Sadílková notes that the situation in Slovakia vis-à-vis attempts to introduce Romani into schools is unique within a European context by virtue of the long-term and relatively widespread support such attempts received from many Roma themselves (Sadílková 2019b). In this chapter I will address language planning only tangentially and will not explore the complexity of the entire debate it has provoked. However, a detailed overview of the

---

92 The continuum of the stigmatised position of Romani has been described on many occasions in different places by Hübschmannová (1999, 2000a). However, it was with a degree of optimism that she looked to the new political order, in which Romani emancipation was born and in which "many Roma found themselves awakening from a bad dream in which they had rejected their own language" (1999: 12).

language situation and its manifestation in a particular region would undoubtedly provide ample material for a follow-up study.

Shifting our attention to the everyday use of Romani, mention should be made of its dialectological classification, since historically speaking individual Romani dialects have been associated with the internal classification of the Roma themselves in Slovakia. At the same time, the speakers of these dialects have found themselves occupying different socio-linguistic roles in particular places. The majority of the Roma in what is today Slovakia (and also the Czech Republic due to post-war migration) are speakers of what are referred to as the "Central"[93] dialects, which are further broken down into South Central Romani (or SCR, influenced strongly by Hungarian) and North Central Romani (or NCR, influenced by Slovak and its dialects). In some areas, however, there has historically been a language shift to non-Romani contact languages. A significant minority of the Roma in Slovakia were speakers of Vlach dialects, who defined their cultural identity in greater contrast to the surrounding non-Romani world while exhibiting a high level of "groupism" (Brubaker 2002). This was largely derived from their distinctive language code (Hajská 2015), which, unlike Central dialects (especially western and central Slovakian), remained full of vitality within the context of its intergenerational transmission (Elšík 2003).

Though they themselves did not use this dialectological classification, the Jolany Roma were ranked amongst speakers of the North Central Romani dialect. As in several other villages in eastern Slovakia, the Romani spoken in Jolany was full of vitality, even though it was heavily imprinted with the dialects of Slovak and above all the local form of Rusyn. The following description of Romani will relate to the predominantly North Central dialects of Slovakia, unless stated otherwise.

The everyday use of Romani in post-war Czechoslovakia was anchored in a traditionally "diglossic situation" (Ferguson 1959, Fishman 1967), in which bilingual speakers use two languages of unequal prestige in different language domains. This was how its use in eastern Slovak rural communities was concretised by Hübschmannová (1979), according to

---

93 As Elšík (2003: 43) points out, this term is not used by Romani speakers themselves and is rooted in the broader linguistic terminology of Romani dialects in the world (see Matras 2002: 5–13; Elšík and Beníšek 2020). The dialectological classification converges only partly with the (self)categories of the Roma. In other words, the categorisation of the Roma can be implemented in different ways on the local level depending on differences in dialect (Elšík 2003: 45–46).

whom Romani was a less prestigious language code restricted to the "private sphere", i.e. for inter-Roma communication. On the other hand, Slovak (or Hungarian or Rusyn) was used by the Roma as a prestigious language code when communicating in the non-Romani part of the village and non-Romani environments in general (even when talking amongst themselves). Hübschmannová's students Pavel Kubaník, Jan Červenka and Helena Sadílková continued their teacher's study of the everyday use of Romani, but focused on the vitality of the language amongst other generations of the Roma who came from Slovakia to the Bohemian lands (Kubaník et al. 2013). As far as Slovakia itself is concerned, Kubaník conducted long-term research into linguistic socialisation amongst the Roma in a specific village in eastern Slovakia (2015, 2017).

Drawing on research in other Slovak villages, Pinter (2011) and Hajská (2015) developed the concept of diglossia. Both authors observed that Romani functioned as a strong marker of group identity in the language communities under examination, and, in contrast to a somewhat fixed concept of linguistic prestige, emphasised its situational contingency with regard to the dynamics of the linguistic attitudes of specific speakers. They pointed to the multilingual character of the villages where they conducted their research as evidence of the possible heterogeneity of the communities in which Romani was to be found in Slovakia. While Pinter observed a community in which Hungarian coexisted alongside Romani and Slovak, Hajská showed that the distinction between two Romani dialects was key to maintaining a historically grounded, internal categorisation amongst the Roma throughout the whole of the region she monitored.

The specificity of the language situation in Jolany resided in the fact that, despite its small population, it was a multilingual community involving several language codes deployed on a daily basis, which included official Slovak, Rusyn, Romani, as well as several local dialects (or varieties) of Slovak. In this chapter I shall focus on language ideologies and concrete linguistic practice. I shall track how the Jolany Roma reflected upon and demonstrated through language their social belonging at various levels, including their belonging to a specific place. I shall show that, although the Jolany Roma were strongly associated with Romani, it was not one distinctive language that was central to their identity so much as an ability to combine individual languages in different social contexts. Similarly, the category of Gypsyness was not only signalled by Romani, but also by a specific (in)competence in other languages. On the other hand, I will show that Romani was not regarded simply as a distinctive characteristic that singled out the Roma within a given place, but, in its specifically linguistic form, as a characteristic by means of which they understood themselves and were in turn understood as being part of said place.

Language acquisition in Jolany

The situation in Jolany was unusual in that three main languages (or its varieties) were used on an everyday basis in the mutual communication that took place within a relatively small population. Before proceeding to a more detailed analysis of the way these languages were used, I shall define their position within the multilingual community under examination. Slovak was the official language and was spoken by all the residents, who came into contact with it at school (lessons in Drevany were taught in official standard Slovak), in the media, and in communication with the authorities. Rusyn was the native language of the Jolany non-Roma and, in its capacity as the locally dominant language, had also been adopted by their Romani neighbours. In contrast, Romani remained primarily a language for the purpose of communication amongst the Roma themselves, and the Jolany non-Roma seldom displayed any knowledge of it. In order to understand more deeply the hierarchisation of these three languages and to address the question of their significance within the structuring of local relations, I shall observe key moments in which the residents of Jolany (especially the Roma) switched between individual languages and faced the dilemma of "language choice" (Fishman 2000). To this end, I will first examine the context within which the individual languages of bilingual (or multilingual) residents of Jolany were acquired.

While the non-Romani native speakers of Rusyn only achieved fluency in Slovak as their second language through school attendance, in Romani families this acquisitional model included yet another language. Romani speakers came into passive contact with Slovak through television, and more active contact through nursery and then primary school attendance in the same building in neighbouring Drevany. Similarly to another village in eastern Slovakia, interactions within individual families also played a role in the acquisition of Slovak in Jolany (cf. Kubaník 2015). In Maroš and Katarína's household I saw how the pre-school children, raised in Romani, were encouraged to practice their Slovak. The adult members of the household would occasionally tell them to name a specific item in Slovak. The children themselves would then spontaneously practice their Slovak in the form of games that consisted of imitating situations at the local authorities or the doctor's surgery, usually under the guidance of older siblings who were by now attending school.[94] The Roma gradually acquired a knowledge of Rusyn mainly through contact with its native speakers, i.e. their non-Romani neighbours, whether at school, work, or during mutual interactions in the village.

However, this model of language acquisition represented an ideal more than it reflected the situation on the ground. Many non-Romani villagers, i.e. Rusyn speakers, spoke Slovak to their children and pushed Rusyn into second place. Since most of the young, non-Romani families no longer lived in Jolany, it was virtually impossible for me to monitor their language use. However, from interviews with older, non-Romani villagers it transpired that a passive knowledge of Rusyn prevailed among such families.[95] In Jolany itself, however, Rusyn continued to be a lively and important language from the point of view of a certain symbolic capital.

Jolany was also home to several linguistically mixed families. Some non-Romani men had married into the village, having arrived during the period of socialism to work in the forestry industry. Most had come from non-Rusyn regions and did not speak the language. There was a similar asymmetry in the knowledge of Rusyn in Romani families, where acquisition of the language depended very much on age and gender. The older generation had had Rusyn classmates at school and had fraternised on work collectives. The increased segregation in education and rising unemployment of the 1990s meant that the younger generation encountered Rusyn far less frequently.

In the case of gender, the asymmetry of competencies was influenced by the fact that many Romani women had married into Jolany from villages where the everyday interaction of the Roma with their Rusyn neighbours (and thus the language) had been far more limited than in Jolany (not to mention those women who arrived from non-Rusyn villages). In

---

94 The important role of children's groups in the acquisition of Slovak has been discussed by Kubaník (2015).

95 Vaňko described the situation of Rusyn in the region similarly: "Due to the fact that north-eastern Slovakia, where the majority of Slovakia's Rusyns live, is among the economically least successful regions of Slovakia, many (chiefly young) Rusyns are forced to leave north-eastern Slovakia and to seek employment in non-Rusyn-speaking regions, which of course removes them from the Rusyn communication networks and fosters their assimilation." (Vaňko 2007: 83).

Jolany itself Romani men interacted with their non-Romani neighbours in the pub and while carrying out odd jobs, which were the contexts in which they not only encountered Rusyn but were expected, as locals, to respond in kind. The Romani women of Jolany, too, entered non-Romani environments when they bought provisions in the local shop, travelled into town, and collected their children from school. However, during the period of my research the frequency of such interactions with the non-Roma was far lower than in the case of the men, as was the use of Rusyn in such situations. The very existence of different expectations regarding communication in Rusyn shows that while language contact is an important condition for the acquisition of a certain language, it does not on its own explain linguistic competence. Native Romani speakers converted a long-term contact with Rusyn into full acquisition of the language, while their non-Romani neighbours, despite coming into contact with Romani every day, remained strangely immune to it. Several residents of Jolany successfully avoided an active knowledge of Rusyn, though all managed to acquire a knowledge of the institutionally required Slovak. It is clear from these examples that language contact was always linked to the hierarchy of socio-economic relations and to certain categories associated with the use of individual languages (the racialised category of Gypsyness, gender or even place).

Slovak

In a step-by-step overview of the languages spoken in Jolany I will first look at official Slovak. During the 1960s, as part of broader nationalist processes that copied ideas of the homogenisation of the nation, culture and place,[96] the teaching language used in the Jolany primary school was switched from Ukrainian[97] to Slovak. Though the villagers would appear to have infringed upon this "national order of things" (Malkki 1995) through their daily use of Rusyn and Romani, during my stay in the village Slovak remained the authorised language (Bourdieu 1991).

---

[96] For more on the linguistic emancipation of Slovak at this time, see Sloboda et al. (2018: 267–269).

[97] Under Soviet policy, the Rusyns were regarded as being part of the Ukrainian population and culture. As Sloboda points out, this Ukrainianising perspective was also adopted by many local elites, and pro-Rusyn activities were subject to severe suppression right up until the end of the communist regime (Sloboda et al. 2018: 273–274).

Roma of all generations recalled the slogan "Slovak in Slovakia" (*na Slovensku po slovensky*), which had been used by primary school teachers when admonishing them for speaking Romani. Though such recollections included an element of mockery of this type of nationalism and the priggishness of the education system, the Roma themselves identified with the slogan and used it to signal both their identification with a specific place and their belonging to Slovak society as a whole.[98]

The Romani villager Churdo was explicit in his support for the use of Slovak, making the point in debates about language use that "we live in Slovakia, not in some flipping Romathan",[99] by which he advocated the necessity to learn Slovak properly for all citizens of the state, including the Roma. He also described Romani as a flawed language in which "you express yourself badly" and "don't say what you mean".[100] This kind of attitude resonates strongly with the idea of Romani as an inferior language, or even just an argot, cultivated (not only) in communist Czechoslovakia (see, for instance, Hübschmannová 1999), a fact picked up on in internalised form by socio-linguists conducting research amongst Romani speakers in the Czech Republic (Kubaník et al. 2010). Churdo himself demonstrated this approach through the systematic use of Slovak when communicating with me. The whole time I was in Jolany we conducted a linguistic tug o' war, with Churdo attempting to persuade me of the inadequacies of Romani by speaking Slovak, while I attempted to prove the opposite to him (and perhaps myself) by doggedly continuing to speak Romani (part of my strategy from the outset to become as fluent as possible).

Churdo's emphasis on the necessity to adapt to the surrounding non-Romani world also corresponded to his positionality within the geographical layout and social hierarchy of the village. As well as living "amongst the *Gadže*", he placed a premium on speaking the *Gadžo* languages, while his attitude toward the Romani language ran in parallel with his belief in the "backwardness" of the Roma in the settlement.

---

98 Admonishing Romani children for speaking Romani in school tended to be associated primarily with the official assimilation policy of state socialism (Hübschmannová 1999: 11). However, Gažovičová has pointed out that similar habits continued to feature in Slovak primary schools even at the start of the new millennium (2015).

99 Interview with Churdo (b. 1960), conducted in Romani and Slovak, 30 March 2015. The portmanteau *Romathan* consists of the Romani words *Roma* ("Roma") and *than* ("place" or "country") and is the title of a popular Romani theatre from Košice in eastern Slovakia. In this instance Churdo used it as the name of a hypothetical Romani state.

100 Ibid.

Churdo recalls that Slovak and Rusyn were spoken at home when he was a child and that he only actively learned Romani in second grade, when he found himself in closer contact with the Roma from surrounding villages (he grew up in the neighbouring Drevany as a member of what at that time was the only local Romani family). It should perhaps come as no surprise that his opinion that Romani was an inferior language was reflected in his preferred choice of language for intergenerational transmission. As he himself said, he spoke Rusyn and Slovak to his children from an early age, while his wife Linda, who herself came from a non-Rusyn village, spoke Slovak. Both deemed it very important that their children be able to communicate fluently with their non-Romani surroundings from an early age, whether this be at school, on the bus, or in the public space of the village.

Some other Romani families in Jolany opted for the same strategy. This of course included Marča, daughter of Churdo and Linda, who lived in the same household along with her husband and three children. As well as Zoralo and Jana, whom I mentioned in the introduction and who lived in one of the council flats, Vašus and Vierka, who lived in their own home "amongst the *Gadže*", prioritised Slovak over Romani for intergenerational transmission. However, the language strategies of all three households included an emphasis on the subsequent acquisition of Romani by all of their children. This was not a problem, since native speakers of Romani prevailed amongst the children and Romani remained a living language and an important characteristic for (self) identification with the category Roma in the local context.

In short, a competence in official Slovak was required primarily for the institution of education, which was equipped with formalised tools for its correction (see Bourdieu 1991). The legitimacy of Slovak as the official language led several Romani parents to prioritise it for intergenerational transmission over Romani and Rusyn (and I have also shown how several non-Romani, Rusyn-speaking parents opted for the same strategy). However, in order to understand the language strategies of the Jolany Roma it is essential we conduct an analysis of the position of Rusyn and Romani in their linguistic repertoire, i.e. languages that were both officially categorised as "minority" languages in relation to Slovak on a national level. Despite possessing the same official status, in Jolany the two languages occupied different positions in the hierarchy of linguistic prestige, and to a certain extent played a part in the additional structuring of local relations.

Rusyn

It is clear from the list of Romani families in which the children learned Slovak as their first language (and Rusyn in the case of Churdo) that this strategy did not replicate the earlier formulated distinction based on the position of the Roma in the geographical layout of the village. This was confirmed by the language strategies operating in the home of Maroš and Katarína (who also lived "amongst the *Gadže*"), which, on the contrary, coincided with the situation in most of the households in the council flats (i.e. in the settlement). Communication in these households was dominated by Romani, which was also the native language of all three sons and the growing number of Maroš and Katarína's grandchildren.

It is interesting that even Maroš defined himself in contrast to the other Romani families in the village on the basis of preferred language strategies, though he saw holes in Churdo's logic: "They teach their children *Gadžo* language, though they can't even speak it themselves."[101] This claim illustrates the phenomenon that I discussed in Chapter One, namely the situational designation of certain Roma who "act like the *Gadže*", even though it is clear that they will forever remain Roma (see Chapter One, and within the context of language use see below).

Although Maroš and Katarína opted for Romani in terms of first language acquisition, even in their household it was linked with particular domains of language use, specifically inter-Roma communication. As such, Romani was later to be supplemented by the acquisition of Slovak and Rusyn. Maroš defended the acquisition of Slovak using the familiar argument that "if a child lives in Slovakia, it should speak Slovak". The importance of a knowledge of Rusyn was then based on a shared idea of the position of the Roma in the local social hierarchy, which Maroš voiced explicitly within the context of language acquisition:

> They say that we Roma come from India, even though I know I was born and bred in Jolany. But if I lived in India and someone came to live with me, then they would have to learn to speak like me.[102]

Maroš's words resonate strongly with the interconnectivity of the main categorisations of the Jolany population examined up till now.

---

101 Interview with Maroš (b. 1967), conducted in Romani, 21 June 2018.
102 Ibid.

Historically speaking, non-Romani villagers were perceived as unproblematic locals and their Romani neighbours as new arrivals, even though most, like Maroš, were born and bred in Jolany. Maroš thus encapsulated the full ambiguity of the local belonging of the Roma, who, despite being "locals", in their capacity as Roma were not "indigenous" (Theodosiou 2004). They may have been "ours", but they were still identifiable as Roma/Gypsies, a characteristic that to an extent set them apart from the local community (Kobes 2012) and turned them into "inappropriate/d others" (Minh-ha 1998).

When Maroš and other Roma declared "We are Rusyn Roma!" (*Amen sam rusňaka Roma!*), they were seeking to ameliorate the exclusory implications of the category "Roma" and highlight their own local and regional belonging. The Jolany Roma did not think of Rusyn as a language that occupied a similar minority status to Romani within the broader national context, but as a language code that symbolised local belonging and was understood as the language of the local *Gadže*, the same *Gadže* against whom they measured themselves and with whom they shared an identity as Jolany residents, even though these *Gadže* were in some contexts immediate reminders of the dominance of the surrounding non-Romani world.

When Jolany Roma described a language as *gadžikanes* (the *Gadžo* language), they were referring to Rusyn, while Slovak was specified as *slovenskones*. Inasmuch as the Roma attempted to live "like the *Gadže*", from a linguistic perspective this life was symbolised by Rusyn, i.e. by the *Gadžo* language.

Rusyn in the local authorities

Rusyn enjoyed a different status to Romani, not only in that it operated as a marker of local belonging, but also that, thanks to the dominance of its primary speakers, it was associated with a wider range of language domains. Unlike Romani, it was often the native language of local employers or gangmasters, as well as doctors, priests and teachers. And therefore my description of Slovak as being the language for official communication is not quite accurate. The Jolany Roma spoke Rusyn at the offices in the county town, usually within contexts where a degree of de-anonymisation of the actors of the communication situation had already taken place. Communication took place in Rusyn with Nurse Mariena, a healthcare worker who came into regular contact with patients at the local paediatrician in Svidník. Rusyn was typically used when communicating with the local authorities or in shops where non-Romani acquaintances worked who had moved to the city from Jolany or one of the surrounding villages. In contrast, Slovak could be heard, for instance, in more anonymous communication at the post office or less frequent visits to medical specialists.

Even in Jolany itself, Rusyn was spoken not only in non-Romani homes and during informal interactions in the public space, but also during more formal events, such as meetings of the local council. At a public session of the local council on the occasion of the handover of the office of mayor, the meeting was formally opened in standard Slovak, after which proceedings continued in Rusyn in the presence of two Romani councillors (of the five-member council). The presence of the Roma, whose representatives had sat on the council since the latter half of the 1980s, did not influence the choice of Rusyn, and it was simply assumed that everyone would understand. This attitude, which made at least a passive knowledge of Rusyn on the part of all the villagers an imperative, was one of the manifestations of difference in status of Romani and Rusyn.[103]

"So the *Gadže* don't say…"

It should be pointed out that Rusyn and Slovak, in their capacity as Slavic languages, enjoyed a high level of mutual comprehension amongst their users (especially so in the case of Rusyn and eastern dialects of Slovak). According to linguistic criteria, Romani was naturally incomprehensible in relation to these languages, even though it borrowed a number of lexical features due to the intense contact between all three languages. However, in addition to structurally linguistic features, the question of intelligibility is always related to the social hierarchisation of a given multilingual community and the linguistic attitudes ensuing therefrom. In other words, those who occupy a higher rung on

---

103 Similarly, Kubaník showed that, though the Roma in the village where he conducted his research were not resistant to the use of Romani in the presence of non-Romani residents, when communicating with a Romani employee of the local authority they switched to Slovak so as not to undermine her authority among her non-Romani colleagues and give the impression that she was discussing something she was not supposed to (Kubaník 2015: 380).

a particular socio-economic ladder are not motivated to make any real effort to understand the language of the people below them (Wolff 1959). We can view the situation in Jolany from this perspective. The local Roma accepted the general assumption of Rusyn comprehensibility, but also ensured that Romani was basically unintelligible to their non-Romani neighbours. Leaving aside Slovak, this constellation of intelligibility presented the Roma (i.e. Rusyn and Romani speakers) with a certain dilemma regarding choice of language when communicating in the presence of non-Romani villagers (i.e. people who spoke only Rusyn). Zoralo formulated the model situation and embellished it with his own assessment of a certain social practice:

> You know what I hate? We go to the pub and some *Gadžo* sits down with us or speaks to us and someone you're sitting with starts speaking Romani. About the same topic you're talking about with the *Gadžo*! I just feel so embarrassed. What does the *Gadžo* think, eh?[104]

In Zoralo's example the *Gadžo* represents the direct actor in the communicative situation and it is therefore necessary that an intelligible language code be chosen if he is to be actively involved in the conversation. However, the Roma would sometimes switch to Rusyn even in situations where the *Gadžo* was not directly involved in the communicative situation but was within earshot and might otherwise suspect that the conversation was about them. In this situation, too, the Roma paid heed to "what the *Gadže* think". They staved off potential conflict and wished to act in such a way "that the *Gadže* don't say…" (see Chapter One). In these situations their fears and thus their policy were clear: "Speak the *Gadžo* language so that the *Gadže* don't think we're bad-mouthing them". This phenomenon returns us to active strategies aimed at preventing the slightest hint of a conflict and the subsequent activation of the category of "problematic Gypsy", this time through appropriate language selection and code switching. However, as I show in the next section, even these strategies derived from the status of individual actors in the communicative situation.

---

104 Interview with Zoralo (b. 1987), conducted in Romani, 17 April 2015.

The Mayoress and Kaleňák

It was Easter and I was with a bunch of Romani in their twenties. We were doing the rounds of the non-Romani homes as part of the traditional Wet Monday *Śmigus-dyngus* [a Catholic celebration held on Easter Monday across central Europe and other places]. We found ourselves standing in the doorway of the then mayoress, Hrickaninka, waiting for her to bring us the obligatory box of treats. One of the Romani men asked out loud where we would head afterwards. However, he asked the question in Romani and was immediately told that he "must not speak Romani so that she [the mayoress] doesn't say..." The mayoress of course had no interest whatsoever in the order of our visits. In other words, it was not that the other lads were keen for the mayoress to understand exactly what they were saying, but to understand what they were *not* saying, i.e. they simply wanted to demonstrate that the content of the conversation they were having was non-conflictual and was not at her expense.

This concern for transparency was all the more necessary when visiting the mayoress, since she personified the non-Romani dominance in the village. It was important to maintain good relations with the mayoress. Most of the Roma lived in the council flats that she was responsible for, and many Roma came into daily contact with her during what was known as "activation work" (see Chapter Four) and required her tacit permission when seeking to release themselves from activities being performed for the village early. They also required her assistance with bureaucratic requirements. In addition, Jarus, the mayoress's husband, was an occasional provider of odd jobs and would sometimes loan money to the local Roma. The Roma practised a similar communicative transparency when performing odd jobs for the non-Roma. If a Roma rang Maroš while he was in the middle of an odd job, he would speak either Rusyn or Slovak. He would never speak Romani on the telephone when in the presence of the person he was working for.

This strategy of transparency was of course a matter for individual Roma, who would decide how important it was depending on the social status of the non-Roma present in a given communicative situation. The caution on display during a visit to the mayoress was in stark contrast to the indifference shown to Kaleňák, who was not only in frequent contact with the Roma, but was actually visited by them in his home. When I was living with Kaleňák, I was a party to situations in which the Roma entered his home without embarrassment and began speaking to me (and amongst themselves) in Romani, thus to a large extent excluding Kaleňák from the communicative situation in his own home.

What these examples show is that the activation of a strategy of open communication is derived from the recognition of certain social hierarchies and power relations. Some of the Roma regarded the non-Roma as important contacts in social and economic networks and tried to maintain good relationships with them. It was when talking of these non-Roma that several of the Jolany Roma would declare "I'm at one with the *Gadže!*" (see Chapter One). On the other hand, some of the non-Roma were not deemed important enough to justify such an adaptation of language choice in their presence.

In short, the Jolany Roma did not switch to Rusyn because of the stigmatisation of their own language.[105] Romani was spoken not only in the Romani households and in the areas around the council flats, but throughout the entire village, in the local pub, on the bus and in the school. The Roma would switch from their incomprehensible language code into Rusyn on a situational basis with regard to the transparency of their communication, especially in relation to their higher status non-Romani neighbours.

New domains of Romani?

While the language strategies deployed by the Roma reinforced established modes according to which Romani was to remain strictly within the domain of intra-group communication, in Jolany itself there were plans for its expansion into other domains. These plans were based on legal measures guaranteeing certain rights to minority languages, which in the case of Slovakia meant Rusyns and Romani.[106] This in turn prompted a national debate on how Romani might be included in the Slovak education system (Gažovičová 2015). Although the primary school in Drevany was attended almost exclusively by Romani children, including those from Jolany, these debates appeared to have no effect whatsoever.

Instead, as the vignette at the start of the chapter shows, it was the right to information or the signposting of the local authorities in the

---

105 In the case of the Roma in the Bohemian lands, Hübschmannová cited internalised stigma of their own language as a reason for switching from Romani in public (1979, 2000a).

106 This involved the European Charter for Regional or Minority Languages and the National Minorities Languages Act.

minority language, speakers of which represented at least 15% of the total population of a given municipality in two consecutive censuses (Sloboda et al. 2018: 279),[107] that had the greater effect. Thanks to this part of the Act, bilingual signs really did appear on the buildings of the local authorities in Slovakia. As well as many Hungarian villages spread across the whole of the southern region of Slovakia, this included districts with the specified share of Roma or Rusyns. Signposts with both the official Slovak and Rusyn variant of names of specific districts could be seen in the region surrounding Jolany, though the same did not apply to the Romani language.

Though entitled to such rights according to the results of the most recent census, neither the Rusyn nor the Roma pursued this claim in Jolany. This is one reason why the mayoress's proposal that the name of the local authority be written in Romani met with incomprehension. When I asked the mayoress (a native Rusyn speaker) why she had not considered a sign in Rusyn, she replied that Rusyn residents did not meet the required percentage of the population in the census. However, according to information available from the previous two censuses, this is not true, which in turn tends to confirm the villagers in their suspicion that the introduction of the sign in Romani was merely a sop to the local Roma. (However, one has to take into account the agency of other actors, in this case the Slovak Government Plenipotentiary for Romani Communities [*Úrad splnomocnenca vlády SR pre rómske komunity*], which oversaw the linguistic rights of Romani speakers and upon whose initiative mayoress Hrickaninka was probably acting.)

The mayoress's request that they translate the wording of the sign into Romani also caused some confusion amongst the Jolany Roma. This was not because they were unable to meet this request, but because the word for "municipal authority" in Romani was a loanword from Slovak. The name given to the municipal authority, *obecno viboris* (from the Slovak *obecní výbor*), was not regarded by the Roma as being "genuine Romani", and they were reluctant to propose it for the official Romani sign. To the embarrassment of the Roma, the mayoress opted for the title provided by the Office of the Plenipotentiary, which in the final version became

---

107 In the amendment to the Act the necessary percentage was reduced from 20% to 15%, though a new requirement specified that this figure had to be recorded in two consecutive censuses. The amendment therefore embodies a focus on how settled a linguistic minority is in the community. I would like to thank Marián Sloboda for pointing this out (personal communication with Marián Sloboda).

Gaveskero urados Jolanos. However, not only did this name not conform to what the Jolany Roma called the municipal authority, but did not conform to the term used in Romani. The Jolany Roma did not call their village *Jolanos* (masculine singular), but *Jolaňa* (feminine singular). For the Roma the clanger in the title was yet another example of cheap electioneering on the part of the mayoress in the lead up to the regional elections that were to take place in November that year. In conversations I had with them, they pointed out that this kind of gesture did not help them in the slightest and that they would rather the mayoress focus instead on the availability or otherwise of housing and work. Similarly, some of the non-Roma criticised her on the municipality's Facebook page and said she should stick to looking after the village. They did not raise the topic of a similar sign being created in Rusyn. These opinions were reflected in the results of the election two months later, in which the mayoress was roundly defeated.

Attempts to provide centralised support for the Romani language caused confusion among the Roma in Jolany. The main problem was that, though the initiative might have come from the Office of the Government, the implementation of individual measures was a matter for mayoress Hrickaninka. The Romani villagers viewed the introduction of their language on the official notice board to be a symbolic gesture related to the mayoress's political ambitions. Moreover, such a gesture was in sharp contrast with their experience of what otherwise had been a highly disciplinary policy she had pursued against the Roma (even in comparison with the previous mayoress Pišťáňa). The form of assistance itself confirmed the asymmetric position of both local "minority" languages. While Romani only appeared on the exterior of the building of the local authorities (for reasons of political expediency according to the Jolany Roma), and even then strewn with errors or in a not particularly reader-friendly form in the case of "information for voters" (see the vignette that begins this chapter), Rusyn was accepted as a communication code inside the building itself.

Bearing in mind these two concrete official applications of the Romani language, we are finally in a position to formulate a different stance vis-à-vis the socio-linguistic situation of this multilingual community. The confusion surrounding the use of Romani completes an important explanatory framework for the language use under examination, namely, the historically shaped status of individual languages and their natural association with certain language domains. As I have shown above, none of the residents of Jolany questioned the normality of the link between Slovak and the bureaucratic and educational spheres (let us not forget that Slovak was made the language of teaching in Jolany in the 1960s), nor did it occur to anyone to point out the artificiality of its standardisation. On the other side lay Romani, the use of which within the bureaucratic domain was viewed as unnatural by the residents of Jolany.[108] Rusyn occupied a position between Slovak and Romani. Under the communist regime it had been subject to a policy of Ukrainisation, and it was only standardised under the new political regime in 1995 (Sloboda et al. 2018). Although there were signs of a shift amongst Rusyn speakers towards Slovak (see above for the intergenerational transmission of language in Rusyn families), Rusyn was still regarded as a natural communicative code in certain official domains (see above), including the sermons given by the priest celebrating the Greek Catholic Mass.[109]

Language as a tool of othering

In addition to their association with specific language domains, individual languages were carriers of other symbolic meanings, i.e. ideas of linguistic (in)competence were linked with certain social categories. Within the racialised hierarchy the Roma were regarded as naturally incompetent speakers of the dominant languages and at the same time bearers of their own specific communication code, i.e. Romani. This situation, accompanied by the dominant requirement to "adapt" (see Chapter Four), led Vargáňa, a non-Romani sales assistant, to try to persuade me not to communicate with the Romani children in Romani but to encourage them to speak Slovak instead. The paradox is that she expected me as a non-Romani Czech speaker to have more success in coaxing Romani children into speaking Slovak than their Romani parents who had passed through the Slovak language education system. This was not because of any real competence I possessed, but simply because I was not a Rom.

---

108 Such an understanding of the locally used languages chimes with the reflections of young Roma, who told me how they would often read the Slovak subtitles to Romani language internet features. They explained this by claiming that the standard Romani spoken was difficult to understand. However, this might again be viewed as an example of a lack of familiarity with Romani as a media-driven linguistic domain.

109 Whether to deliver the sermon in Rusyn was a matter for each priest. The priest in question left his parish in 2015 and his successor preferred Slovak. One should not overlook the fact that the formal liturgy is sung in Old Slavonic.

Vargáňa made it abundantly clear that the Roma operate according to a different language code even during specific social interactions. As the owner of the local shop (adjoined to the pub), she would travel to Jolany every morning from Svidník. When Romani children entered the shop, she would greet them in Romani with the words *So kames, mandro?* ("What do you want? Bread?"). This was the extent of her knowledge of Romani. Similarly, Viktor, a non-Romani villager, would use a corruption of a vulgar address in Romani when greeting the Romani men who would occasionally join him for a drink in the pub. Though these minor linguistic efforts might be accompanied by a friendly gesture, they could not be interpreted as representing adaptation to the Romani communication code (as when the Roma switched to Rusyn), but more as a symbolic reminder of difference. In Viktor's case this was obvious. His garbled greeting meant nothing in terms of content and was purely symbolic. In Vargáňa's case, though the query possessed a degree of relevance, even here it was clear that it was mainly symbolic in intent. The Romani children did not interpret the question as a genuine invitation to speak Romani, something which in any case Vargáňa would not have been capable of. In fact, the children tended to react with an element of embarrassment and would immediately specify the goods they wanted in Slovak.

These ideas regarding linguistic competencies take us back to Fanon's analysis of the racialised relationships in the (post)colonial situation (see Chapter One), in which a different linguistic (and more broadly cultural) code was expected from the colonised Blacks.[110] Fanon observed that the white colonisers instilled these ideas in the colonised Blacks by simplifying the language code used when communicating with them. A recognition of the quality of French spoken by certain Black intellectuals served the same purpose. Fanon showed how an enthusiastic admiration for language competence was based on an entrenched idea of linguistic incompetence. Something similar could be seen in Jolany. This is how the former mayoress Pištáňa reported the statement by the delegation of the Office of the Government that visited the village in connection with the construction of the council flats:

> They said to me: "But they speak Slovak really nicely, you could even talk about politics with them. After all, they know who the president is, who

---

110 Oravcová and Slačálek (2019) also make reference to Fanon's emphasis when analysing the position of Romani youth on the Czech rap scene.

the prime minister is, who the minister for construction is, they know everything. You can have a conversation with them about culture, sport, everything."[111]

Pištáňa used this quote, in which the local Roma are credited with exceptional linguistic and cultural competence, as proof of their integration, and it formed part of her patronising narrative already referred to (Chapter Two). This was again based on a shared assumption of the linguistic (and cultural) incompetence of the Gypsies.

Language and inter-Roma relations

In light of what I wrote about Fanon's conclusions in Chapter One, it is not surprising that the Jolany Roma came to share this conviction that they were naturally incompetent in non-Romani languages. In addition to persuading some of them to relegate Romani to the status of second language (so that their children had "no difficulties" with a non-Romani language code), references to specific examples of linguistic (in)competence were part of the way that relations between the Roma themselves were defined. As I have already indicated, Churdo and Maroš had pointed to certain language (in)competencies when distinguishing between the other Roma. The former was keen to put a distance between himself and the Roma of the settlement, whose children, so he claimed, "couldn't even buy butter in Slovak"[112], while the latter defined himself in opposition to those Roma who, with regard to intergenerational transmission, gave priority to non-Romani languages that "they themselves couldn't speak"[113].

In the scheme of symbolic meanings and the prestige of individual languages, official Slovak (not its eastern Slovak dialects) was deemed the language of socio-economic mobility and a certain level of education. It functioned in a similar way within the delineation of local relations. When Maroš spoke of his late brother Ivan, he recalled how Ivan spoke such a precise form of Slovak that it was admired "even by the [Jolany] *Gadže*". Before returning to his native Jolany (where he lived with Maroš) a few years before his death, Ivan had spent some time in Trenčín, a city

---

111 Interview with Pištáňa (b. 1953), conducted in Czech and Slovak, 3 July 2015.
112 Interview with Churdo (b. 1960), conducted in Romani and Slovak, 17 April 2015.
113 Interview with Maroš (b. 1967), conducted in Romani, 14 May 2015.

in western Slovakia. Maroš claimed that his brother's alleged linguistic competence placed him within a higher social bracket than that of the geographically, socially, economically and linguistically[114] marginalised region of north-eastern Slovakia.

However, though there was some degree of situational overlap with the symbolic importance of Slovak, it tended to be references to a person's competence in Rusyn that served to delineate local relations in Jolany. As I have already shown, Rusyn was symbolically linked to the local *Gadžo* cultural code and an individual's ability to establish themselves within the local socio-economic networks. In addition to being obliged to understand Rusyn and to use it as a transparent language code, the Roma activated its symbolic meaning during statements regarding language competences. A shared identification with the category of "Jolanian Roma" (see Chapter Two) was accentuated in situations in which the Jolany Roma differentiated themselves from the Roma in the surrounding area on the basis of language. They would point to the incompetence of other Roma in particular Rusyn-speaking villages when they wanted to emphasise their own inability to adapt to the local culture.

However, there was an internal categorisation among the Jolany Roma themselves that was activated in a similar way. This took the form of Romani men citing the incompetence of the local Romani women in Rusyn. During such exchanges the men would distinguish between "locals" and "outsiders", reframe the question as one involving gender, and then point out that it was the Romani women who had moved into the village and had generally limited contact with the "local" non-Roma.

Shared ideas of the natural (in)competence of differently categorised residents of the village in locally used non-Romani languages and the symbolic content of the languages in question allowed language to be included in discursive practices when defining a person's own position within the local social hierarchy. In this respect Romani was presented as a language with limited domains of usage and offering the lowest social status. Nevertheless, in Jolany it still maintained its position as a fully vital language code.

---

114 Leaving aside the fact that the region in question was dominated linguistically by Rusyn, even the eastern Slovak dialects, unlike those of the west, differed considerably from official Slovak.

Subverting linguistic dominance

The vitality of the Romani language in the village remained not only undisturbed, but was boosted by the increase in the percentage share of its speakers ensuing from the dynamic of demographic change. In fact, the aim of the local Roma was not to rid themselves of everything Romani in a desperate attempt to "live (or speak) like the *Gadže*". The situation described in the first chapter, in which someone "reached out to Gadženess" or "made out they were a *Gadžo*" in an undesirable way, could also be perceived on a linguistic level. Though non-Romani language codes possessed a degree of symbolic capital, capitalising on this was subject to certain limits even amongst the Roma. Churdo was proud of the linguistic abilities of his children and grandchildren. Nevertheless, when he stubbornly insisted on speaking Slovak with me, the other Roma averted their gaze, including his wife, who during one of our conversations suddenly flashed at him: "Why don't you speak Romani when he's speaking it to you?"[115]

The Roma of nearby Lackovce were sometimes praised for living a respectable life and being "accustomed to living with the *Gadže*", a fact demonstrated by reference to their use of Slovak when communicating with their children. However, for the Jolany Roma these language preferences showed that the Lackovce Roma "took themselves too seriously" and, it was said, could not be induced to join in shared wisecracks predicated upon the use of Romani. Helena, Maroš and Katarína's daughter-in-law, came from Lackovce. Though she spoke Romani, she communicated with her family back in Lackovce in Slovak. Demeter, her father, was a Rom, who was said to enjoy great "respect" (*patïv*). However, he was also on occasion the target of derision, such as when he organised a celebration of a milestone birthday, had gifts brought to him "à la *Gadžo*", and had everyone sing "Happy Birthday to You" in Slovak (*veľa šťastia zdravia*).

As I showed above, even though Maroš himself was in favour of a knowledge of non-Romani languages, Romani was spoken in his home. The lack of competence in Slovak displayed by Janík, one of Maroš's grandsons, who at the beginning of my stay was about to start school,

---

115 Interview with Churdo and Linda (b. 1960), conducted in Romani and Slovak, 30 March 2015. As a non-Rom who spoke Romani I found myself in a somewhat strange position. Outside of his own home and family I did not hear Churdo use a non-Romani language code when communicating with other Roma.

was more a source of merriment than concerned attempts to educate the little boy. This example indicates that merely switching from Romani to non-Romani codes did not necessarily symbolise an acceptance of non-Romani dominance, but, on the contrary, could be used to undermine it. The situational use of set idioms expressing courtesies in Slovak were a source of great amusement amongst the Romani. Such idioms were either lacking in the local variety of Romani or were created by means of semantic calques or direct loanwords from non-Romani languages that sometimes jarred in Romani. When visiting their relatives the Roma would sometimes use, with an irony they clearly relished, the formal Slovak greeting *dobrý deň* ("good day").[116] I myself was witness at Maroš's to the way that even young children had picked up this way of using non-Romani courtesies, when they would use the Slovak[117] expressions for "please" (*prosím*)[118] and "thank you" (*ďakujem*), also heavily laden with irony, to the great amusement of those in earshot.[119] Romani

---

116 The greeting *servus* was commonest amongst Romani peers, though given the openness of Romani households (especially those of the council flats in the grounds of the former settlement) greetings were often omitted altogether. Sometimes, instead of a greeting, the conversational question "What are you up to?" (*So keres/keren?*) would be used, and in the case of meetings outside the household the question "Where are you headed?" (*Kaj džas/džan?*). During the time I spent in the village I was unable to free myself of the habit of greeting people, and upon entering a room would often resort to the somewhat forced *lačho džives*, a direct translation of the Slovak *dobrý deň* (*good day*). Similarly, I was often teased upon entering Romani households for the simple fact that they knew who was arriving because I had bothered to knock on the door.

117 They used the Slovak words because Romani children acquired a knowledge of Rusyn at a later age. It is also obvious that the school (Slovak-language) environment is crucial to the acquisition of such expressions of courtesy.

118 Instead of the usual "please" (*prosím*), the children used more formal (and therefore more ironic) variations such as "I beseech you" (*prosil/a by som si*).

119 An expression of thanks in Romani is *paľikerav* ("thank you"), though this is less often used than in the social contexts in which Slovak or Rusyn is used. The same is true of its reply *nane vaš soske* ("my pleasure"). This is also related to the maintenance of solidarity networks and the daily sharing of food and various objects (see Chapter One). This is exemplified by the common expression *me tuke dava pale* ("I'll make it up to you"), which did not necessarily mean returning a specific item (or smaller sums of money, cigarettes, etc.), but more to an ongoing sense of reciprocity and solidarity among the Roma. Hübschmannová offered a similar explanation for the absence of thanks among the Roma in a chapter with the telling title "Don't thank me, you're not with the *Gadže* now", a section from her book written for a non-expert readership on multicultural understanding (Hübschmannová 1993). It should be emphasised, however, that thanks were not absent altogether from the Romani spoken amongst the Jolany Roma and could also be a matter of individual taste. Usually, however, it was restricted to contexts that went beyond everyday sharing. On the other hand, there was no direct equivalent in Romani to the Slovak word *prosím*, which expressed a request. Instead, a request would be voiced in other descriptive ways, such as the phrase *Av ajso lačho* (literally "Be so good as to...") or through the particle *oča*, which is used at the start of a sentence in order to moderate the force of a particular request (e.g. *Oča, Moňo, ker mange kava* – "Moňo, could you make me

of course has its ways of expressing courtesy. However, this is done in a different way and sometimes within different contexts (see the previous footnotes).

However, amusement was also the response to the situationally incompetent use of language in traditionally formal language interactions. In the Rusyn region, the customary Eastern greeting is *Christos voskrese!* ("Christ is risen from the dead!"), the answer to which is *Voistinu voskrese!* ("Verily he was resurrected!"). However, one of the Romani women was not aware of this, and in answer to the greeting from her local priest replied with the simple *ďakujem* ("thank you"). When this story was being told, it was not the specific faux pas that was relished so much as the framework of an encounter between the Roma and a non-Romani formalised situation. This was the usual context within which these amusing episodes were set by the Roma themselves. The Roma would offer similar examples with a degree of self-irony when speaking not only of an individual's incompetence in non-Romani languages, but their broader incompetence within the locally embedded culture. Again, this was not in order to intensify the distinction between Roma and non-Roma, but between local and outsider by means of cultural incompetence (in the example given above the distinction was in addition gendered).

The examples of language deployment given above remind us that the Jolany Roma were not necessarily imprisoned within an emphasis on due competence in non-Romani languages. Self-deprecation apparent in references to their own linguistic and cultural (in)competence was one of the strategies by which the seemingly unambiguous distribution of prestige within the framework of the linguistic schema was disrupted.

Romani: the Roma's shared cultural code

Inasmuch as the Jolany Roma were able to capitalise on exhibiting the features of a non-Romani way of life on condition they confirm their belonging to the local Romani community (see Chapter One), it was also appropriate to display a due competence in non-Romani languages while retaining a competence in Romani as the shared language code of the Roma. As I have already shown, even those Roma who had decided their

---

a coffee please?"). Hübschmannová addressed similar ways of expressing a request in Romani in a text co-authored with Hristo Kyuchukov (Hübschmannová and Kyuchukov 2009).

children would learn Slovak as their first language (or in Churdo's case Rusyn) reached the same decision, and relied on their children picking up Romani through hanging out with their native Romani-speaker friends. Some even expressed the conviction that the Roma had an innate disposition to acquire Romani and therefore had no reason to doubt the ability of Romani children to acquire their native language later in life. These were the same people who decided to transmit Slovak as the primary language to their children. They included Churdo, who, despite flaunting his family's *Gadžo* way of life, nevertheless knew that his grandchildren, whose primary language of socialisation was Slovak, remained Gypsies (using the Slovak word *Cigán* to convey this idea):

> He'll pick up Romani naturally. No school, no textbooks. When I hear my grandson speak Romani... And who taught him? No one. It simply happened of its own accord. [...] How? Because he's a Gypsy, he has something in him. I don't know, without writing, without grammar, they simply know.[120]

However, the Jolany Roma would regularly encounter other Roma who did not speak Romani or only had a passive knowledge of it. This might involve relatives who had grown up outside of a Romani language environment and only visited Jolany occasionally, or Roma who lived in the surrounding villages. When judging these individuals, the Jolany Roma usually took into account the particular circumstances of their lives.

One of the Roma who did not have an active knowledge of Romani was Feri, a forty-year-old living in nearby Drevany. Feri grew up in a children's home in the Czech Republic and only moved to the region when he was older. He learned Rusyn perfectly, but never used Romani. He had many friends in the neighbourhood, both Roma and non-Roma, many of whom admired him for his musical talent. When I debated the issue of language use with the Roma, they often referred to Feri in order to show that if someone does not speak Romani, it does not mean automatic social stigma and ostracism from Romani social networks.

However, Feri himself felt caught between two stools. He confided in me that he still felt like a Gypsy when amongst the non-Roma, but did not fit in completely to the Romani community. He illustrated this sense of straddling two worlds by means of his lack of Romani. He had

---

120 Interview with Churdo (b. 1960), conducted in Slovak, 30 March 2015.

apparently in the past made an effort to learn the language, but had the feeling that the other Roma were making fun of him. And so he gave up and since that time had not spoken any Romani whatsoever[121]. Though welcomed by the Roma around him, the fact that he did not speak Romani limited him in social interactions. Romani was not simply a tool for the self-identification of the Roma, but a form of capital that offered the Roma, unlike their non-Romani neighbours, a wider selection of possibilities for combining different language codes depending on the social context.

Romani amongst the *Gadže*

However, not even the non-Romani villagers remained entirely immune to a certain competence in Romani. According to the Jolany Roma, their non-Romani neighbours had acquired a little of the language. In conversations I had with them they would remind me that "here [in Jolany] all the *Gadže* understand [Romani]" (*Kadaj sa o gadže rozuminen*). Maroš told me that even some of the teachers in the Drevany primary school had an active knowledge of Romani.

Kubaník (2015: 378) observed the same phenomenon, namely, the attribution of a degree of competence in Romani to certain non-Roma, in another village of eastern Slovakia. In both the village examined by Kubaník and in Jolany, it would appear that the belief in an active knowledge of Romani was more a symbolic formulation of an individual's positive relationship to the non-Roma being spoken of than an accurate description of their linguistic competence. At the same time, it became apparent that most non-Roma only knew the meanings of certain oft-used words and idioms (typically the vulgar ones). Some of them displayed a very limited active knowledge, which in any case, as I showed above using the case of Viktor and Vargáňa, they used more for its symbolic value.

At the same time, I have already shown that the expression of language (in)competencies must simultaneously be understood within the context of anticipated (or assumed) competencies. The comments made by my Romani friends were based on the general assumption that the non-Roma had no interest in Romani and were naturally incompetent

---

121 Interview with Feri (b. 1970), conducted in Czech and Slovak, 26 September 2019.

in it. Within such a context, any degree of knowledge, whether active or passive, could be seen as exceptional. And so when the local Roma declared that "all the *Gadže* here understand", they were referring to a particular place where the language competence of "our *Gadže*" (see Chapter One) illustrated the professed historical embeddedness of the Roma within the local community.

Determining just how good the non-Romani villagers were at Romani was possible via the concept of intelligibility. It is no coincidence that it was those villagers with the lowest social status who were better at Romani. Their status was such that Romani speakers were more careless as to the language they spoke, their closer links with the Romani social networks meant greater exposure to the language, and they had greater motivation to understand Romani. It was not surprising, therefore, that my first host, Kaleňák, along with Juraňák, husband of Ľuba, the Romani woman from neighbouring Maslovce (see Chapter One), possessed a superior (albeit passive) knowledge of the language. In this respect Mára, Juraňák's son from his first marriage, was exceptional. At school he had been the only non-Romani boy in his gang of schoolmates and communicated in Romani without difficulty.

This overview of language competencies in Jolany shows that the association of individual languages with particular locally highlighted categories does not map completely onto the genuine competencies of the Jolany residents thus designated. However, the links between individual languages and specific categories was key to understanding how certain language competencies between Jolany residents were understood. Romani was bound up directly with the category of Roma/Gypsy, and so certain competencies in the language possessed by non-Romani villagers could be used to express historical links with the Romani residents, while in the case of the Roma a poor knowledge of Romani could arouse feelings of not belonging (as in the case of Feri).

"Original" Romani

In order to indicate the complexity of ways in which the Jolany Roma related to a particular place, I would like to focus on Romani itself in the conclusion to this chapter. In Jolany, Romani was basically used for communication by the Roma with other Roma, usually within Romani households, in the area in front of the building of the local authorities, and during ordinary communication in the village, in the pub, at Romani parties, on the bus, etc. It was also used when communicating with Roma from the surrounding villages or the wider region. Romani functioned as a common communicative code with Roma from different parts of Slovakia, with whom the Jolany Roma often came into contact as migrant workers in the Czech Republic. The Jolany Roma would sometimes (albeit rarely) communicate with Roma from Poland[122] or Romania, who made regular trips to Slovakia to sell textiles. From this perspective, the Romani language, which symbolically segregated the Roma from the community of a particular place, connected them with other Roma regardless of local identification (see Conclusion). However, as I shall show, the Jolany Roma also understood belonging to a specific place through Romani itself.

Like other varieties of North Central Romani, the Romani spoken in Jolany contained a high number of easily identifiable lexical (and other) loans from the surrounding non-Roma languages thanks to long-term, intensive linguistic contiguities in what is today Slovakia (cf. Elšík 2003). In Jolany, the structural linguistic impacts of the interaction of the three local languages reproduced their previously established hierarchy. Standard Slovak had basically been immune to any influence of Romani and Rusyn. On the other hand, Rusyn had been strongly influenced by Slovak, especially in the form of its eastern dialects, and contained no loanwords from Romani (with few exceptions). In contrast, Romani exhibited significant traces of Rusyn and Slovak, especially their local dialects.[123]

The Jolany Roma were aware of the extent of loanwords in their variety, which they regarded as a contaminated variant of "genuine" or "original Romani" (*original romanes*). It was on the lexical level they identified most of this contamination. When I attempted during the period of my research to expand my vocabulary through the inclusion of specifically local Romani words, the Roma would warn me against expressions clearly borrowed from Rusyn: "But that's not original Romani [*original romanes*], we now express it in the same way as the *Gadže*." My experience was similar to that of Theodosiou when she was researching the Roma (*Yifti*) in Greece. Like the Roma of Parakalamos, those of Jolany were

---

122 In addition, for historical (and now forgotten) reasons, several of the Jolany Roma shared the same surname with many Roma from the neighbouring Polish region, a fact they enthusiastically interpreted with the claim that "We are a family" (*Amen sam narodos*).

123 In light of this hierarchy, it is difficult to determine whether a feature was introduced into Romani from the dialects of Slovak or Rusyn.

keen to remind me that "they did not provide sufficient 'difference'" for my research (Theodosiou 2004: 45). The Jolany Roma would comment that they shared many characteristics of the way of life of the *Gadže*, thus highlighting their historically embedded belonging to a particular place. At the linguistic level, the shift from the category "Roma" to "local" was manifest not only by means of a competence in Rusyn as a marker of local culture, but also in the form of a particular variety of Romani in which many Rusyn loanwords were easily identifiable.

Nevertheless, as I showed in the previous chapter on the negotiation of an understanding of the space of the village, the Jolany Roma did not become "local" simply by means of the characteristics of a non-Romani way of life (i.e. despite their Gypsyness), but in their capacity as Roma (i.e. inhabitants of the [Romani] settlement). Similarly, Romani was not connected to a specific place merely by virtue of its identifiably "non-Romani elements", but also via the complex characteristics of its local variant. In this respect it should be noted that the Jolany Roma did not associate "genuine" or "original" Romani, which they contrasted with their "contaminated" Romani, simply with (anonymous) Roma elsewhere in Slovakia,[124] but with the life of the Jolany Roma "back in the day" (*darekana*). For them, life "back in the day" did not mean only severe poverty (cf. Chapter One), but also a certain "honour" (*pativ*), which, it was said, symbolised specifically Romani values (communality and solidarity in particular). They viewed the Romani spoken by the older generation in a similar way, as "pure" Romani, not only with regard to its lexicon (the presence of "original" Romani words and idioms), but also a certain affective level (its ability to express courtesy, complaints, etc). For the Jolany Roma the Romani language was as deeply embedded in a particular place as they considered themselves to be.

In addition, the Roma were able to reveal certain distinctive features in their own variant of Romani (on the level of lexicon, phonology or style of expression), and these distinguished their language variant from that of the Roma of other places. They pointed to differences on both a regional and national level, as well as to significant differences from

---

124 These were often categorised as "Vlachs" (*o Vlachi*). In Jolany, this designation did not necessarily refer only to speakers of Vlach Romani (see Elšík 2003), but was a broad category that referred more to anonymous Roma living in isolation from the non-Romani world. This category often included Roma in highly segregated eastern Slovakian Romani settlements, and the reference to *o Vlachi*, in this case implying "Gypsy backwardness", might to an extent overlap semantically with the designation *o degeša* (see Chapter One).

the language spoken by the Romani textile retailers from Romania (with whom they had to use a very limited vocabulary if they were to make themselves understood). The Roma I met during my research respected my interest in Romani and encouraged me to visit other places in the region where "they [the Roma] speak completely differently" (*vakeren caľkom inakšeder*). Spotlighting differences in individual dialects of Romani in Slovakia was a favourite pastime of the Roma during interactions with other Roma from all around Slovakia, with whom Romani men especially would come into contact during trips to the Czech Republic for work.

Finally, the Romani women who had married into Jolany could be identified not only by virtue of their rudimentary knowledge of Rusyn, but also the different variety of Romani they spoke. This was particularly so in the case of Jana, wife of Zoralo, who had married into Jolany from a distant region. However, the differences in the Romani spoken could be heard even in those Romani women who had moved to Jolany from villages within the district of Svidník. From this perspective, it was more the form of Romani itself rather than a competence in non-Romani languages that indicated who belonged to a particular place. At the same time, belonging to place was one of the core categories using which the Roma identified those around (as "Jolanian Roma" [*Jolaňakere Roma*], Maslovcian Roma [*Maslovciskere Roma*], Lackovcian Roma [*Lackovciskere Roma*], Bukovcian Roma [*Bukovciskere Roma*], etc.)[125] and attributed to them other characteristics (e.g. the intensity and quality of their interaction with the local *Gadže*).

Romani as a cryptic code

In winding up this chapter, I would like to return from a consideration of Romani as a marker of belonging to a particular place in interactions between different Roma to its use in practice. I have already shown that under certain circumstances the Jolany Roma opted for a strategy of communicative transparency in the presence of their non-Romani neighbours, which led them to switch to a generally intelligible non-Romani language code. In other situations, however, they preferred to use

---

125 Depending on context it was possible to use only the local modifier (e.g. *Bukovciskere*) and it was immediately clear that the conversation was about local Roma.

a cryptic code, and this was the function that Romani performed. It should be noted that these two strategies did not encompass anywhere near all the contexts of the communicative situations of Romani actors, which in some way the non-Romani villagers also participated in. The strategy of linguistic transparency complemented numerous other situations in which the Roma switched to a non-Romani language code, not "so that the *Gadže* don't say...", but simply in order to direct a specific communication to the *Gadžo*. Similarly, in many situations the Roma communicated amongst themselves in Romani while in the vicinity of non-Romani villagers without intentionally activating its cryptic function. I shall focus on the cryptic function of Romani even though it was only used sporadically in comparison with the everyday use of the language. I shall do this in order to show how the Roma balanced non-conflictual relations with their non-Romani neighbours through deliberate manipulation of the Romani lexicon.

The "contamination" of Romani by loanwords from other languages had implications for certain language interactions. The Jolany Roma knew that obvious loanwords in Romani could be identified and potentially understood even by their non-Romani neighbours, and were concerned that they might decipher the contents of their interactions through leveraging certain key words. It was these words that the Roma attempted to replace with the lexicon of "genuine" Romani.

A good example of this would be the verb "to understand", which in the Jolany variant of Romani was expressed using the loanword *te rozum-inel* (Slovak *rozum-iet'*, Rusyn *rozum-iti*), clearly intelligible to the non-Romani villagers. However, if a Rom wanted to convey that a non-Rom present (e.g. sitting at the next table in the pub) had a greater proficiency as regards conversation in Romani, instead of the easily decipherable *jov rozuminel* ("he understands"), they would use the older Romani verb and inform their Romani listeners that *jov achal'ol* ("he understands"). The situational enclosure within their own world in the presence of non-Romani surroundings through activation of the cryptic function of Romani was characteristic of its "purification" from the identifiable features of non-Romani languages.

A typical context in which cryptic variants of Romani were used involved the odd jobs carried out for non-Roma, during the performance of which the Roma would discuss how to set about the work and grumble at the demands it was making. This led not only to the revival of Romani words that in other contexts were disappearing, but also the creation of completely new terms and the expansion of the semantic range of existing words. Some Roma referred to five euros as *jekh čhajori* ("one little girl"),[126] mostly when agreeing amongst themselves on the rate of pay they would ask from the person they were working for. The reason for this was that numerals from eleven upwards in the local variety of Romani are expressed by loanwords from Slovak or Rusyn. And so, for instance, rather than using the intelligible numeral fifteen, the Roma used the designation *trin čhajora* ("three little girls") for a similar amount in euros. Other potentially intelligible words that could be crucial in deciphering the content of a conversation had their own cryptic equivalents. The cryptic equivalent of the *Gadže* (*o gadže*) was *o gore* (and less frequently *o chale*), so that the non-Roma in question did not suspect that they themselves formed the topic of juicy gossip. The verb *te peťarel* (originally meaning "to burn") occupied a special place in the cryptic language, and popped up in various different forms and meanings, functioning as a kind of universal cryptonym. The word for the hard liquor that was expected as part of the remuneration (usually *e thardïmol* or simply *e thardï*) could be replaced by the substantivised *e peťardï* (feminine singular), and a cryptic allusion to money might take the form of the substantive *o peťarde* (plural) instead of the more universally comprehensible *o love* ("money").

The significance of the social context of the work carried out for non-Romani employers demonstrates that the cryptic function of Romani was activated more in the presence of higher status non-Roma. As I have shown, not much in the way of linguistic consideration was shown lower status non-Romani villagers in the form of a strategy of communicative transparency, and it was not deemed important to hide things from them using cryptic idioms since it did not matter much what these non-Roma might think of the Roma. On the other hand, when communicating with potentially important socio-economic allies, a certain linguistic caution was warranted. The coexistence of different communicative strategies when in the presence of non-Romani villagers shows that the switch was not simply mechanical. Instead, it depended not only on social status, but also on an evaluation of the attention being paid to the communicative situation in question, the risks involved in activating the category of Gypsyness, the appropriateness of allowing the content of a conversation to be understood, and the social status of the Romani actors themselves.

---

126 This habit goes back to the earlier designation of five Slovak koruna, originally no doubt derived from the little girl depicted on a Slovak five-koruna banknote dating back to 1945.

Conclusion

In an article on Roma belonging, Scheffel concluded that in Veľký Šariš a certain group of Roma had achieved the status of "autochthonous", which historically underwrote their right of domicile (Scheffel 2015). In the previous chapter I showed that the Jolany Roma maintained their position in the geographical layout of the village in a similar way. However, I believe that in this respect the full implications of Scheffel's argument have not been fully teased out. Though he recognises the unequal status of the Roma in the local social hierarchy, in his view the terms "autochthonous" and "local" blend into one, which prevents him from analysing in further detail the quality of Romani belonging to place.

While Scheffel based his argument on an examination of right of domicile, I opted to analyse language ideologies and use in order to acquire a more detailed understanding of the ambiguous relationship of the Roma to place.

I observed the position of the three languages used in this multilingual community: Slovak, Rusyn and Romani. I showed that degrees of competence in these languages were not associated only with different social categories, but also linked to different levels of belonging. However, I have shown that language competence cannot be explained simply by the symbolic significance of individual languages, nor by language contact, but that these are closely linked to the existing socio-economic hierarchy.

Returning to the question of local Roma belonging, we may conclude from the above that, given the natural association of Romani with the category Roma, the Roma themselves were separated from a community that linguistically was mainly characterised by Rusyn. However, for a more detailed analysis of the ambiguous position of the inhabitants of Jolany thus identified, one must examine each language in practice. Though I have shown that language ideologies impacted the form of intergenerational transmission, in this chapter I have focused much more on situational code-switching. In this sense I have followed up on the phenomenon of "silencing Gypsyness" already referred to, which here was linked to a strategy of linguistic transparency. It did not represent an attempt to avoid at all cost the use of Romani as a stigmatised (and stigmatising) language code, but rather a broader strategy aimed at not offering any excuse for the situational activation of the category of Gypsyness (see Chapter One).

The language into which the Roma tended to switch in these situations was Rusyn. The use of Rusyn as a marker of local belonging was related to a situational attempt to emphasise self-identification with the category of "local" resident and downplay the category of Gypsyness. I also showed in this chapter that the negotiation of belonging to a specific place was to an extent gender dependent. This was caused on the one hand by a general tendency to maintain virilocal post-marital residence, and on the other by the relatively higher participation of Romani men in interactions with their non-Romani surroundings.

However, given the fact that Romani flourishes in Jolany, one must reject the logic by which all actions of the Roma would be seen as representing an attempt to "silence Gypsyness" and speak and/or live "like the *Gadžo*". On closer examination it is also possible to specify in greater detail the entire scheme hitherto formulated not only of language competencies, but the interweaving of language with different levels of social belonging. Inasmuch as I have shown that the Jolany Roma experienced a sense of togetherness regardless of local identification with other Roma via the Romani language (inter alia), equally it should be noted that they emphasised their belonging to a specific place via the specific form of their own variant of Romani. There were obvious loanwords from contact with non-Romani languages that supposedly foregrounded the historical embeddedness of the Roma in local socioeconomic networks.

This in itself shows that the language codes discussed thus far cannot be understood in isolation, but must be thought of as a dynamic field of language competencies and repertoires. In addition to the fact that the local variety of Romani contained many features identifiable as "non-Romani", it should be noted that some of the non-Romani villagers also displayed a competence in Romani: often limited, but not always. Such a linguistic environment was an important context for the use of the cryptic function of Romani in which the Roma actively manipulated the lexicon and, in contrast to the strategy described of linguistic transparency, situationally intensified blurred cultural boundaries by means of language.

Though the Jolany Roma sometimes deliberately avoided certain easily identifiable loanwords from the local non-Romani languages, they viewed even this purified form of Romani in relation to a specific place. In other words, as far as the Romani language was concerned, the Jolany Roma did not understand their local belonging only via its clearly "non-Romani" elements, but also via those elements that they understood as being distinctive in relation to non-Romani languages.

This linguistic analysis leads me to agree with Theodosiou that "otherness [...] is not only something that enters [...] from 'outside', it grows within it too" (2004: 38), or, as Olivera says on the basis of research conducted among the Gabor in Romania, "the social organisation and culture of a Gypsy community does not necessarily have to come from elsewhere to be 'original'" (Olivera 2012: 32). Like the Romani settlement, though the Romani language to some extent symbolically separated the Roma from the rest of the village, at the same time it was historically entangled in it. One is thus entitled to view Jolany similarly to Parakalamos as a "doubly occupied place" (Theodosiou 2004, see Stewart 1996), which arose historically as a place shaped, inter alia, by the relationships between Roma and non-Roma, a place formed by the village (implicitly named) and settlement, as well as by the Rusyn and Romani languages.

The evolving dynamic of language use by the Jolany Roma ultimately suggests another interpretation, to wit, that the very strategy of "silencing Gypsyness", as well as being balanced, for example, by the deployment of Romani's cryptic function, was not necessarily a poorly thought out attempt to acquire the characteristics of a non-Romani way of life, but may have contained within itself a certain subversive element that shifted the logic of (linguistic) "adaptation" to the level of a kind of game. Though when playing this game the Roma sought to act in such a way "that the *Gadžo* don't say...", they did not attain this objective by means of a necessarily one-sided attempt to adopt the characteristics of a *Gadžo* way of life. I shall elaborate on this theme, especially in respect of economic strategy, in the next chapter, in which I show, inter alia, how the concept of "Gypsy work" was negotiated in Jolany.

Chapter Four
Gypsy Economy in Jolany

During my time in Jolany I would often visit Churdo and Linda, both in their fifties. Churdo was a great musician and would sometimes play the accordion for me. Mostly, however, all three of us would sit on their veranda and enjoy long chats over coffee. There was a good view of the council flats in the settlement from their balcony, and it was here that Churdo and Linda formed many entrenched opinions of the Roma of the settlement as linguistically incompetent and culturally backward. They enjoyed good relations with the other two families living "amongst the Gadže". Churdo considered Maroš his cousin and visited him often, while Linda was the sister of Pavlína, who had moved with her husband Miro into a house located "amongst the Gadže" in the 1980s.

Despite making clear their differences, Churdo and Linda were on friendly terms with the occupants of the council flats when they met them during what was known as "activation work" for the local authority. It was the domain of work that, in Churdo and Linda's opinion, showed how backward the Roma from the settlement were. They were convinced that unemployment amongst the Roma was a natural consequence of the fact that "they had never been used to working" (na sas sikhade te kerel), whereas they regarded their own unemployment as a well deserved breather before entering retirement following a life that had largely been spent working in the Bohemian lands, later the Czech Republic.

Maroš, Churdo's cousin and seven years his junior, carried out a lot of odd jobs in the informal economy, and was occasionally joined by his sons and grandchildren. Once, when we were helping out in the garden of Maroš's neighbour Marek, a non-Romani villager, Marek began to complain that a trailer he had loaned to the Roma had been returned to him with a broken tail light. Maroš immediately began a chorus of "you know how it is, the Gypsies don't value anything". A moment later one of Maroš's grandchildren knocked over a shovel that had been lying against the wall, which fell heavily onto the concrete pavement. Maroš's ten-year-old grandson immediately began to reprimand his four-year-old cousin. "Peťko, take care for heaven's sake," he scolded the little boy, repeatedly cuffing him, albeit symbolically, while checking that Marek had noticed his attempts to educate.

Not only Maroš and Churdo, but the other Jolany Roma too, possessed a strong work ethic, and this played a large part in the creation of relations in the village, not only between Roma and non-Roma, but between the Roma themselves. It was above all in respect of work ethic on which Churdo and Maroš based their reservations regarding the other Jolany Roma, especially in conversations with me, though ideally in the presence of non-Romani villagers. Both Maroš's observations regarding the other Roma, and the actions of his older grandson, showed that economic strategies were always embedded within a certain social context. Maroš and his grandson set out to signal their own credibility and break free from stereotypical ideas of Gypsies (as people who did not know the value of things and were ill-mannered and uncouth). In this chapter I shall show firstly how interactions related to the Roma's economic strategies were an important context for negotiating an understanding of the category Gypsyness, and secondly how, thanks to migration as one of the key economic strategies of the region's population, these same strategies were an important factor in understanding the relationship of the Roma to place.

The Roma and work in Slovakia

In the period prior to the Second World War, the Roma were an integral part of the local socio-economic structures of eastern Slovak rural areas, though their inferior status meant they were economically dependent on their non-Romani neighbours (Hübschmannová 1998). Their practice was to combine various different economic strategies. The men were often musicians, for whom playing at village weddings and parties was an additional source of income (Horváthová 1964), unlike their higher status counterparts in the cities, who played in cafés. Another position often occupied by a Roma was that of "Gypsy blacksmith", who was a cheap alternative to their non-Romani counterpart, often regardless of the quality of work (Hübschmannová 1998). In the patron-client relationship, the non-Romani villagers would often pay "their Gypsies" in kind (ibid.). This was basically the situation in Jolany prior to the war, where both the blacksmith and musicians plied their trade.

In the post-war period, a large number of Roma left Slovakia for the Bohemian lands (see Sadílková 2020), not only in search of work in industrial cities, but also hoping to leave behind their inferior status and find a more dignified position in society (Sadílková 2016, 2020; Synková 2006). Although post-war migration to the Bohemian lands was not restricted to the Roma, it was the mobility of the Roma that caused the central authorities of the socialist state to resort to terminology like "uncontrolled" and "undesirable" (Guy 1998 [1975]). Leaving aside the fact that the movement of the Roma made it considerably more difficult for the central authorities to control them, it was not seen as normal economic mobility, but as a sign of a "backward Gypsy way of life" (ibid.), which was to be resolved by transforming the "backward Gypsy" into a regular socialist worker (Donert 2017: 48–53). The government decree on "controlled dispersal" of the Gypsies, 1965 (ibid.: 159–168, see Chapter Two) also aimed to oversee the movement and inclusion of Gypsies in the work process. Though the final wording of the Act did not specify them by name, an attempt had already been made to control the movement of the Roma under the terms of Act 74/1958 on the Permanent Settlement of Nomadic People.[127] As its implementation in the Svidník district and in particular Jolany shows, the "list of nomadic people" included the Roma who had been living on a long-term basis in particular municipalities, thus confirming the confusion endemic to any understanding of the categories of Gypsies and nomads on the local level (see Ort 2022).

On the other hand, taking as his example one of the eastern Slovak villages where the Roma were traditionally involved in migratory activities, Grill spotlights the agency of the Roma themselves. According to him, the local Roma were able to avail themselves of certain aspects of the socialist policy regarding "citizens of Gypsy origin" in order to raise their standard of living (availability of work, housing construction, greater social participation) without succumbing to the pressure to culturally assimilate (Grill 2015a,b). This is a fair description of the situation of the Roma in Jolany, who associated the period of socialism (specifically the 1970s–80s) with their own significant material progress.

However, it was also the Roma who were most affected by the political and economic transformations of 1989, since they were usually the

---

127 Regarding the genesis of the wording of the Act see Zapletal 2012: 26–57, see also Sadílková 2013).

first to be made redundant in the wake of the privatisation of key enterprises. As far back as the 1990s, the gloomy economic prospects and the outbreak of open anti-Gypsyism goaded many eastern Slovakian Roma to submit applications to western European countries for asylum (Grill 2012, Dobruská 2018). This then provided the impetus for more extensive labour migration, especially to Great Britain and Canada, ensuing from the neoliberal social reforms of the start of the new millennium (see Marušák and Singer 2009) and the opening of the borders after Slovakia's accession to the European Union in 2004 (Grill 2012, 2017, Dobruská 2018, Uherek 2018).

The Jolany Roma were not part of the migration of the Roma from eastern Slovakia to the West. Their own migration was limited to short-term trips to the Czech Republic in search of work, and there was no suggestion that they had upped sticks and left Jolany for good. However, in this chapter I shall examine migration as one of many economic practices of the Jolany Roma. I will be interested how the idea of a "Gypsy economy" was manifest in the village (Brazzabeni et al. 2015), i.e. I shall examine what was included under the rubric of Romani economic strategies, and above all how the Roma themselves viewed their position in the locally negotiated network of actors and relations through such practices. I shall show that the concept of "Gypsy work" (*cigánska robota*) was associated in Jolany, as elsewhere in Slovakia, mainly with the naturally poor work ethic of the Gypsies. Given the deep-rooted work ethic, this characteristic of Gypsyness was an important factor in the sense of moral superiority experienced by the non-Romani villagers over their Romani counterparts and offered a certain justification of the exploited position of the Gypsy within local economic relations.

Finally, I shall show that, although the Jolany Roma conceded their marginalised status within the network of economic relations, by and large they accepted the concept of "Gypsy work". On the one hand, they drew on this concept in order to define themselves in relation to other Roma (either in the village or elsewhere), while on the other they used it to formulate their own ability to adapt to functioning in a society characterised by anti-Gypsyism and non-Romani dominance.

Historical overview of economic strategies in Jolany

As I have already pointed out, the pre-war situation in Jolany was basically the same as that in other villages of rural eastern Slovakia. In Chapter Two I noted that the Roma in Jolany included blacksmiths and musicians, and the records of property ownership point to significant economic inequality between the Romani and non-Romani villagers. In addition, the designation "Gypsy worker" (*cigánsky robotník*) again brings to mind the racially defined position of navvy or day labourer (see Chapter Two). This economic dependence on their non-Romani neighbours featured in the (generationally transmitted) recollections of Jolany residents. Margita, a Romani villager born before the war, recalled how as a young girl she worked for a non-Romani family and how many Romani women would walk around begging. Mayoress Pišťáňa, a non-Roma, would recount stories told to her by her grandfather, according to whom the Roma worked for the local Jews,[128] while the Romani women cleaned out ovens for non-Romani villagers in the lead up to Easter or put their cattle out to graze.

From at least as far back as the 18th century, the non-Roma in Jolany had made a living as lumberjacks, with many of them later employed at the sawmill and a local match factory. However, during the First World War the factory burned down and was never put back into operation. There is no evidence of the Roma migrating from Jolany right up to the Second World War. However, the migration of non-Romani villagers is documented in part and indicates the economic hardship suffered by the region at the beginning of the 20th century. Many non-Romani families formed part of the broader phenomenon of migration to America (cf. Zahra 2016), where some remained, while others returned to build new homes in Jolany. The Bohemian lands were another destination, to which, according to mayoress Pišťáňa, mainly non-Romani men travelled to study during this period, with many remaining there.

Evidence of migration as a Romani economic strategy goes back to the immediate post-war period, when several left Jolany for northern

---

128 According to mayoress Pišťáňa, the non-Romani villagers recalled two Jewish families living in Jolany prior to the war. One family hid in the woods with the aid of the local people, and when the war ended moved to Israel. The fate of the second family is not known. On the basis of the recollections of Romani witnesses, Hübschmannová (2000b, 2005) described the more permanent socio-economic relations between the Roma and their Jewish neighbours in the pre-war east Slovak countryside, based primarily on the assistance of the former provided to the latter.

Bohemia, only to return after a few years, so contemporary witnesses say, and build the wooden shacks of the settlement with the money they had earned (see Chapter Two). However, references to migration pepper the period lasting from the early 1950s to the period of my research. They appear in various archive materials, according to which entire families would up and leave for several years, while male work gangs would be gone for shorter periods. The experience of Romani men living in the Bohemian lands was bound up with compulsory military service, which for many of them became an opportunity to find a job upon being discharged. It is clear from what the Jolany Roma said that many families remained permanently in the Bohemian lands, though the members of the first generation of such migrants were already deceased when I was conducing my research and had not maintained contact with their descendents in Jolany. The high level of migratory activity on the part of Romani and non-Romani villagers (non-Romani villagers also left for the Bohemian lands, now the Czech Republic, during the period of state socialism, and even later at the turn of the millennium) was not exceptional in this region, and its depopulation at the start of the new millennium represented a kind of continuity with the rich migratory history of (north)-eastern Slovakia.

Despite the ongoing migration, during the period of socialism a reliable economic strategy pursued by the Jolany Roma involved employment in the wood processing factory (the sawmill) in neighbouring Drevany. The sawmill figured in the narratives of the Jolany Roma as a symbol of their involvement in the formal economy and of the golden age of their wider social participation. An anecdote recounted in the archived materials reveals to what extent the sawmill represented security in life. A Romani school pupil allegedly refused to study at school, explaining that "in any case I'm going to work at the sawmill".[129] Let us not forget that it was the sawmill that in the mid-1980s offered many Romani families company apartments (see Chapter Two). Another important local business at that time was the Odeva clothing factory in Svidník, where both Roma and non-Roma from Jolany often sought and found employment.

It was during the period of state socialism, particularly the 1970s and 1980s, that narratives were situated in which the Roma accentuated the contrast between the destitute lives they had lived "once upon a time"

---

129 ŠA, Svidník, f. MNV v [Jolanech], "Kniha prestupkov [Jolany]".

and their newfound material progress, a progress symbolised by the purchase of a first car or television. According to these recollections, even some of the non-Roma who lived near the settlement and did not own televisions would visit their Romani neighbours in the settlement to watch ice-hockey. However, other memories confirmed the continuity of economic strategies with the pre-war period. Long after the war, Maroš's father Jozef, employed at the sawmill, earned a little extra on the side as a blacksmith, and along with other Jolany-based Romani musicians played at weddings, parties and public festivals. Both Romani and non-Romani villagers recalled how, even under communism, relations were maintained within the framework of the informal economy, with the Roma visiting their non-Romani neighbours on a Saturday to help out with odd jobs.

"Gypsy work"

The sawmill was privatised in 1992. Several of the Jolany Roma were still working there during the 1990s, before it was closed down completely. The clothing company in Svidník was also privatised, and though it remained open and still employed some of the Roma from Jolany and surrounding villages during the period of my research, it was well known for its poor working conditions and late payment of wages. In Jolany, an economically marginalised region within Slovakia as a whole, the post-revolutionary increase in economic uncertainty led to the exodus already referred to of young, non-Romani families in search of work to Svidník, Bratislava, towns and cities in the Czech Republic, and even to Great Britain in the case of one family. Many of the non-Roma who remained in Jolany were older villagers now collecting a pension. The vast majority of the non-Roma of economically active age had permanent jobs and would commute to Svidník, and one of them would regularly travel to the Czech Republic for weeks at a time. The owner of the local shop, Vargáňa, commuted every day from Svidník to Jolany, and employed Juraňák, a non-Romani local (see Chapter One). The latter's brother Rasťo, along with Kaleňák, were the only non-Romani villagers who would meet their Romani neighbours during "activation work" (*aktivačná práca*).

Within the context of a strong social emphasis on manual labour traditionally present in the rural areas of Slovakia (cf. Kandert 2004), it was a poor work ethic that was claimed to be the main characteristic of Gypsyness. From the perspective of the non-Roma in Jolany, this supposedly symbolised the ingrained cultural "backwardness" of their Romani neighbours. A similar narrative drove nostalgic recollections of the communist period, when "everyone had to work", including the "naturally lazy" Roma.

It was within the context of a strong work ethic that what was known as "activation work" was introduced as part of neoliberal reforms in Slovakia, the aim of which was to maintain the work habits of the unemployed. As Grill has noted, given the socially entrenched ideas of the Roma's approach to work, and the high unemployment rate in their ranks, the introduction of this measure had a strong racist undertone (Grill 2018). Similarly, van Baar notes that this programme in practice was highly dehumanising, especially of the Roma (van Baar 2012: 1296–1299).

In Jolany itself, only two of the non-Romani locals participated in the "activation work". The rest were Roma. However, according to the logic already discussed (see the case of Kaleňák in Chapter One), these two non-Roma were deemed the exception that proved the rule of the working non-Roma, while the participation of the Roma was confirmation of their naturally lax approach to work. As I shall show, even the Roma themselves shared this perspective to an extent. In addition, the content of this mandated work programme by no means coincided with general ideas of what constituted proper work. The entire project, which was always implemented under the aegis of the relevant municipal authority, required 20 hours of work per week from each participant and provided a contribution of EURO 64 a month on top of unemployment benefit. Work would typically involve tidying up public spaces, i.e. sweeping the road, mowing grass, leaf raking, snow clearing, painting the railings on the bridge, etc. The way "activation work" was targeted reinforced ideas of the absence of any work ethic amongst the Gypsies, while the jobs that needed doing confirmed the subordinate position of the Roma in economic relations in which they performed work that was poorly rewarded, both financially and in terms of social prestige.[130]

---

130 In the village where he conducted his research, Grill noticed that non-Romani participants in the activation work were usually assigned more qualified work and enjoyed a greater flexibility of working hours (Grill 2018). I did not observe such differences in Jolany. More qualified work (such as operating the brush cutter) was usually taken care of by Maroš, who also carried out the majority of odd jobs for the non-Romani villagers. Both non-Romani participants (Kaleňák and Rasťo) tended to keep to themselves within the overwhelmingly Romani collective. Grill also remarks that activation work served as a form of exploitation and was used as a cheap option on various construction and repair projects aimed at modernising the village.

Inasmuch as the aim of "activation work" was to prod the unemployed into finding employment, its implementation was thwarted not by their allegedly poor work ethic, but by the economic marginalisation of the region, and, in the case of the Roma, severe discrimination on the labour market (cf. Grill 2018). Rather than being a stepping stone to permanent employment, for the Jolany Roma "activation work" became one of the potential sources of income that they factored into their considerations when selecting economic strategies and juggling the household budget. As well as other state contributions (unemployment, housing, and parental benefits), such income usually included temporary formal employment in unskilled positions in the region (e.g. roadworks) or outside it, usually in the Czech Republic, but sometimes in Germany or Austria. Income from the grey economy typically included odd jobs for the local non-Roma or the collection and sale of wild mushrooms, beechnuts and occasionally forest fruits. This way of combining different sources of income was a daily reality for the Jolany Roma and bore witness to their highly precarised status and never-ending economic uncertainty.

The situation in Jolany was very similar to that in Tarkovce, where Grill conducted his research, where there was no designation of "Romani work" in the sense of specifically Romani economic practices (cf. Abu Ghosh 2008, Horváth 2005, Solimene 2015, Stewat 1997; see also Grill 2015a: 92). However, in both villages there existed a dominant term "Gypsy work" (*cigánska robota*), which non-Romani villagers used when referring to work that was poorly performed (ibid.)[131]. As I shall show below, even the Roma used this term in a particular way. However, inasmuch as a distinctive Gypsy economy existed, the Jolany Roma associated this more with an ability to live on little and to combine different sources of income within a single household considered as an economic unit.

Non-Romani actors of the Gypsy economy

This, then, was the economic situation at the end of my stay in the village at the beginning of the summer of 2015, when a one-off regional project co-financed from European funds and the Slovak state budget was launched. The main aim of this ecologically oriented project was to

---

131 I did not notice "activation work" being used in this way in Jolany. In a small village, which Jolany was in comparison with Tarkovce, where Grill conducted his work, both mayoresses in office during my research had problems in finding enough work to go round.

initiate preventative measures against drought and floods in the region "using the potential of the long-term unemployed", as the project documentation put it.

Representatives of almost all the Romani families (all men except for one woman) availed themselves of the employment opportunities on offer, while neither of the two unemployed non-Roma did so. They commuted to various places along the local River Ondava, where they carried out soil water retention work. The residents of other villages in the region, mostly the Roma, were also employed on the project, which offered them work for eight months from spring to autumn. They received the minimum wage, at that time EURO 320, for about 24 hours of work a week. For the Jolany Roma this was a welcome increase in their monthly income. Furthermore, now armed with a job contract they were in a position to take out bank loans.

However, the actual implementation of the project was very much in line with the idea of "Gypsy work", with the unskilled labour being carried out by the Romani villagers and supervised by their non-Romani foremen, often the local mayors. These entrenched ideas regarding the menial work carried out by the Roma were then confirmed by comments made by the non-Roma. This usually took place in the pub, where we would sit over a bottle of beer after digging ditches all day (an activity I participated in for a while). On these occasions the Romani employees would speak of the difficulty of the work they were doing, not made any easier by the hot sunshine. The non-Romani men present would respond with considerable scepticism and remind their listeners of the full-time jobs they were holding down in contrast to the seasonal work being carried out by the Roma. Above all, they insisted on reminding the Roma that "someone's making money out of them [the Roma] again" by pointing to the low wages and supposedly opaque financing from the European Union.

In my opinion, this kind of interaction was indicative of more general aspects of the dynamic of local relations. On the one hand, there was a certain shared experience of demanding, poorly paid work, which in a socio-economically marginalised region affected not only the Roma, but many of their non-Romani neighbours. However, during encounters in the pub the non-Roma activated the category of Gypsyness by referring to how their Romani neighbours only ever worked on an intermittent basis. They expressed a degree of solidarity when referring to the corruption of the European Union and, from their marginalised and peripheral position, formulated a situational coalition with the Roma against the state/European power apparat. All in all, the non-Roma peppered their doubts regarding the commitment of the Roma with scepticism regarding unemployment policies being implemented from afar, whether this be the state's social security provision or the regional projects being financed by the European Union.

Looked at from this perspective one sees that the non-Roma did not deploy only a disciplinary narrative against the Roma, but also cooperated with them on the circumvention of the formal regulations of external authorities and the diversion of economic practices towards the informal economy. A good example of such a coalition was to be found in the figure of mayoress Pišťáňa. Despite harbouring doubts regarding what she called the "staying power" of the Roma, Pišťáňa was nevertheless prepared to assist them in their attempts to increase their income. For example, at the very start of my research, while she was still mayoress, she allowed Maroš to report for "activation work" and then slip off in order to perform an odd job. Another time, when there was to be a regional inspection of personnel, she personally rang around the Roma informing them of the fact and instructing them to appear before the authorities and avoid being taken off the programme for absenteeism. In an interview with me, Pišťáňa expressed her belief that it is difficult to live purely on unemployment benefit, which was why she always attempted to be receptive to the needs of the Roma (Grill observed something similar in his research referred to above [2018]).

However, there were credits to be earned from such cooperation with the Roma (or "assistance" to the Roma as Pišťáňa put it, subtly emphasising the unequal status). In the case of Pišťáňa this took the form of an appreciation of her "work for the Romani community" (see Chapter two), but also won her the covert political support of specific Roma in Jolany. For other non-Roma, such benefits were more tangible. The doctor based in Svidník would write sick notes for the Roma in return for a backhander when those working in the Czech Republic wanted to spend a week at home and earn a bit of extra money on the side, or when they needed to explain their absence from "activation work" so as to avoid being thrown off the programme.

"Gypsy work" and inter-Roma relations

Unlike those Roma who rejected the dominant concept of work and placed a distance between themselves and the non-Romani world by means of their own concept of "Romani work" (*romani butji*) (cf. Stewart 1997),[132] in the case of the Roma in Slovakia the dominant narrative regarding work ethic was to an extent accepted (cf. Grill 2015a).[133] The Jolany Roma also acquiesced to this narrative, even as they denied strongly that they themselves were lacking in this respect. They recalled state socialism not as a regime that obliged the Roma to work, but as one in which they could finally realise their own work abilities. As well as the usual references to work at the sawmill, they would point out that it was the Roma who built a large part of the newly created, county town of Svidník after the war. And in contrast to their socio-economic participation under communism, the Roma would cite the increased economic marginalisation they suffered from subsequently, which they associated mainly with the privatisation of key enterprises in the 1990s and the social reforms enacted at the beginning of the new millennium (see Marušák and Singer 2009). From their point of view a significant deterioration in living conditions was symbolised by the transition from the Slovak currency (koruna) to the European (euro) in 2009. In conversations with me the Roma were united in citing the historically entrenched asymmetry of economic relations in which, they claimed, the non-Roma always benefited from inherited economic assets, leaving the most demanding labour that the non-Roma did not want to perform for the Roma.

However, a rejection of the stereotypes clustered around "Gypsy work" was only part of the narrative by which the Roma reacted to the dominant discourse. In addition to declaring their own readiness to work, the Jolany Roma attempted to shift the concept of "Gypsy work" over to a different group of Roma. There were several paths along which the Jolany Roma situationally threaded this narrative. Members of the older generation of Roma would recall their own work during the socialist period and point out that the "young Roma" were "no longer used" to such work. On other occasions the Roma in Jolany would contrast themselves with those in neighbouring Maslovce, whom they used as a local example of the general category of "problematic Gypsy", or would point

---

132 For more on this, see, for instance, Horváth (2005).
133 Things might have been different in the case of the Roma of eastern Slovakia, who identified as *vlachika Roma* ("Vlach Roma", see, for example, Hajská 2017).

to the lax approach to work of unnamed Roma from poor settlements in eastern Slovakia.

For the purposes of this kind of self-definition they drew on the terminology of the dominant discourse, evaluating the degree of alleged backwardness according to who was "used to working" (*sikhado te kerel*) and who "knows how to manage their affairs" (*džanel te chulajinel*). The use of such language was the outcome of a day-to-day negotiation of dominance and marginalisation, as the Roma sought to identify more closely with the dominant position of the workers and to redefine the group of marginalised non-workers.[134]

The close of the second chapter (housing) and the vignette that opens this one suggest that in Jolany itself such self-identification mainly took place on the basis of the position of the Roma in the geographical layout of the village. The Roma living "amongst the *Gadže*" availed themselves of the clear-cut boundaries of the settlement in order to reinforce its "territorial stigmatisation" and to condemn its inhabitants as "backward". A person's work ethic was supposedly the best guide to the degree of their "backwardness". Churdo and Maroš, though keen to set themselves apart from such Roma, did not deny the discrimination faced by the Roma on the labour market and corroborated it with recollections of their own personal experiences. However, they also claimed that anyone who wanted to work could find work, and that, in the words of Churdo, that "you can't just keep whining 'they won't take me because I'm a Gypsy!'"[135].

In other words, when underlining their own healthy work ethic the Roma completed in narrative form the process of setting themselves apart from other Roma. They did this with the aim of escaping the stigma of Gypsyness and establishing themselves in non-Romani networks of socio-economic relations. It was therefore natural that it was the non-Roma who decided just how successful such a strategy would be. And so although the Roma were happy to speak of their own work ethic in conversation with me, what was crucial for them was the public deployment of such narratives in the presence of the non-Roma.

In the previous chapter I showed how, when communicating with important non-Romani villagers, the Roma opted for a strategy of linguistic transparency in order to dispel suspicions of any subversive or

---

134 Howe describes such a dynamic on the basis of research amongst the unemployed of Belfast, Northern Ireland (1998).
135 Interview with Churdo (b. 1960), conducted in Romani and Slovak, 17 April 2015.

incorrect content in what they were saying (Chapter Three). However, I suggested that switching from Romani when communicating with the non-Romani villagers was not simply a case of conflict management and prevention, but a way of "being heard" by the right people. In the local pub the Roma usually spoke amongst themselves in Romani. Switching to Rusyn was a signal that what was being said was also being addressed to non-Romani villagers. Such communication typically involved work-related narratives, focused either on their efforts to find work or on the performance of a particular job, such as when they recounted how difficult the work was on the flood prevention project.[136]

Being a trustworthy worker

In addition to these and similar claims, it is important to look at the specific social practices that accompanied them, not in an effort to evaluate the "genuine" work ethic of the Jolany Roma, but in order to show how dominant ideas of so-called "Gypsy work" were incorporated into these practices and how the Roma explained their relationship to the surrounding non-Romani world through such actions.

When I participated on the activation project with the Roma, I was admonished by the other members of my work gang for working too hard and laughed at for my naive determination to perform the task assigned me.[137] The Roma were well aware that they were being paid just over one euro per hour, and did not consider this sufficient reward to justify expending huge amounts of energy. I have shown that the non-Romani villagers were similarly sceptical regarding the activation project. Both mayoresses admitted in conversations with me that it was virtually impossible to find enough new work every day. However, the situation was completely different in the case of the odd jobs performed for the non-Roma. These were fully in line with the tradition of economic relations in the (eastern) Slovak countryside, in which the Roma worked for the non-Roma and had the opportunity to establish a good name for themselves as trustworthy workers in the eyes of influential villagers.

---

136 Howe (ibid.) has previously highlighted the significance of relating stories in public about work in the structuring of relationships between the unemployed in Belfast.

137 A similar experience was described by Grill, who was reminded by the Roma that it was necessary to work in such a way that "it is good" (Grill 2018).

Representatives of basically all the Romani families in Jolany carried out odd jobs at some time or another. However, the most active in this respect was my host Maroš, for whom this form of labour had sometimes provided a key source of income for his household. To a certain extent Maroš was cashing in on the status his father had already carved out for himself among the non-Romani villagers. His father had operated as a blacksmith and had done the rounds of his non-Romani neighbours performing odd jobs. Maroš inherited from his father not only a house on land "amongst the *Gadže*", but also the reputation of a trustworthy worker.

The almost eighty-year-old, non-Romani village woman that lived next door but one to Maroš told me that Jozef (Maroš's father) used to help her husband, and that after both had died, Maroš helped her son. Maroš had a good reputation among the non-Roma, and he in turn passed on this status to succeeding generations. Some of the odd jobs were now being carried out by his sons on their own, and Maroš would sometimes put even his grandsons to work carrying chopped firewood. As I showed in the introduction, this meant that the little boys not only participated in the work itself, but were at the same time being socialised into strategies for signalling one's trustworthiness to the non-Romani neighbours.

Maroš would be asked to perform the largest number of odd jobs at the end of summer as the non-Roma began replenishing their woodpiles for winter. Maroš and his group would be requested to saw, chop and stack the wood. It was with this in mind that Maroš invested in a good quality chainsaw during my stay, a decision that paid off handsomely. Maroš did not only carry out odd jobs in Jolany, but, thanks to his extensive contacts, in other villages in the region too. These contacts piled up, one after the other, as I saw for myself during one odd job in Svidník, when the wife of a local parish priest observed us for a while over the fence of her garden, before plucking up the courage to ask Maroš if he would come and chop and stack her wood too.

Maroš was living proof of the efficacy of the accumulation of a combination of social and economic capital. Unlike some other Roma in Jolany, he was able to invest in a chainsaw, which then allowed him to acquire other odd jobs, and these helped him strike up contacts with non-Roma, leading to yet more odd jobs and more social contacts and financial remuneration.

Shifting the logic of adaptation

The subsequent visit to the wife of the parish priest provides a good opportunity to highlight other aspects of the social interactions that took place while the odd jobs were being carried out. Since this was the first time that the priest's wife had invited Maroš and his sons to work for her, it was clear from the outset that she was unsure as to what their respective roles entailed. To begin with she had prepared some sandwiches, over which a conversation took place between her and Maroš. To the huge amusement of his sons, Maroš conducted a conversation with their host in fluent Rusyn on the theme of faith. Having explained to her that he and his sons were used to receiving something more fortifying than mere sandwiches, she finally got the hint, brought out a bottle of spirits, and, having asked timorously if we really wanted to drink alcohol in the morning, poured each of us a small shot.

The work involved was the same as usual at this time of year. Maroš sawed the trunks of beech trees that had been transported to the garden, after which his sons and I chopped the blocks into logs and stacked them in the shed. After about an hour of work, Maroš switched off the saw and warned me in Romani that we weren't obliged to carry out our client's instructions to the letter. She had specified the maximum size of the logs, but according to Maroš it would suffice if I placed smaller logs on top of larger ones in the wheelbarrow we were using to transport the wood to the shed. That way our client, who would wander past occasionally, would not notice anything. His son Tomáš looked on with amusement and offered me the following friendly advice: "You have to learn not only to speak like a Rom, but to double-cross too" (*Mušines te sikhľol romanes na ča te vakerel, aľe the te obuľedkerel*). It is highly unlikely that these "everyday acts of resistance" (Scott 1985) were a specifically Romani practice, even at the local level. What is interesting is that Tomáš framed things in this way, thus indirectly acknowledging a degree of relevance to stereotypical notions of "Gypsy work" in the sense of jobs that are shoddily performed.

Maroš repeated what Tomáš had said to his Romani friends for the rest of my research period, and would often remind me of it in other situations when he wanted to draw my attention to what he saw as characteristically Romani behaviour. The remark itself and its later iterations bore witness to an overview that poked fun not only at the economic strategies of the Roma but also my own interest in Romani. However, the situation as framed in this way must be viewed within the entire context of the odd job, which, as I have shown, could not be reduced simply to the performance of the commissioned work, but represented a specific (and, given the asymmetrical relationships, typical) context for social interaction between Roma and non-Roma.

When the Jolany Roma spoke of the "backward Roma" (*degeša Roma*) to be found elsewhere in Slovakia, they often maintained that the latter "were unable to adapt" (*na džanen pen te prisposobinel*). The Jolany Roma themselves claimed that they were able to "adapt" thanks to the intense contact they had with their non-Romani surroundings, especially while performing odd jobs. The behaviour so designated included not only deciding on the appropriate level of effort to be expended (we really did process all the beech trunks in a single day at the priest's), but also displaying an ability to "speak with the *Gadže*" (*te džanel te vakerel le gadženca*), something Maroš managed by using *Gadžo* language (i.e. Rusyn: see Chapter Three) and addressing certain themes (faith in God during the conversation with the priest's wife). However, such strategies also created a space in which those performing the odd jobs were able to formulate their own interests and establish certain "working conditions", as we saw when Maroš managed to negotiate the brandy and agree on a favourable price.

There was still room for subversive practices. When Maroš urged me not to follow the priest's instructions to the letter regarding the size of the logs I was chopping, and this encouragement was then framed by the stereotype of Romani "double-crossing", this represented the ironic expression of a distance from the dominant discourse of a strong work ethic. This distance was reinforced not only by the Romani language, which was used situationally to supplement the dominant Rusyn during odd jobs (often through the targeted activation of its cryptic function: see Chapter Three), but also by the amusement with which Maroš's sons later returned to the way he had introduced the theme of God when speaking with the priest's wife. In this instance they did not dwell on the declaration of faith in itself, since in Jolany such faith was deemed natural amongst both Roma and non-Roma. What amused Maroš's sons more was by what means and how often Maroš returned to the theme in this particular conversation.

The amused reactions to Maroš's behaviour during the performance of an odd job resonate with the humorously framed stories of situational manifestations of the linguistic and cultural incompetence of certain Roma during interactions with their non-Romani surroundings (see Chapter One). In this sense the Roma accepted the dominant requirement "to adapt" (as expressed in the racist notion of the Roma as being naturally "unadaptable": for the Czech and Slovak context see Čada 2012, Powell and van Baar 2018, Walach 2014), though they then reframed this "adaptation" as a kind of game (see Scott 1985). Within the dominant discourse thus modified, the call on the part of the Roma to "adapt" to the non-Romani way of life was simultaneously the subversion thereof. One might look anew from this perspective at the slogan "so the *Gadže* don't say...", which we now see does not necessarily express complete submissiveness to non-Romani neighbours and an anxious attempt to avoid being identified with the category Gypsy, but rather a selective acquiescence to non-Romani requirements while maintaining a space for the formulation and consolidation of one's own interests and cultural identity (cf. Grill 2015a). Maroš had not been anxious or submissive when talking to the priest, but, on the contrary, socially competent. It was perfectly clear he knew very well how to "talk with the *Gadže*" and how to act in such a way that "the *Gadže* don't say...". However, his ability to "adapt" did not represent total acquiescence to non-Romani supremacy, but an appropriate demonstration of its characteristics while retaining a space for the formulation of his own distinctively understood economic (and, more broadly, cultural) practices. As part of the Romani concept of "adaptation", the non-Roma themselves were required to adapt in part (see Brazzabeni et al. 2015: 11), for instance, by acquiescing to the working conditions requested or, in the case of language, accepting the use of Romani, unintelligible to them, in public. In this respect the phrase "so the *Gadže* don't say..." was more a corrective to the negotiation of self-interest aimed at maintaining harmonious relations than the expression of an ongoing, anxiety-ridden attempt to "escape Gypsyness".

The Gypsy economy in Jolany

When Tomáš reminded me of the need to learn how to "double-cross like a Roma", he was affirming dominant ideas of poor quality "Gypsy work" and indirectly referring to the ability of the Roma to circumvent the rules of the formal economy. However, contrary to the idea of a lax approach to work on the part of the Roma, the Jolany Roma basically accepted this aspect of their own economic strategies. They formulated such a strategy against the backdrop of their historical experience of life on the fringes of society, in which, according to them, they had to combine various economic strategies in order to survive. By formulating

such a strategy they were not denying their own work ethic, but showing that, though the Roma were always being asked to take on the most
demanding work, they were usually paid peanuts. In the conversation
in which Maroš, Churdo and Katarína claimed that the "Gypsy steals
iron and a *Gadžo* steals millions" (Chapter One), all three agreed that the
Gadže would not be able to survive on the paltry amount the Roma were
forced to live on.

This entrenched economic strategy was articulated directly by Zoralo.
When speaking of the ability to combine different types of income, he
declared that "we [Roma] are dab hands at such things". The list of different economic practices pursued by the Jolany Roma that opened this chapter does not have to be seen only on a descriptive level. Given their location on the border of the formal and informal economy, these strategies
can be seen as the essence of what in Jolany represented the "Gypsy economy" (Brazzabeni et al. 2015), i.e. certain economic practices or strategies
by means of which the Roma understood their position in the non-Romani world. As in another eastern Slovak village (Grill 2015a), so in Jolany,
the Gypsy economy was not tied to a specific type of work, but more to
the ability to combine skilfully various economic and social practices.

In this respect, though the Roma were sceptical regarding the topic
of "activation work", they nevertheless included the money they earned
performing it in their calculation of the monthly family budget. Though
the soil water retention project offered formal employment for several
months and enabled many Roma to increase the level of their bank loans,
some deliberately opted not to apply for it, since, combined with the
family budget, it would not pay off. On the other hand, Zoralo's wife
Jana opted to join the programme, since if Zoralo were to participate on
his own it would paradoxically lower their household income, because
they would see their unemployment benefit cut. Some of the Romani
wives in Jolany would seek short-term employment in the *Odeva* clothing factory in Svidník for a similar reason, even though the company
was otherwise spurned due to its poor pay and conditions. On the other
hand, those Roma who enjoyed a more stable position in the informal
economy, e.g. Maroš, did not participate in the soil water retention programme, since were they to find temporary formal employment, they
would risk severing their contacts with the non-Roma in the area, who
would then find others to do their odd jobs.

The ability to combine different types of income included several casu-
al, more marginal economic practices. In a collaboration with Vargáňa,
the local shopkeeper, several members of Maroš's family traded in

tobacco, which they sold to the other Roma in Jolany (without any lasting economic success). Anyone with a car could earn a bit on the side by ferrying other Roma to the district town of Svidník, for instance, if they needed to visit the doctor or the local authorities.[138] The Roma were able to obtain larger amounts of money by taking out a bank loan, though more often by borrowing from private companies. For this reason the pawnshops in Svidník were popular. Looked at from this angle, Maroš's investment in a chainsaw made perfect sense, not only in light of the odd jobs he was able to accept, but because of the large sum of money he would receive immediately were he to pawn it (cf. Hrustič 2015a). Furthermore, such items could be bought on higher purchase, i.e. without having to shell out a large amount of money in one go.[139] Unlike many other villages, interest was not charged on unofficial loans in Jolany (cf. ibid.). The Roma lent and borrowed amongst themselves (usually from their relatives, often from surrounding villages) and also from selected non-Romani villagers. At the end of the month they would often ask Vargáňa the shopkeeper to put the goods they had bought on their tab.

Taking Maroš and his odd jobs as an example, I have showed that the strategy of combining different economic practices included certain social skills. Having a name for oneself amongst the non-Romani villagers was important if these strategies were to prove successful, either in finding more odd jobs or borrowing money. I have also shown that many non-Roma, e.g. the mayoress Pišťáňa and the doctor, cooperated with the Roma on these practices. However, the very ability to shuffle economic practices in the space between the formal and informal economy was seen as typical of the Roma/Gypsies. The non-Roma perceived it in this way and included it in the concept of "dishonest Gypsy work", and this interpretation was even accepted by the Roma themselves. As they saw it, their ability to juggle diverse money-earning activities was a response to their socio-economic marginalisation, in which a commitment to work was simply not enough.

---

138 At the beginning of my research, only a few families owned a car, though gradually almost everyone bought one. Occasionally cars would break down, and so the role of driver, who for a small fee would drive other Roma families into the city, was passed from one person to another.

139 Investment in similar items (e.g. televisions) involved a system previously known as *včelička* or "little bee". A group of people would decide on a fixed amount that each would contribute every month to a joint bank, usually for a year. Each of the Roma would withdraw the entire amount from the bank on the basis of a sequence decided by lottery. The Jolany Roma had already consigned this system to the periphery since it was allegedly impossible to rely on everyone being able to make payment every month.

Visibility of the Gypsy economy

An economic strategy based on a combination of different income streams, some less secure than others, had its visible manifestations. For instance, Zoralo maintained that at some point in the past suddenly almost all of the Roma bought a Škoda Felicia, since everyone having the same car made spare parts more accessible. However, this also meant that a repaired Felicia, on which the repair work was clearly visible due to the different body paints used, became associated with the Roma (as a product of the Gypsy economy) and as such became the target of frequent police traffic checkpoints in the region.[140] Zoralo maintained that, in an endeavour to escape not only the stigma of the Gypsy economy, but also the consequences thereof (e.g. police checkpoints), the Roma began buying different car brands.

The way the Jolany Roma changed their telephone numbers so frequently could be seen in the same light. The Roma themselves regarded this as the sign of a Gypsy economy, as well as an attempt to reduce their footprint and become less easy to trace by institutions (e.g. debt collectors, lenders or government agencies).[141]

Visible signs of the Gypsy economy were particularly associated with the housing situation (Chapter Two). When the villagers claimed, on the basis of families living outside the settlement, that the Roma were congenitally incapable of "living like the *Gadže*", they did not point only to the growing number of people in these households, but above all to the distinctive physical appearance of entire backyards. Two young Roma, Zoralo and Martin, defended the anti-Gypsy attitudes of non-Romani villagers vis-à-vis the sale of building land by claiming that, even were only a single building in the entire village to be inhabited by Roma, it would be instantly recognisable as such. This was not only a reference to the way that multiple buildings had a habit of arising on a single building plot, but also the way such buildings were constructed. Vašo, the son of Miro and Pavlína, built a brick house from breezeblocks that stood out from the other houses in the village by remaining without

---

140 According to the Jolany Roma, the automobile brand Lada/Žiguli, known as the *žigulík*, had been previously considered the "Gypsy car". This was the case in many villages of eastern Slovakia. I would like to thank Petra Dobruská and Jan Grill for pointing this out (personal communication with Jan Grill and Petra Dobruská).

141 Similarly, Abu Ghosh examined Roma strategies aimed at escaping the reach of disciplinary practices on the side of state institutions (Abu Ghosh 2008).

any facade. Maroš was forever trying to build or refurbish something. The construction of the last building in his garden lasted almost two years, during which the process sped up or slowed down depending on whether Maroš was able to get his hands on wooden beams, roofing materials and windows. The ongoing construction work taking place in Maroš's yard and the visible disparity of materials and garden equipment was a tangible manifestation of the combination of different sources of household income.

Yet things were not always this way in Maroš's yard. He and Katarína would recall spending several years in the Czech Republic and investing the money they earned in repairing their house in Jolany. As Katarína put it, "nobody would have believed that it was Roma living here"[142]. The words used by Katarína to describe the outcome of that previous construction work pointed to the entrenched expectations surrounding visible signs of Romani life and its low status. However, contextualisation of the statement also reveals the potential for social mobility that migration had embedded within it as a specific type of economic strategy.

Migration

Migration was an important economic practice in Jolany that was always factored in when the Roma were combining different income sources. Its importance was due its being traditionally associated with socio-economic mobility and having the potential to redefine the hierarchy of local relations.

As I showed in the introduction to this chapter, migration possessed a continuity in Jolany among both the Roma and non-Romani villagers. At the start of the 20th century, the non-Roma left for South and North America (cf. for instance Čulen 2007), and in the lead up to the Second World War to the Bohemian lands. From the early 1950s, if not before, and right up to the period of my research, the Roma from Jolany also migrated to the Bohemian lands, later to the Czech Republic. The migration of the Jolany Roma can be divided roughly into long, medium and short-term. Long-term migration included examples of families who moved to the Bohemian lands and never returned. As I showed in the chapter on housing, this type of migration mostly involved families

---

142 Interview with Katarína (b. 1967), conducted in Romani, 27 September 2016.

who left the country during the period of communism. At the start of the new millennium, Metres, the son of Churdo and Pavlína, remained permanently in the Czech Republic. He visited his parents regularly (unlike many others, with whom contact had been broken off entirely), and found seasonal work for other Jolany Roma in the Czech Republic. During the course of my research he was joined by his brother Jaňo, who also moved permanently to the Czech Republic.

Medium-term migration involved several years spent by entire families in the Czech Republic. In Jolany this applied above all to Maroš and Katarína, who moved to the Czech Republic at the start of the millennium with their children and grandchildren, before returning to Jolany just a few years before I began my period of research. Zoralo, who was single at the time, lived for a few years with Maroš and Katarína in the Czech Republic, which is where he met his future wife Jana.

However, the most frequent form of migration was short-term and consisted of a three-week period in the Czech Republic and a week at home in Slovakia. These work trips were undertaken by groups of Romani men, while their wives and children remained at home. In exceptional cases married couples would travel for work leaving their children in the care of their grandparents. Although it appeared that migration was no longer a preferred economic strategy as I began my first stay in Jolany, shortly after it ended many Roma began once more to shuttle between the Czech Republic and Slovakia for work. The intensity of such trips always depended on several different factors: the availability of work at any given time in the local region (including the informal economy); the feasibility of balancing the household budget; and of course the availability of (ideally verified) work in the Czech Republic.

The availability of work also to some extent depended on a person being established within local relations. If Romani workers wanted to minimise the insecurity concealed behind the offers of less salubrious job agencies, they relied instead on their own socio-economic networks. As well as contacts in the Czech Republic such as Churdo's son, certain Jolany Roma families were able to find work via the Roma living in neighbouring villages, as when men would join a work gang made up of their wife's relatives. In other cases, however, work was acquired through regional non-Romani employers, either through formal employment (highway maintenance in the region, which some Roma would then follow up with the same work in the Czech Republic), or odd jobs (Maroš and his son found work in the Czech Republic through a non-Romani villager whom they regularly visited in order to help out with chores).

Roma as "(semi)nomadic Gypsies"?

One factor that distinguished Romani and non-Romani migration in the dominant popular discourse was the traditional idea held by the non-Roma of the Roma as a people naturally on the move (Guy 1998 [1975]). Historically, this idea had been baked into specific, nationwide measures, especially the First Republic Act on Vagrant Gypsies (*Zákon o potulných cikánech*) of 1927 (Baloun 2019) and the law pertaining to "the Permanent Settlement of Nomadic Persons" (*Zákon o trvalém usídlení kočujících osob*), which came into force in socialist Czechoslovakia in 1958 (see Donert 2017: 115–143). Drawing on archives, it is possible to track the creation of a list "nomadic persons" (*kočujúce osoby*) on the basis of the second law referred to for the district of Svidník, i.e. including Jolany.[143] The Department for Internal Affairs (*Odbor vnútorných vecí*), which was in charge of the register, basically conflated the categories "(semi)nomadic persons" with "persons of Gypsy origin" in instructions addressed to individual local committees. As in other villages in the region (see Ort 2022), in January 1959, on the basis of this register, the Jolany local committee submitted their own list of "Gypsy residents" (*cigánski obyvatelia*). Of the fifty-six Gypsies listed in total, the local authorities included twenty on the list of "nomadic persons" (comprising three families) in a clarification dated February of the same year, the official reason given being that "they cannot be found permanent work". Such persons were to be prohibited from continuing to travel and the local authority was to provide them with work and accommodation at the place specified in the register.[144]

What key was to be deployed when deciding which Gypsies were to be deemed "nomadic people" is not entirely clear. Even so, the creation of the list suggests that from the perspective of the local authorities (staffed by non-Romani villagers), certain Romani families were perceived as being more mobile (even though other Romani families were

---

143 ŠA, Svidník, f. ONV vo Svidníku I. (1945–1960), "Súpis kočujúcich a polokočujúcich osôb v okrese (cigáňov)", 1959 [without further specification of the date].

144 The question arises as to what extent the local authorities complied with the Act. As we saw in Chapter Two, adequate housing was not provided for these families, and archived materials from the following decades show that the migratory activities of these (and other) families did not stop. A number of requests for exemption from the register have been preserved from other villages in the district (as well as from the whole of Slovakia, see Donert 2017), due to the possibility of continuing to travel in search of work (see Ort 2022). I did not find any such requests relating to Jolany itself, though this does not necessarily mean that none were submitted and/or dealt with.

openly migrating at that time) or less anchored in local socio-economic structures. It is significant that one of the families in the list was that of Štefan and his two brothers, who moved out of Jolany for good during the 1980s (see Chapter Two).

As has already been noted by several authors, although the law contained no mention of Gypsies, its implementation reflected the racist discourse of that time, according to which the Roma were identified as Gypsies, and by extension as "drifters" and "fluctuants", regardless of their actual way of life (see Donert 2017: 115–142, Sokolová 2008: 91–102, Guy 1998 [1975]). As I have shown in the second chapter, it was more the related idea of the deracination and hence ease of "evictability" of the Roma (cf. van Baar 2016) that was manifest in Jolany itself over the following decade, during which the local committee repeatedly proposed resettling all Romani families (or rather those living in the settlement) in Bohemia. Notwithstanding the fact that the Jolany Roma, in their capacity as "our Roma", were to some extent exempt from the general category of Gypsies (see Chapter One), the idea of the Roma as "not indigenous" continued to draw on a historical understanding of their deracination. This was above all reflected in the narratives surrounding the arrival of the first Rom to the village, invited to be the blacksmith by the non-Romani villagers. While the Roma *arrived* in the village, the non-Roma had historically always already *been* there.

However, another important contextual framework for understanding Romani migration was the historical continuity of the socio-economic marginalisation of the region as a whole, in which the migratory experience was shared between Roma and non-Roma. The demographic change that culminated during the period of my research represented a kind of historical continuity in this respect. While I was living in Jolany, Romani movement was seen as normal labour migration rather than an offshoot of the Gypsy way of life. In some cases, even during the communist period, the interconnectedness of Romani and non-Romani migration was manifest within the context of specific working groups, in which Romani and non-Romani individuals would meet and share their experience as migrant workers.

Based on this I shall show that, despite a historically embedded popular discourse on the Gypsies as nomads, in Jolany itself Romani migration differed from its non-Romani counterpart not so much in terms of a different conceptualisation of movement, but more by virtue of how it reacted to the entrenched idea of "Gypsy work", i.e. how the relationship between the Roma and labour was understood. For the Roma, work offered a particular kind of experience that allowed them to re-examine their position in the social hierarchy of the Jolany community. In addition, both these aspects of Romani migration complement the entire discussion on Roma belonging to place.

Contesting Gypsyness through migration

Just as mobility outside the local Romani settlement was seen as a move away from a supposed "Gypsy backwardness", so migration was perceived as a demonstration of work commitment in contrast to the stereotype of "Gypsy work", and as such associated with a certain socio-economic mobility. When the non-Roma were explaining the relatively higher status enjoyed by Maroš's family among the other Jolany Roma, they cited the fact that "he spent some time in the Czech Republic". In contrast, the non-Romani villager Čirčáňa, when speaking of Zoralo, claimed that though he had spent a protracted period of time in Czechia, he remained imprisoned by "cultural backwardness" and the economic marginalisation of the settlement: "I thought he'd think differently. He was in the Czechia, he even lived there"[145].

These examples show that in order for migration to be perceived as successful and to impact positively on locally negotiated social status, it had to be capitalised on in Jolany itself (cf. Grill 2012). The acquisition of new social and economic capital could also, understandably, have been achieved by the Roma who remained in the Czech Republic. However, if they gradually severed links with the home community, they realised such capital in the new socio-economic networks concentrated in and created by their new place of abode. In contrast to movement out of the settlement into the village and "amongst the *Gadže*", which took place before the eyes of the local inhabitants (see Chapter Two), decisions related to migration to the Czech Republic remained concealed from the Jolany population.

Capitalising on such mobility in Jolany itself could take place through the investment of money earned in visible status symbols. Maroš and Katarína made this point when recalling the refurbishment of their house in Jolany. However, while I was living in the village the possibilities for such capitalisation were very limited. Home improvement

---

145 Interview with Čirčáňa (b. 1950), conducted in Czech and Slovak, 12 June 2015.

investment (e.g. a new shower or furniture) remained concealed, especially in the case of the monotone form of the council flats in the settlement. For this reason, capitalising on migration was played out in Jolany to a large extent on a narrative level (cf. for instance Gardner 1993).

Though members of basically all the Romani families in Jolany had experience of travelling for work to the Czech Republic, migration served to reinforce the distinctions previously referred to between individual Roma depending on where they lived, i.e. their location in the geographical layout of the village. Churdo, Maroš, and even Vašus, i.e. the main male representatives of the families who lived "amongst the Gadže", pointed to their own migratory activity and also to the fact that the Romani men living in the settlement had never lasted long in the Czech Republic or "had had their fingers burned" by their own incompetence and had returned home empty-handed.

While I was living in the village, my host Maroš had a longer spell during which he did not travel to seek work. Nevertheless, he even managed to turn this situation to his advantage. In conversations with me he put a distance between himself and the other Roma, who, according to him, travelled to the Czech Republic "like runaways", only to return home empty-handed. He, on the other hand, had no need to travel, so he claimed, since he had sufficient odd jobs with the non-Roma in his home region.

The relations thus structured are fully in line with my previous conclusions, namely, that the Roma living "amongst the Gadže" were fully capable of utilising the territorial boundary and the ensuing stigmatisation of the settlement to smear with the term Gypsyness a group of Roma defined differently (by their position in the layout of the village). In certain respects the Roma from the settlement were in a no-win situation. If they did not migrate, they were called "lazy Gypsies" who were unwilling to travel in search of work. And if, on the other hand, they did migrate, they were again labelled Gypsies who were unable to "adapt" and acquire contacts (and thus work) "amongst the Gadže" in their home region around Jolany. Regardless of the specific circumstances, the Roma living "amongst the Gadže" were always able to attain for themselves a superior position based on a shared understanding of the territorial stigmatisation of the inhabitants of the settlement and the figuration of established/outsider relations (Elias 1994).

These attitudes also reflected the higher social capital of the "established" Roma and their position in the structure of local socio-economic relations. I drew on the example of Maroš in order to illustrate the historically contingent accumulation of a certain symbolic capital and material security, which Maroš was able to achieve by exploiting the position that his father Jozef had created for himself "amongst the *Gadže*". The relatively higher status he enjoyed within local social and economic networks provided Maroš greater room for manoeuvre when combining different economic practices. In the case of migration, it allowed him more space to decide whether an offer of work in the Czech Republic (or sometimes in more distant towns in Slovakia) was credible and lucrative. At the same time, these two levels of testimony offered by Maroš and the other Roma living in Jolany "amongst the *Gadže*" can be seen as being interconnected. The acquisition of greater room for manoeuvre so as to combine diverse economic practices shows that these Roma were able to profit in concrete ways by differentiating themselves from the Gypsies in the settlement.

Escaping everyday racism

However, based on their experience of migration, the Jolany Roma (regardless of their position in the geographical layout of the village) were in a position to review their own unequal status amongst the non-Roma in Jolany and beyond.[146] Katarína put it succinctly:

> If you go somewhere in the Czech Republic, they don't humiliate you. But here? For instance, you go to the doctor... He talks to you with such disrespect it's weird. You don't even know how you're supposed to respond he's so rude. They just strut their stuff. But not in the Czech Republic, there they tell you what you need to know politely and that's that.[147]

Zoralo recounted similar experiences and claimed that within the context of migration one's relationship even with one's non-Romani neighbours was transformed:

> A local *Gadži* from Svidník worked with me in the Czech Republic, plus another girl from Bardejov. I had a lot of fun with them, I can tell you

---

146 Other authors have examined this aspect of migration of the Roma from Slovakia to Bohemia, as well as to countries of Western Europe (e.g. Grill 2015b, 2017; Kobes 2012; Synková 2006, Ort and Dobruská 2018).
147 Interview with Katarína (b. 1967), conducted in Romani, 27 September 2016.

Jan! Time passed quickly on the night shift. In the Czech Republic we were just good pals. And then she saw me in Svidník and completely blanked me. If she did that here, people would call her weird. Here it's simply ingrained in the *Gadže* that a Gypsy is a Gypsy. When she's in the Czech Republic there's no one to see her, you get my drift? She can act how she pleases. She's not repelled by the Roma and has nothing against them and behaves normally.[148]

Whereas Katarína was keen to highlight the difference between the Czechs and Slovaks in respect of how they acted towards the Roma, Zoralo ventured to suggest that the different experiences he had had in the two respective countries might be due to the migratory situation itself, and that even those non-Roma who would ordinarily disdain the Roma at home were now friendly towards them. Zoralo's comments on his experience of migration is an insightful observation regarding the role of a specific place in structuring social interactions between the Roma and non-Roma. It shows that place was an independent actor in these situations, and that the interactions of the exact same people could take on a different form depending on the specific place. Interactions in Jolany or its surroundings were different to those that took place, for instance, in a hostel or factory in the Czech Republic.

However, migratory narratives also clearly revealed a gender-based element to this economic strategy. Short-term work migration was exclusively a male business, and stories about migration were to a large extent the shared frame of reference for men (see Grill 2008). However, according to the Jolany Roma, migration itself had the potential to redefine gender relations. The Roma associated a conservative conception of gender relations not only with the traditional Romani family setup, but also with the specific social space of Jolany. Zoralo and Jana pointed out that the anonymity of the Czech town where they lived and worked meant that they were able to visit the pub together, something that was not deemed acceptable in a small village like Jolany.

The Jolany Roma saw migration as a temporary escape from the asymmetry of relations that were contingent upon local social control, just as Zoralo and Jana were forced to adopt a more conservative definition of gender roles upon returning to Jolany. I was able to observe this transformation in behaviour within the context of migration when

---

148 Interview with Zoralo (b. 1987), conducted in Romani, 11 May 2015.

I met up with some Romani men in the Czech towns they had travelled to for work. Interactions with the non-Romani villagers in Jolany, largely subordinated to the maintenance of harmonious relationships ("so that the *Gadže* don't say..."), were in sharp contrast to the informal way the men behaved to the waitresses in Czech pubs, where they soon became regulars, or the demonstratively disdainful way they treated Vietnamese shop assistants in grocery stores.

Jolany as a safe space

However, the experience of escaping from unequal relationships remained linked to the context of short-term migration, which, during the period of my research, none of the Roma attempted to transform into a longer-term stay in the Czech Republic.[149] Though the Roma found temporary refuge in the Czech Republic from the everyday paternalism they experienced in Slovakia, and migration offered them the opportunity for socio-economic mobility, they also associated it with the insecurity of precarised work and the absence of established socio-economic, family, and other close networks. They even expressed uncertainty in respect of their own children, and were fearful of including them in a collective of Czech children, not necessarily because of racism, but more because of the rumours they had heard of drug use in small Czech towns.

It was against this backdrop that they refused to participate in the phenomenon of migration to the West. Some of the Romani families had relatives in Great Britain, above all the women who had married into Jolany. Nevertheless, they saw migrating to England as a step into the vast unknown. Maroš's daughter-in-law Klára (the wife of his oldest son Vlad) had her stepfather in England, whom she and Vlad had planned on visiting. They had even given thought to settling in England. However, Maroš was dead set against the idea and their trip was abandoned. Maroš, for whom Klára's stepfather was not a sufficient guarantee of functioning socio-economic networks, put himself in their shoes when explaining his objections:

---

149 The only exception was Churdo's son Jaňo, referred to above, who followed his brother Metres to the Czech Republic. However, neither of the brothers had grown up in Jolany (Churdo and Linda had only moved to Jolany at an advanced age) and both travelled to the Czech Republic to be with their partners, Czech women in both cases (Romani in one case, non-Romani in another).

What if there were a problem? How would I get home? It's not like the Czech Republic. If I have to I can hitchhike home. But how would they get back from England? In the Czech Republic there's every likelihood you'll meet someone you know, with whom you used to work. If it comes down to it, someone will always help me. But who will help me in England?[150]

Migration amongst the Jolany Roma was oriented on safe places. The Czech Republic was first and foremost – indeed almost exclusively – the target destination, which, even bearing in mind what Maroš said, demonstrates that the historically formed, transnational social networks between the Roma of the former Czechoslovakia were to some extent still relevant for the Jolany Roma during the period of my research. Despite the asymmetry of relations that the Roma were made aware of on the basis of their experience of migration, their home community remained for them a safe space where they were strongly embedded in the local socio-economic networks. Migration remained primarily a form of socio-economic mobility that could be above all capitalised on "at home" in Slovakia.

Flying in the face of the historically entrenched notion of the "natural" mobility of Gypsies (Guy 1998 [1975]), it seemed that it was the Roma, in other respects excluded from the category of "locals", who displayed a greater continuity of belonging to their home community than the non-Roma, who left for the cities in search of work (some to the Czech Republic, one family to Great Britain). Given the absence of research amongst the non-Roma who quit Jolany, we may conclude, albeit with caution, that although they probably found themselves in the position of immigrant in these new places (e.g. as eastern Europeans in Great Britain, cf. Grill 2017), the contrast between local belonging and non-acceptance beyond the borders of the village was in all likelihood not as great as in the case of the Roma, who were largely accepted in the village as "our Roma", whereas beyond those borders they became simply Gypsies (cf. Kobes 2012). As I showed in Chapter Two, even when looking for housing in the district, the Roma placed an emphasis on remaining in their home village, sometimes even at the cost of worse material conditions.

---

150 Interview with Maroš (b. 1967), conducted in Romani, 6 March 2015.

Conclusion

The authors of the introduction to the anthology *Gypsy Economy* expressed their belief that "an adequate political response to the problems that Roma and Gypsy populations face should not result in treating people as passive victims by denying them their creativity and capacity for struggle on their own terms" (Brazzabeni et al. 2015). For the Jolany Roma, this struggle did not constitute a preference for subversive practices that would mount an unambiguous opposition to the dominant economic strategies (cf. Stewart 1997). Instead, dominant ideas of work morale were formulated more or less explicitly in opposition to "Gypsy work" (Grill 2015a), which was associated with gaming not only a particular job of work, but the entire formal economy.

For a better understanding of the way the Roma responded to the dominant discourse of "Gypsy work", one might cite Howe's analysis of the dynamics of unemployment and the policy of resistance in Belfast (Howe 1998). On the basis of ethnographic research, Howe shows that the unemployed did not necessarily adopt a strategy of resistance to the dominant understanding of work ethic, but attempted to disrupt the logic by which they would be categorised as "welfare scroungers". The long-term unemployed in Belfast attempted to reframe relationships in such a way that they themselves were located on one side of the dominant discourse in the role of the "'deserving unemployed", while shifting the category of "scroungers" to other unemployed people.

I have shown that a very similar dynamic of relationships was in operation in Jolany, with the difference that the perception of the unemployed as being "welfare scroungers" was solidified through the racialised category of Gypsyness. On the one hand, the Jolany Roma rejected the dominant discourse as unfair, while on the other they accepted it, but only to the extent that it applied to a differently defined group of Roma. This had the effect of foregrounding the territorial boundary between the settlement and the rest of the village, which, according to the distinction described by Elias, then distinguished the "established" Roma from the "outsiders" (Elias 1994, see Chapter Two). This approach to the discourse of so-called "Gypsy work" and the work habits of the Gypsies is a further addition to what I have described in previous chapters as the negotiation of the category of Gypsyness and the characteristics associated with it.

An important aspect of the strategy aimed at evading identification with the "lazy Gypsies" in Jolany was its narrative form. Like the long-term unemployed in Belfast, the Jolany Roma talked about their own work commitment and the efforts they had made to find work. These sorts of narrative were important, mainly in contact with their non-Romani neighbours (especially those possessing higher social and economic capital), and involved the use of a comprehensive language code (see Chapter Three). A key role was played by similar narratives within the context of labour migration, the success of which was measured above all by an individual's ability to capitalise on the migratory experience in their home community (cf. Grill 2012).

However, I was able to observe the complexity of the Romani response to the dominant discourse of "lazy Gypsies" and "Gypsy work" through a confrontation of the narratives with the concrete economic practices of the Roma, above all in the home region, where their conduct was subject to greater control on the part of both the non-Romani and Romani surroundings.

Unlike the "activation work" and the short-term European project, which were not perceived as proper jobs, the attention of the Roma in this regard was focused more on odd jobs and providing assistance to the non-Roma in Jolany and its environs. In this context, because of the cumulative character of social and economic capital that I demonstrated using the example of Maroš, it was deemed wise to give the impression of being a reliable worker and to differentiate oneself from the rest of the Roma. It was also important not only to show oneself to be an efficient worker, but someone able to "speak with the *Gadže*", i.e. discuss suitable topics in the appropriate language while implicitly or explicitly setting oneself in opposition to the general category of Gypsyness or to specific Roma. This skill set possessed by the Jolany Roma was sometimes referred to as the art of "adaptation", itself based on a dominant discourse in which the Roma were seen as "unadaptable". However, the Roma subtly reinterpreted the meaning of the concept of adaptation, shifting it away from the dominant discourse. From their point of view, adaptation was understood to involve displaying the characteristics of the desired way of life, while retaining a certain distance and space for sporadic subversive practices that were in themselves deemed specifically Romani. The term "adaptation" now meant not only adaptation to the *Gadžo* order, but its assimilation into Romani (economic) strategies (cf. Brazzabeni et al. 2015: 11), in which there was space for the Roma to formulate their own interests.

By unravelling the discourse of adaptation, which the Roma have in part reshaped, it is finally possible to summarise the ambiguity of the negotiation of what in Jolany formed the concept of the Gypsy economy.

Although I showed that the Jolany Roma were involved in shaping and maintaining the discourse of "Gypsy work", they denied being work shy. On the contrary, the Roma usually framed this discourse in terms of their always being on the receiving end of the most arduous and worst paid work, as opposed to the *Gadže*, who, they claimed, benefited from their historically accumulated capital and the ability to "manage their affairs". Given their experience of historically entrenched marginalisation and direct discrimination on the labour market it might, finally, be possible to place a positive gloss on the dominant concept of "Gypsy work". The Roma viewed gaming the system and circumventing the formal economy to be an integral part of their economic practices in a world of non-Romani dominance.

It should be noted, however, that these practices were not inherently "Romani". The experience of economic marginalisation was common to the entire region. The Roma themselves, in going about their business, relied heavily on non-Romani actors who participated in circumventing the social system and undermining the power of the authorities both in respect of their conduct (as in the case of mayoress Pištána, the GP and informal employers), and the sharing of a certain narrative (as in the case of the regionally implemented project, when non-Romani visitors to the pub would encourage their Romani neighbours not to allow themselves to be "fleeced" by the European Union). However, though the non-Roma in this instance availed themselves of the tension between periphery and centre, in relation to their Romani neighbours they were without doubt on the side of dominance as established by the highly racialised hierarchy of relations. And it was according to the logic of these relations that a consensus existed in Jolany that the practices under examination were typically Gypsy in character.

In this chapter I have analysed economic strategies in order to observe not only the negotiation of an understanding of the category Gypsyness and the structuring of a social hierarchy based on it, but also a second key theme, namely, the ambiguous relationship of Roma to place. In this respect I was assisted by viewing labour migration as a historically significant economic practice of the inhabitants of the region. Migration was a strategy shared by both the Romani and non-Romani population, and the ongoing demographic change wrought by the migration of (above all) the non-Roma into towns and cities forms an important backdrop to the entire research project.

Within eastern Slovakia, Guy pointed to the asymmetric belonging of the Roma to place through the paradox of "settlement": "When – after how many years of being settled – do you cease to be 'sedentary' and just become 'normal'? If you are a Rom, the answer seems to be – Never!" (Guy 1998 [1975]: 29). I have shown how this discourse applied in Jolany. Historically speaking, the Jolany Roma have to an extent found themselves in the position of the "evictable" (van Baar 2016), with their relationship to place undermined by discriminatory policies enacted by the local authorities (or the implementation of centralised policies on a local level).

However, I have shown that the conceptualisation of Romani migration in this region did not necessarily ensue from the dominant idea of locally deracinated Gypsies. It was also understood as an integral part of a shared economic strategy in what has historically been a highly marginalised region. I suggested that the migration of the Roma might differ as regards their experience of the transformation of relationships with their non-Romani surroundings. This then returned me to my methodological starting point, according to which the concept of place was not simply a pragmatic delineation of the terrain in which my research was to be conducted, but an actor in its own right that bore powerful witness to the character of the negotiated relationships. I showed that the Roma themselves were, on the basis of their migratory experience, able to reflect upon the asymmetry of relationships in their home village in Slovakia and view the much vaunted harmony of local relations as illusory (cf. Grill 2015b, Kobes 2012). When speaking of migration, the Jolany Roma pointed to a certain emancipatory potential in addition to the possibility of socio-economic mobility. Nevertheless, despite the visibility of the asymmetry of relations in operation, Jolany, and by extension the entire region, remained for the Roma a safe place, to which their sense of belonging formed an important part of their identity.

Finally, even in respect of the situation in Jolany, an important factor in the changes taking place was the marked increase in the ratio of Roma within the population, not only of the village, but in the region as a whole. Following what I wrote earlier on the politics of place (see Chapter Two), the insistence of the Roma on belonging to a given place (cf. Sadílková 2017) could be viewed as a specific type of agency that to some extent sets them apart from their non-Romani neighbours, many of whom are caught up in an ongoing rural-to-urban pattern of migration. As in the case of the *Yifti* of Parakalamos, who were willing to undergo religious conversion and a change of name in order to retain their relationship to place (Theodosiou 2004), the Jolany Roma maintained a powerful continuity of identity through a belonging to place.

Conclusion
The Roma as Locals

"In my opinion they [the *Gadže* in Jolany] are satisfied with us [the Roma] because there are plenty of worse Roma than us."[151] This was how my friend Zoralo brought to an end one of our conversations on the position of the Roma in the local community. Of course, not every Rom in Jolany would buy in to such a statement, which is captive to the dominant logic of Gypsyness and the structure of anti-Gypsyism baked into it. Zoralo was in this respect possibly more submissive than other Roma, who set greater store by their own unqualified belonging to the community. Nevertheless, for me, Zoralo's statement revealed starkly the extent to which a notion of the status of the Roma as a naturally "alien" element, with which the "indigenous" non-Romani population of Slovak villages had had to learn to coexist, could take hold and become internalised. Quite simply from this perspective, the Roma were seen as a source of problems, some of them large, and some of them, as in the case of the Jolany Roma, not so large.

Zoralo's comment is fully in line with one of the key arguments of this book, namely, that the figure of the Gypsy in Jolany was not simply emblematic of certain popular stereotypes or evidence of the cultural diversity of society, but fundamentally inscribed within the structure and hierarchy of social relations as a highly racialised category within the local context. However, the aim of this book was not only to offer further evidence of the anti-Gypsy racist structures entrenched in European societies (see for instance van Baar, Kóczé 2020), but to reveal

---

151 Interview with Zoralo (b. 1987), conducted in Romani, 27 September 2016.

their instantiation and negotiation in a specific place, above all with an emphasis on the experience and agency of the Roma themselves. I am of the opinion that it is this kind of focus that will assist in opening up new topics. It will feed not only into research in the social sciences, but also broader social narratives centred around the status of the Roma in society and its historical development. It is this approach that will help us avoid viewing the Roma as being merely imprisoned within the logic of anti-Gypsyism (see Olivera and Poueyto 2018).

However, focusing on a specific place was not simply a pragmatic way of delineating the research situation. I viewed place as an independent and important agent in its own right, one that necessarily participated in the form of negotiated relations. As Theodosiou points out (2004), in traditional ethnographies of the Roma the analytical category of place is often overlooked, or merely forms the backdrop against which the Roma negotiate their position in non-Romani society. Leaving aside the few exceptions that accentuate the agency of the Roma (e.g. Olivera 2012, Racleş 2018, and from a historical perspective for the Slovak context Sadílková 2017, Scheffel 2015), the category of place vis-à-vis the Roma was only addressed through an emphasis on their *displacement* as a consequence of neoliberal politics imported from western Europe (e.g. van Baar, Kóczé 2020). With this in mind, several authors speak of the construction of the Roma as "Europe's perennial 'outsiders'" (Powell and Lever 2017), and refer to their ghettoisation (ibid..), nomadisation (e.g. van Baar 2011) and evictability (van Baar 2016). As Fotta had previously observed, the authors of many other works (see for instance Berland and Rao 2004, Bhopal and Myers 2008, Myers 2015) held similar views, and examined the Roma through the lens of Simmel's concept of the "stranger" (Simmel 1950). Fotta notes that these types of analyses reproduce methodological nationalism (Wimmer, Glick-Schiller 2003) and essentialise the position of the Roma as "foreigners" (Fotta 2018: 212–218).

Although this book takes into account the important context of policies aimed at the Roma/Gypsies and the discourse of the locally deracinated Gypsies, in its ethnographic focus it monitors their implementation not only in a specific place, but *in relation to* that specific place. I believe that shifting the emphasis onto the agency and experience of the Roma themselves can help disrupt the homogenising image of the Roma as "European Other", which is the inevitable consequence of a primary focus on the politics of displacement. In the final analysis, even Zoralo's apparent acceptance of the position of the Roma as outsiders within the eastern Slovak countryside was only part of a complex image of the relationship of the Roma to place as understood by the residents of Jolany. At the end of this book I will summarise certain moments that encapsulated the importance of tracking the negotiation of the position of the Roma in Jolany, which at the same time I believe could provide inspiration for continued comparative research into the (self)identification and sociability of the Roma in eastern Slovakia and elsewhere. I will address the following conclusions in subsections:

1. One of the key experiences that the residents of Jolany spoke of (especially the Roma) was that of the harmonious relations between the Roma and non-Roma. However, I have shown that such a concept, which was reflected in a specific social practice, arose from racist assumptions that individual actors then reproduced in their actions.

2. The Romani response to the existence of entrenched racist structures did not merely involve the passive internalisation thereof. On the one hand, the Roma created their own counter-narratives, in which they highlighted their resistance to non-Romani dominance; and on the other, they accepted the dominant requirement to adapt to the *Gadžo* way of life, all the while reshaping it, assimilating it into their own strategies of sociability, and in part filling it with subversive content.

3. In their response to the dominant narrative, which positioned them as the "excluded Other", the Jolany Roma emphasised their belonging to a specific place. In this respect they sought to overlay the category of Gypsyness with that of "local" residents. However, although "place" was to a large extent defined by "non-Romani normality", in many respects the Roma sought to belong to said place by means of, and not despite, their Romani-ness. In this respect, the Roma did not necessarily have to be seen as a foreign element within the place in question, since the very distinction between Roma and non-Roma (including the harmonious coexistence of the residents thus categorised) was inscribed within said place as one of its key components.

4. In another two subsections I will elaborate on the complexity of the relationships studied and recall other social categories that have remained somewhat sidelined throughout this book. As part of some observations on gender and kinship, I point out that these categories not only played an important role in negotiating who was local, but also provided a framework for identifications that might transcend the distinction between Roma and non-Roma and the logic of location-based identification.

Harmony as narrative and social practice

I believe that statements regarding the harmonious relations between Roma and non-Roma must be taken seriously, since they reflect the lived experience of the local population. Nevertheless, it is impossible to overlook the fact that such statements may also encompass other meanings depending on the social context in which they were uttered.

Firstly, I showed that the broader narrative of harmonious relations in Jolany represented a certain political agenda, and was presented in the media (and elsewhere) as a distinctive characteristic of the place in question. Yet participation in this narrative on the part of the inhabitants of the village itself could only be understood with regard to their position in the strongly racialised social hierarchy. In this way the Romani residents declared their own relatively higher status by implicitly or explicitly contrasting themselves with the Roma in other places (defined in various ways). They activated this narrative in conversations with me in my capacity as newcomer in order to make it clear that "here it's different to elsewhere". However, they also channelled this narrative in contact with representatives of non-Romani institutions in the region (the local mayors, doctors, civil servants, etc.), reminding them that they were from Jolany and thus demonstrating their ability to "adapt" to a *Gadžo* way of life.

The non-Roma were less keen on this narrative. In accordance with the logic of racialised hierarchy, they naturally found themselves on the side of dominance and basically did not need to prove their own status through forms of relationship with the Roma. Moreover, the non-Roma had no interest in highlighting the presence of the Roma in the village, whatever their relations with them. The very presence of Roma in the village was perceived more as a stigma, with the rise in the number of Roma within the population of the village as a whole viewed as being directly responsible for its socio-economic stagnation (or decline). The media image of the village was the business of a small group of residents (and strongly associated with the then mayoress), while the other inhabitants of the village only gave their assent to such a narrative in conversations with me due to my status as a researcher. As I mentioned in the introduction, within this context the non-Roma tended to comment on relations with the Roma perhaps primarily in light of my research objectives and my direct association with a specific Romani family. Participation in the narrative in question could be seen as a denial of racial inequality in the village and a way of defining oneself in relation to the human-rights discourse surrounding the racial discrimination of the Roma. However, even such sentiments continued to confirm the entrenched nature of racist structures. This was reflected in those statements that directly labelled the racially derived distinction between "black" (i.e. Roma) and "white" (i.e. "normal" or "white" inhabitants), for all that those making such statements would in the next breath emphasise that "skin colour doesn't matter here [in Jolany]". However, something similar was to be seen in situations in which the non-Roma referred to their neighbours as "our [i.e. more civilised] Roma", thus making them the exception to the rule of "problematic Gypsies". The non-Roma therefore relied on the existence of this racialised category, which they understood as generally accepted and intelligible and continued to reproduce in accordance with the logic of their own discourse.

However, I showed that harmonious relations in Jolany were not simply a matter of narratives, but represented a concept that was inscribed in specific social practice. Strategies for maintaining harmonious relations, whether from the point of view of the Romani or non-Romani residents, shared a common emphasis on "silencing the difference" (Horváth 2012). In this respect the Roma attempted to conceal characteristics of Gypsyness and, on the contrary, to uphold the social and economically advantageous position of "our Roma". For the non-Roma, on the other hand, the strategy of "not naming the Gypsies" (ibid.) was a way of sidestepping accusations of racism. In other words, the non-Roma tried to preserve the existing social hierarchy in which they naturally enjoyed a superior status. I also showed that a similar historically embedded strategy was pursued by the non-Romani representatives of the local authorities, who, even while perpetuating the marginalisation of the Roma (e.g. by rejecting applications for building land in the village), avoided formulating anti-Gypsy attitudes and activated other types of argument (usually by citing various administrative obstacles).

All these characteristics of the concept of harmonious relations (whether at the narrative level or the level of concrete practice) share something in common, namely, that they acknowledge the relevance of the category of Gypsyness and are therefore firmly rooted in an asymmetrical power hierarchy of relationships structured according to a racial key. In other words, the entire concept of harmonious relations was built on racist assumptions. It arose from a natural association of the Roma with the category of "problematic Gypsies". In this respect the harmonious relations between Roma and non-Roma in Jolany were far from embodying a multicultural understanding of the equal coexistence of different ethnic groups exhibiting mutual respect. All the more so given that even the Roma themselves were able put a name to non-Romani dominance and their own social marginalisation. However, it was significant that despite their experience of concrete examples of racial discrimination, the Roma did not turn their anger against the non-Roma involved, but against those Roma who, face to face with the non-Romani environment, situationally or more permanently displayed characteristics of the category "problematic Gypsies" and thus consolidated the poor reputation of the Roma in general. They did not regard such Roma as merely empirical proof of the validity of the discourse of "problematic Gypsies", but also as a reason for understanding and even sympathising with publicly articulated anti-Gypsy attitudes. In this way, concrete examples of non-Romani dominance did not conflict with the concept of harmonious relations, but became part thereof.

"So the Gadže don't say..."

Nevertheless, in this book I have tried to avoid a dichotomous understanding of social space in which different forms of identification are neatly separated by fixed boundaries. Similarly, I have shown that the very distinction between Roma and non-Roma was of a positional/situational character, given that in other respects the villagers thus categorised shared, for instance, the experience of belonging to a historically marginalised social periphery, the experience of migration, and to some extent the shared languages and characteristics of the local culture. In light of the methodology and indeed the ethics of the entire research project, we must for this reason reject any understanding of the Roma as primarily the "eternal outsiders", since this would contribute to the essentialisation of this position.

Regarding the inhabitants of Jolany, we cannot therefore think in terms of two clearly distinctive ideologies (Roma and non-Roma) that together maintain the equilibrium of harmonious relations. The Roma saw themselves as a fully-fledged part of the community and attempted to display this belonging in how they acted. The fact that situationally they found themselves outside of the community as understood in this way can ultimately be seen in two ways: on the one hand, as the outcome of exclusion based on a racial key; and on the other, from the Romani perspective, as the maintenance of a certain distance in which dominant accusations of Gypsyness could be incorporated as an active part of a more complex strategy of sociability in the *Gadžo* world.

In focusing on the agency of the Roma I have observed how, though the Jolany Roma strongly internalised their subordinate position within the racialised structure of social relations, their actions and statements did not indicate that they accepted without reservation the logic of non-Romani dominance. I have shown that the Roma created counter-narratives to the dominant narrative of harmonious relations based on the civilised traits of "our Roma" in comparison with other Roma, and that in these counter-narratives the harmonious relations were the outcome of their own agency, resulting from a resistance to certain manifestations of non-Romani superiority and an ability to maintain their position in particular socio-economic structures linked to the place in question. Moreover, the Jolany Roma did not enter into relations with their non-Romani neighbours with an unbridled determination to rid themselves of all the potential characteristics of Gypsyness. I believe that, unlike the Roma in the Hungarian village, the Jolany Roma did not entertain the illusion that, if they were simply to conceal their Gypsyness, they would become non-Romani villagers (cf. Horváth 2012: 129). Not only did they uphold distinctive features (e.g. language) in contact with their non-Romani surroundings, but they also allowed themselves space for individual acts of subversion of non-Romani "normality". To grasp the complexity of the Romani responses to non-Romani domination, I would like to focus on a phenomenon that conceals within itself both an acceptance of the established order, and the reframing thereof.

I have shown that the attitudes of the Roma to their own conduct in contact with the non-Romani surroundings were largely motivated by the wish that "the *Gadže* don't say…" and variations thereon. A few examples, chosen at random. The Roma did not want to participate at the farewell banquet for the priest "so that the *Gadže* don't say we just came for the free food". On the other hand, one explanation for their full participation in Christian festivities was that, if they did not, "the *Gadže* would say 'they don't have the money to prepare a basket for consecration'". When one of their number spoke Romani in an inappropriate situation, the other Roma would warn him that he should "speak *Gadžo* language, so that the *Gadže* don't think we are taking the piss out of them". In Maroš's yard, the children were occasionally told to behave themselves or not to cut wood on a holiday, both injunctions issued "so the *Gadže* don't say anything". When little Janík secretly accompanied me to mass at church, his mother was terrified of "what the *Gadže* must have said" when they saw how he was dressed. Fear of "what the *Gadže* will say" was primarily an expression of the desire not to provide their non-Romani neighbours any excuse to activate the stigmatised category of Gypsyness. As I showed earlier on, from the vantage point of the Roma, this active "silencing of Gypsyness" (Horváth 2012) was an important element in the creation and maintenance of harmonious relations in Jolany.

The phrase "so the *Gadže* don't say…" cemented an understanding of the *Gadže* as naturally "local" guardians of the established order and primary beneficiaries of social and economic capital, which was why it was advantageous to maintain good relations with them. The Jolany Roma believed that it was this strategy that had ensured for them the status of "our Roma" (i.e. Roma who do not present a problem and are conscientious workers, etc.) among their non-Romani neighbours, along with the advantages ensuing therefrom.

On the other hand, I have shown that the precept "so the *Gadže* don't say…" does not necessarily reflect an uncritical adherence to "*Gadžo* normality". If we understand it as a manifestation of the strategy of sociability of the Roma in a non-Romani world, then in addition to the sometimes anxious "silencing of Gypsyness" and a signalling of the characteristics of a non-Romani way of life it contained within itself a subversive element by which the Roma themselves indexed such conduct as a kind of game and kept their distance from the world of "*Gadžo* normality". I have illustrated such a shift in the concept of "adaptability", which in the dominant racist discourse stemmed from the designation of the Roma as "unadaptable". However, an important development had taken place in the Romani concept that set it apart from the dominantly formulated discourse. The Romani concept of "adaptation" was not aimed at full acceptance of a way of life that from their view was regarded as characteristic of the *Gadže*, but more at the selective acquisition of certain of its traits. There remained space in such a conception for the activation of specific practices that the Roma themselves understood as both distinctively Romani in nature and as subversive strategies that helped them endure the ubiquity of non-Romani dominance.

In accordance with the methodological appeal voiced above, I do not think that we should reframe the entire participation of the Roma in the dominant discourse as one big act, the purpose of which was simply to conceal their subversion of the *Gadžo* order. Instead, their concept of adaptation reflected a sharing of the ideology of a certain lifestyle, which was then supplemented by the formulation of their own, specifically Romani, interests. This did not involve a unilateral process of adaptation on the side of the Roma, but also compromise on the part of the non-Roma, who were to accept specific working conditions during the performance of odd jobs, certain concessions, the use of the Romani language in the public space of the village, and even the presence of particular families in the non-Romani residential areas. From this perspective, the phrase "so the *Gadže* don't say..." expressed a kind of corrective to the strategies thus configured that was intended to ensure the maintenance of harmonious relations. However, a key element in all of these negotiations, and one that this book has been keen to emphasise, is that adaptation to a non-Romani way of life, which at the same time the Roma were forever fashioning in their own image, was firmly tied to a specific place.

Place

The inclusion of place makes it possible to unravel the dynamic of the complex (self)identification of the Roma in Jolany. The inclusion of the category of place permitted me to disrupt the apparent pervasiveness and dominance of the distinction between the Roma and non-Roma, and to show how various categories and identifications could coexist and how individual actors might situationally negotiate them. Jolany was not simply one of the places where it was possible to observe the relationships between Roma and non-Roma: on the contrary, it exerted a direct influence on the form of these relationships. When reflecting upon the category of space, in this book I did not only examine the general relations pertaining between the Roma and non-Roma, but also the relations between the villagers who were understood to be "our Roma" and "our *Gadže*". Through such designations, in which the possessive adjective "our" expressed not only a certain relationship, but also belonging to a specific place, the category of place became highly relevant to the entire concept of harmonious coexistence earlier summarised.

The ambiguity of the local Roma belonging in Jolany resided in the fact that, though they themselves strongly identified with a specific place and were included in its community by their surroundings, they were at the same time excluded as historically "new arrivals" by means of the category Gypsyness. The strategy outlined above of "silencing Gypsyness" to a large extent consisted of overlaying the exclusionary category of "Gypsy" with the integrative category of "local" resident.

The category of place played an important differentiating role between the Roma. While the non-Roma activated the basic distinction between "our" and "other" Gypsies (although they were able to differentiate in more detail between "other Gypsies" on the basis of local affiliation), the Roma themselves tended to activate categorisation on the basis of an identification with a specific village ("Jolanian Roma", "Bukovcian Roma", "Maslovcian Roma", etc.). At the same time, the characteristics of the Roma thus categorised evolved depending on how they related to the category of Gypsyness. From this perspective the Roma were regarded to varying degrees as either "backward" (*degeša Roma*) or, conversely, as excessively "reaching out to Gadženess" (*cirdenas pen gadženge*). The frequent activation of the category "Jolanian Roma" was a way of signalling a relatively higher status based on an ability to "live with the *Gadže*". In the case of the Roma of Jolany, a belonging to place was inscribed in social status by means of its natural association with a non-Romani way of life.

In this book, however, I am less interested in observing the importance of place for the self-identification of the Roma in general, but more in tracking the processes by which the Roma negotiated their own belonging to place. It was therefore necessary to move from an understanding of place as a general category to the specific characteristics thereof. I examined the specificity of place, inter alia, through its language diversity. In a multilingual community, individual languages indexed certain types of social belonging that could be negotiated by means of situational code-switching. Rusyn operated as a marker of belonging since it was the language associated primarily with "our *Gadže*" and referred to by the Roma as a *Gadžo* language. At the same time, focusing on language made it possible for me to interrogate ideas of Jolany as a naturally "non-Romani" place. The Roma themselves did not understand belonging to place merely in terms of a competence in Rusyn ("*Gadžo* language") and an ability to utilise it, but also by means of Romani itself: not only its "*Gadžo* aspects" (local loan words), but also the locally embedded "original" Romani associated with the category of "Jolanian Roma". I described a similar model in the chapter on the politics of space. The Jolany Roma confirmed their belonging to the village not only through their drift away from the Romani settlement into the non-Romani part of the village, but also through the very fact of remaining in the settlement and thus maintaining what, within the context of eastern Slovakia, was its surprisingly central position within the village.

In light of these examples, it was impossible to view Jolany as exclusively defined by the non-Romani way of life, but also by the distinction between Roma and non-Roma, or the relationship between "our Roma" and "our *Gadže*". At the same time, this shift illustrates an earlier thesis, according to which the Roma were not necessarily seeking absolute acceptance and the signalling of the characteristics of a non-Romani way of life when overlaying the category of Gypsyness with the category of local residents. For them, local belonging did not stand in opposition to (self)identification with the category of Roma. They understood themselves as part of the place in question *because* they were Roma, and not *despite* that fact. In this respect this study of the importance of the category of place for the self-identification of the Roma in Jolany could be seen as an appeal for caution when reproducing an interpretation of the position of the Roma as "eternal outsiders" in the communities of eastern Slovakia, among others.

However, in the case of Jolany, we must not forget another important characteristic of place that was significantly reflected in the negotiation of local relations and their transformation in time. Jolany belongs to a region of Slovakia that has long been marginalised socio-economically and from which the local inhabitants have often travelled far and wide in search of work. For the Jolany villagers themselves such migratory tendencies go back to at least the beginning of the twentieth century, when many non-Roma participated in the broader phenomenon of migration from eastern Slovakia to south and north America. The Romani villagers also participated in this movement, and from the post-war period onwards would travel to the Bohemian lands in search of work, and to the Czech Republic after the division of Czechoslovakia. As in Parakalamos (Theodosiou 2004), in Jolany the movement of the Roma was not necessarily in conflict with local belonging, but sometimes even confirmed it. Firstly, the migration of the Roma was usually firmly anchored locally and their movement could be seen as a way of reinforcing their own position in the socio-economic networks that were concentrated in Jolany and therefore as a way of confirming their belonging to place. Secondly, within the context of migration, place played the role of independent actor that impacted the form of situationally negotiated relations. Relationships between the same people could take a different form under the influence of different places. At the same time, however, the Roma themselves were capable of casting a new eye on relationships in Jolany, i.e. in the place within which they identified primarily, thanks to their experience of other places. However, though they were able to enumerate the mechanisms of locally realised non-Romani dominance in their new outlook on place, an outlook that originated from their experience of migration, Jolany remained a safe social space in which they were able to benefit from the trustworthy position of "our Roma".

Focusing on the relationship of the Jolany Roma to place leads us to a possibly unexpected conclusion. For the Roma, who, as Gypsies, were regarded by their surroundings as not being locals (see, for example, Guy 1998 [1975]) and referred to in terms of nomadism in centralised policies and in popular discourse (see, for example, Sokolová 2008), being rooted in a specific place was key to their self-determination. Their emphasis on local belonging becomes all the more visible by virtue of the way that the residents of Jolany thought of the place as one of socio-economic stagnation, especially with regard to the dearth of job opportunities. However, while the vast majority of young non-Roma upped sticks and left the village, the Roma usually remained and were increasing their share of the total population of the village relatively rapidly. Though the way the Roma remained living in the village was sometimes activated (even by the Roma themselves) as a supporting argument in the dominant discourse on "passive Gypsies", I have shown that from the perspective of belonging to place, the Roma viewed their reluctance to leave the village as the outcome of their own agency, by means of which they maintained and consolidated their position in what for them was a safe and familiar social and physical place. As in the case of the Roma in Parakalamos, place became a defining feature of the continuity of their self-identification (Theodosiou 2004). But what Theodosiou did not remark upon in her work, and what I have observed only patchily up till now in this book, is the question of how gender was reflected in the negotiation of local belonging as another important category of social relations.

Gender

A brief summary of the above: the category of place was closely linked with the concept of harmonious relations; it was important for the (self) identification of the Roma in Jolany; it played a significant role in the negotiation of the category of Gypsyness; and as such it participated in a more detailed differentiation between the Roma themselves. However, in order to achieve a comprehensive understanding of the relationship of the Roma to place, other social categories and identificatory axes must be taken into account. This is important for two reasons. Firstly, various other types of categorisations are involved in determining who is local and who is not. Secondly, these categories will help show that the self-identification of the Roma themselves did not follow the logic of place unconditionally.

In this respect the category of gender is particularly worthy of attention. I have shown in this book that, inasmuch as belonging to a specific place was a strong part of the identity of the Jolany Roma, the separate category of "Jolanian Roma" was underpinned to a significant extent by gender. In a highly patriarchal society, it was men from whom the local belonging of specific families primarily derived. In this respect it was crucial that, when creating new families, the men remained in their native community, while the women moved to their partner's place of residence (the concept of virilocal post-marital residence). In the chapter on the politics of place I showed that women had been very neglected in the entire historical narrative of the "Jolanian Roma". The backdrop to this story involved the wholesale movement of young Romani girls from Jolany to other villages, where they became part of the story of the Roma in a different place. Conversely, the origin of Romani women who lived in Jolany faded in significance when compared to the local belonging of Romani men. Jozef provides an ideal example. The local authorities indirectly designated Jozef as "alien", part of the argument they used when refusing to grant him building land in the village. Let us not forget that the local authorities ignored the local origin of his partner Haňa, which not even Jozef deemed worthy of mention.

However, the example of Jozef also illustrates how the categorisation of "other Gypsies" versus "our Gypsies" was not necessarily fixed. During the 1960s, Jozef was declared "other" by the local authorities, someone who had a "poor reputation" among "citizens of Gypsy origin" and "local" residents. However, by the time of my research, the residents remembered Jozef as a Rom who had the strongest links within the local non-Romani socio-economic networks, and during the process of obtaining his own housing "amongst the *Gadže*" best met the criteria of "our [civilised] Roma".

The case of Jozef, who was politically active and worked as a local blacksmith, musician and odd-job man, also reveals how it was above all men who participated in the public life of Jolany and signalled their local belonging in contact with their non-Romani neighbours. I was able to observe this during the period of my research, when the women tended to remain at home while the men were expected to be the breadwinners. In the vast majority of cases it was they who performed odd jobs for the non-Romani villagers, travelled in search of work to the Czech

Republic, and regularly met up with other male villagers (both Romani and non-Romani) in the local pub. It was also exclusively Romani men who, from the 1980s onwards, regularly held one or two places on the local council, where they were perceived above all as representatives of the *local* Roma. In this respect it was mainly men who were the guarantors of local belonging and the social status of specific Romani families.

It is clear from the above that the category of gender played an important role in the internal differentiation of the residents of Jolany. Though I have showed that the hierarchy of social relations was to a large extent structured in accordance with a racial key, the category of gender was able to disrupt or overlap situationally the distinction between Roma and non-Roma. This could be seen, for instance, during the regular meetings of the men of Jolany (both Romani and non-Romani) in the local pub, where the presence of women was perceived as inappropriate, or during work trips, where Romani and non-Romani men from around the region often met.

One should also point out, however, that the category of gender also influenced not only the negotiation of the distinction between Roma and non-Roma, but the understanding of the category of Gypsyness. During situational formulations of their moral superiority over the world of the *Gadže*, the Roma would point out that "Romani women are faithful to their husbands". Divorce and broken families, which the Roma observed in Jolany and amongst their relatives in other villages, were regarded as a *Gadžo* phenomenon and as typical products of *Gadžo* individualism.

On the other hand, the Roma associated references to specific realisations of gender with the category of "backward Gypsyness", a term they used to label the Roma in surrounding villages or those living in the Jolany settlement. The "backward Gypsyness" of the Roma thus described was seemingly manifest in the exaggerated shame of the women, who bathed in a nearby stream fully clothed even on hot summer days (in reality I never saw a single Roma woman from Jolany bathe in the stream or anywhere else in public), or the excessive jealousy of the men. In general the Roma linked the shift from such manifestations of "backward Gypsyness" to acceptance of the features of a *Gadžo* way of life, which they associated in particular with migration to the Czech Republic inasmuch as it did not relate exclusively to male working groups, but entire families or married couples. Couples with such experiences spoke of their own emancipation from traditional gender roles, while at the same time saying that upon returning to Jolany, these roles returned to a certain extent to their former state (e.g. in an anonymous location in the Czech Republic they were able to visit the pub together, something that in Jolany was basically impossible given the strong social control of a small village). Their experience of migration thus formulated showed that place impacted significantly not only on the form that relationships took between Roma and non-Roma, but also on the nature of their gendered relationships.

Roma and kinship

Another category I would like to draw attention to here that was not treated in detail in the rest of the book is kinship. One should start by noting what I observed in the first chapter, namely, that family ties were important alongside other characteristics (e.g. skin colour, surname or language) in identifying specific people as Roma or Gypsy (cf. Grill 2017), who were viewed in this way because, inter alia, they had been born into a Romani family. At the same time, I showed that such a connection could be looked at from the other side. Inasmuch as certain people were identified as Roma on the basis of specific characteristics, while other key features of this category were lacking (typically when they had a very light complexion or lived a generally "*Gadžo* way of life"), speculation would be rife among the local population that their ancestors had included non-Roma.

However, kinship as a category was reflected not only in the negotiation of Gypsyness, but in the nature of local belonging. The sociologist Kobes, whom I have cited several times already, observed the mechanisms of local belonging in a different village in eastern Slovakia. He showed that, in the absence of the appropriate family relations, the Roma were excluded from the local community, defined, inter alia, by means of the concept "single *fajta*" (clan or lineage) (Kobes 2009, 2012). Kobes further states that they were able to be included in a community understood in this way, but asymmetrically (paternalistically), via unilateral (non-reciprocal) godparenthood (2012).

Social relations operated in a similar way in Jolany. Separate circles of kinship networks confirmed the distinction between Roma and non-Roma. However, for the former they also meant partial separation from the locally realised socio-economic relationships. I have shown that, though Kaleňák's economic situation and housing conditions were worse than all of the Roma in the village, he was nevertheless perceived as naturally local because of his origin in a local non-Romani family, even though in the eyes of the other non-Roma he had failed to display the character-istics of the appropriate "way of life". Ľuba and Juraňák were the only people in Jolany who disrupted the separate kinship ties of Roma and non-Roma. However, their marriage did not guarantee Ľuba, a Roma-ni villager, inclusion in the local "one family": on the contrary, it was regarded as confirmation of Juraňák's downward social mobility.

However, the categories of kinship and place did not only signal the distinction between Roma and non-Roma, but came into contact during other types of differentiation between the Roma themselves in Jolany. This could be seen to an extent in the case of Jozef, who was perceived by the local authority as "other", not only on the basis of his origin in another village, but also the absence of the appropriate family ties (spe-cific mention was made of the absence of a "legal marriage") that would bind him to Jolany. At the time I was conducting my research, the Roma were calling for a category of kinship that would confirm the deeper validity of the distinction between the Roma living "amongst the *Gadže*" and those in the settlement. When signalling a relatively higher status, the former would draw attention to the origin of their family in another municipality. For instance, Maroš and Churdo situationally made ref-erence to the category of the "Sl'ivanian Roma", who were supposedly "more used to living with the *Gadže*" than the Roma in Jolany. The same logic was used by several Roma who no longer lived in Jolany but drew attention to their self-identification with the category "Jolanian Roma". This was so in the case of Zoralo's brother Robo, who set himself apart in this way from the Roma in Maslovce, his new place of residence.

In addition to participating in the creation of the locally nested cat-egory of "Jolanian Roma", kinship links provided the Roma of Jolany a network of relationships that transcended the logic of an exclusive identification with place. Family ties that went beyond the borders of place, and in which local identification was not emphasised, involved primarily the maintenance of contact and mutual solidarity between siblings, i.e. men and women who lived in different places within the region or even far beyond its boundaries (e.g. in the Czech Republic). Maintaining such relationships could take the form of ordinary every-day communication, as well as more formal meetings on the occasion of important events. The guests at a baptism, wedding or funeral would be invited not on the basis of local affiliation, but above all on the basis of family ties.

Returning to gender, kinship relations also provided important soli-darity networks to Romani women, who in the vast majority of cases had moved to Jolany from their home communities. Several of these women had sisters in the village and were therefore able to form coalitions within Jolany itself (most of the women had moved to Jolany from neighbouring Maslovce). However, many women were not in this position, and in conversation with me they spoke about their difficulties adapting to the way of life of the Jolany Roma. Pavlína, for instance, recalled how, when she married a man living in the settlement at the end of the 1970s, the Roma were living "like sardines in a tin". Zoralo's wife Jana spoke of the language barrier formed by different varieties of Romani, as well as her difficulty in understanding Rusyn. Kalo's wife Marga told me how unused she was to the open-door policy of the Roma households in the settlement. Whenever these women distinguished themselves from the "Jolanian Roma", it was by means of kinship that they drew attention to their own belonging to another village in the district (or in Jana's case beyond its borders).

I believe it is important to recall such types of bonds in a book in which I have focused on the strong identification of the Roma with place. It was not only the links with close relatives that transcended the logic of an identification with place. When the Roma spoke of encounters with Roma on the Polish side of the border, which Jolany was close to, they spoke of how these Roma had the same surnames as them (adapted to Polish pronunciation and spelling) and of how they were probably related to them (*jekh narodos*, or "one kin"). However, as well as the (declared) kinship links, there was obviously the identification with the category of Roma, which transcended the logic of local identification. Perhaps slightly hyperbolically the Jolany Roma would tell me that they would never get lost in the world because "they had acquaintances everywhere" (i.e. there are Roma living everywhere in the world). Similarly, despite the significant differences in Romani dialects, they declared that any Roma could always get on with another, a claim they would back up by referring to their regular contact with Romani tradespeople from Romania. However, these examples must not be seen as being in conflict with the local identification of the Roma, but rather as showing that Romani identity was constituted situationally from several elements. Sometimes this would involve an identification with place, other times kinship, and finally it might take the form of an "imagined community" (Anderson 1983), or, on the contrary, a supplement to the comprehensive negotiation thereof.

In Jolany these identifications were combined and dynamically negotiated in various situations. Romanian Roma were ordinarily perceived as being "other". However, during their visits to Jolany a shared identification was activated of a broader "imagined community". Under certain circumstances the Jolany Roma would identify with the category "Jolanian Roma", while on other occasions they would define themselves on the basis of kinship and draw attention to their belonging to a family in a different village in the region. The Romani families that moved into Jolany from other villages (see the Epilogue) were able to declare an affiliation with the "Jolanian Roma" thanks to their newly acquired building plots, as well as to the fact that they had family ties with several Roma in Jolany. In certain contexts the other Roma recognised them as "Jolanian", while in others they would remind them of their difference on the basis of their strong association with the village from which they had moved, etc.

In other words, this book does not seek to emphasise place as the exclusive category of Romani identification in Jolany. Instead, by comprehensively monitoring the relationship of the Roma to place, it accentuates an important part of their identity that has been and continues to be neglected in both popular and academic discourse on the Roma.

Epilogue
Is Old Jolany Slowly Disappearing?

At the end I would like to recall the temporal level, not only of the relationship I have examined, but of the entire research setting of this book. I have tried to draw attention to the historical dimension of the relationships I have examined, which have, of course, developed dynamically over time. In this respect, the book might serve, inter alia, as an ethnographic corroboration of the claim of those historians who have showed that the racialisation of the Roma, whatever the official ideology of equality, was deeply embedded in the functioning of the society of state socialism, and was not therefore a phenomenon associated with the transition to capitalism (see Sokolová 2008). I demonstrated this continuity in the spatial segregation of the Roma, which was based on the logic of the category Gypsyness and drew basically on a racial key. And so on the one hand, there was racialised land ownership, with physical space and Jolany qua village being defined as non-Romani by virtue of the ownership of land (cf. Kobes 2012). On the other, there was the racialised category of Gypsyness that historically had made access to village land virtually impossible to specific villagers (i.e. Gypsies). However, while the territorialisation of the Gypsies had taken place during the era of state socialism in the face of an official ideology that promoted their "dispersal" among the rest of the population, in the new political order that arose in the wake of the Velvet Revolution their territorialisation was preserved in accordance with the state housing policy towards the Roma. I have also shown that, notwithstanding the fact that the ethnic category of Roma was publicly named in the official ideology of the new political order, on the contrary, during the negotiation of everyday relations and interactions in Jolany a bilateral strategy predominated of "silencing the difference" (cf. Horváth 2012). Such a strategy, which to a large extent conserved the racialised relations between Roma and non-Roma, traced its roots back to the ideology of the previous regime, which, by introducing the designation "citizen of Gypsy origin" (*občané cikánského původu*), provided for the complete erasure of the characteristics of a "Gypsy way of life" by regarding Gypsyness as a category of social deviance (see Sokolová 2008).

It is important we be reminded of such continuities in order to disrupt ideas of the sudden end of social equality and the associated radical transformation of social relations. However, an emphasis on historical continuity should not be allowed to obscure the relevance of certain historical milestones. The form of negotiating social relations in Jolany did not, it goes without saying, remain immune to the broader political and economic development of society. The Roma themselves cited their own material progress during the period of socialism, which they specifically dated to the 1970s and 1980s. This shift was in stark contrast with the life of the Roma "back in the day", i.e. with life prior to the war, but also immediately after it, a period that they themselves characterised by their almost complete economic dependence on their non-Romani neighbours. According to the Roma and their non-Romani neighbours, however, a significant change took place in local relations during the 1990s, when the socio-economic marginalisation of the entire region increased as a consequence of the political and economic transition. When reflecting upon these events, the residents of Jolany would refer to the closure of the local factory and the decline in the public life of the village. It was these factors that led to the deeper demographic change that, as I have already mentioned, became an important context for my entire research project.

From the very start of my research it was the case that, while the vast majority of the young non-Roma left Jolany permanently in order to find work in the county town or beyond the borders of the region, the Roma mostly remained. However, this trend, which saw the percentage of Roma of the population of Jolany as a whole increase, continued not only during the course of my research, spread over several years, but while I was putting the finishing touches to this book. In order to illustrate this development, I would like to focus on the continuation of the story of the dynamic development of the position of the Roma in the geographical layout of the village. Following on from the story that I left hanging in the air at the end of the second chapter will allow me to show both the rising presence of Roma in the public space of the village and the potential for greater social change that such a development promises in the future. Another open continuation is also a reminder that this book is primarily a reflection of the researcher's experience and situated in a specific time. The publication of this experience should definitely not be understood as a timeless description, not only of the relations between Roma and non-Roma, but also of the more broadly understood situation in the region under examination.

When Jozef, a Romani villager, finally managed to acquire a building plot in the village "amongst the *Gadže*" in the 1960s, he encountered significant resistance on the part of his future neighbours while building his new house. According to the dominant discourse, shared by Romani and non-Romani villagers, this conflict above all represented the efforts of the non-Romani villagers to prevent a Gypsy from living in the village. Until then the Roma had only lived in the local settlement the other side of the river. In the end, Jozef successfully completed the construction of a home for his family and was accepted by the non-Romani villagers as someone who knew how to live among "white people". The territorial boundary between the "settlement" and the village once again remained intact for a long time. At the start of my research, the settlement was still regarded as a naturally Romani space, even though three Romani families now lived "amongst the *Gadže*". With the demographic changes taking place referred to above, other Romani families gradually dissolved the historically entrenched idea that the Roma from Jolany lived in a settlement.

I ended the chapter on the negotiation of the position of the Roma in the geographical layout of the village at the moment when Kalo finally refurbished his house "amongst the *Gadže*" and Tomáš and Helena moved into an unoccupied council flat in June of 2020. However, Kalo and his family were not the only Roma who had managed to find housing in the village. In spring 2018, one of the non-Romani villagers died and his survivors, who had no links to Jolany, sold his house to a Romani family from neighbouring Maslovce. While the property owned by Maroš and Katarína, Miro and Pavlína, and Churdo and Linda was located on the outskirts of the village, two new Romani houses now stood in the very heart of the village immediately opposite the local authorities and the pub. One reaction to the presence of the new Romani families in a "non-Romani residential area" was given by the non-Romani villager Viktor, who, during a conversation with me held over his garden fence, pointed to a group of Romani children playing in front of the house of the family from Maslovce, with the comment that "old Jolany is slowly disappearing". It is significant that it was Viktor who spoke of "old Jolany", since he himself had only moved to the village fewer than ten years before the start of my research and had lived in Jolany for a significantly shorter time than Kalo, for instance, a native born and bred.

However, Viktor was not the only non-Romani who felt the need to make such comments regarding the changes underway in the geographical layout of the village. During conversations with other non-Romani villagers it became clear that several felt nervous, and spoke of a feeling of alienation from their native village when referring to yet another Romani family living outside the settlement. Reflecting on the arrival of a Romani family from Maslovce, they wondered aloud why the previous owner's heirs had sold the house and land to the Roma, "foreign Roma" no less, who were not "from here" and were therefore not ranked amongst "our Roma".

While the movement of the Roma to the non-Romani part of the village was regarded mainly as a manifestation of individual activity that would not disrupt the idea of the "cultural backwardness" of the Roma/Gypsies, the influx of Romani families into the village led to a fear of losing control of non-Romani territorial hegemony. The circumstances by which the Roma began to acquire their own buildings and property in the village may have contributed to such concerns. The ageing non-Romani population and the decline in its numbers was mainly due to the departure of young non-Romani families to the cities, and those who already lived outside the village had no problem selling an unoccupied house to a Romani family, wherever they might be from. These non-Roma no longer had to worry about whether the sale of the building or land would impact negatively on relationships "in such a small village" (see Chapter Two), since they no longer lived in the village and in many cases had no ties to it whatsoever.

In August 2020, as I was putting the finishing touches to this book, I paid a brief visit to my friends in Jolany. This trip was purely for pleasure and had nothing to do with my research. As we sat drinking coffee in Maroš and Katarína's garden, Maroš happened to mention that another Romani family had moved into the village, this one from nearby Bukovce. I learned to my surprise that the family had bought the house previously owned by former mayoress Pišťána, who had recently moved into a town in eastern Slovakia. The sale of the house, which had been part of the post-war reconstruction project, marked the definitive severance of her ties with the village, with which not only she, but her forebears too, had been closely associated. When I asked Maroš what the people in the village thought about this, he looked at me with incomprehension and replied: "What do you think they said? Everything was above board, they [the Romani family from Bukovce] paid up. What could people possibly say?" With these words Maroš unambiguously rejected the relevance of the territorial distinction between the naturally "Romani" and "non-Romani" parts of the village and declared it a matter of course that Romani families would buy houses "amongst the *Gadže*". Though this was a situationally contingent statement made by a single individual without any backup in research, it was clear that the presence of the Roma in what had previously been regarded as exclusively "non-Romani" residential areas was gradually becoming the norm. The ongoing demographic changes taking place meant that this was no longer an isolated example (in August 2020 there were six extended Romani households in the "non-Romani" part of the village, as opposed to eight households in the council flats in the grounds of the old settlement), but a clear trend that promised the further dynamic development of social relations in Jolany and possibly a more permanent breach of the logic of non-Romani territorial hegemony.

Though the purchase of a house and grounds by a Romani family from Bukovce held out the promise of a continuation of this trend, at the same time it brought to an end another story. With the sale of her house, mayoress Pištáňa had symbolically terminated her close connection with her native village where she had been mayoress for twelve years, during which time she was largely responsible for the promotion in the media of the narrative of harmonious coexistence as an important aspect of the village.

Bibliography

Published documents

Jurová, A. 2008. *Rómska menšina na Slovensku v dokumentoch, 1945–1975.* Košice: Spoločenskovedný ústav SAV.

Archives

Štátny archív v Prešove, pracovisko Archív Bardejov
Štátny archív v Prešove, pracovisko Archív Svidník

Internet sources

Grill, J. 2008. "Mange mište pro Čechy" (Mně je v Čechách dobře): slovenští Romové na českých stavbách, *migraceonline.cz* (online), 21 November 2008. https://migraceonline.cz/cz/e-knihovna/mange-miste-pro-cechy-mne-je-v-cechach-dobre-slovensti-romove-na-ceskych-stavbach.

Minh-ha, H. T. 1988. Not you/like you: post-colonial women and the interlocking questions of identity and difference, *Feminism and the Critique of Colonial Discourse. Inscriptions* 3-4 (online), accessed 10 January 2020. https://culturalstudies.ucsc.edu/inscriptions/volume-34/trinh-t-minh-ha/.

Mušinka, A. et al. 2019. Atlas rómskych komunít na Slovensku (online), accessed 23 January 2020. https://www.minv.sk/?atlas-romskych-komunit-2019.

Sadílková, H. 2019a. Holocaust of the Roma and Sinti on the territory of Czechoslovakia, *Roma Facts* (online), accessed 14 January 2020. http://romafacts.uni-graz.at/get_pdf.php?file=pdf_docs/ROMANI_HISTORY/English/H_5.6_holocaust_czechoslovakia.pdf

Synková, H. 2006. In the Czech Republic they call you 'Mister': The migration of Slovak Roma as a tactic to overcome exlusion. *migraceonline.cz* (online), 10 April 2006. https://migrationonline.cz/en/e-library/in-the-czech-republic-they-call-you.

Roma Spirit. 2020. Accessed 23 January 2020. https://www.romaspirit.sk/roma-spirit-2019/.

Journal issues

Romano džaniben. 2006. *Romano džaniben* 13 (1).

Literature

Abu Ghosh, Y. 2008. "Escaping Gypsyness: Work, Power and Identity in the Marginalization of Roma." PhD diss., Univerzita Karlova.

Anderson, B. 1983. *Imagined Communities: Reflections on the Origins and Spread of Nationalism.* London: New Left Book.

Baloun, P. 2019. "We Beg You not to Equate the Names of Gypsies and Knife-Grinders with Honest Traders" Itinerant Trade and the Racialisation 'Gypsies' in the Czech Lands between 1918 and 1938. S. I.M.O.N. *Intervention. Methods. Documentation* 6 (2): 44–55.

Barth, F. 1969. Introduction. In *Ethnic Groups and Boundaries: The Social Organization of Culture Difference*, ed. F. Barth, 9–38. London: George Allen & Unwin.

Belák, A. et al. 2017. "Health-Endangering Everyday Settings and Practices in a Rural Segregated Roma Settlement in Slovakia: A Descriptive Summary from an Exploratory Longitudinal Case Study." *BMC Public Health* 17 (128): https://doi.org/10.1186/s12889-017-4029-x

Belák, A. et al. 2018. "Why Don't Segregated Roma Do to More for their Health? An Explanatory Framework from an Ethnographic Study in Slovakia." *International Journal of Public Health* 63: 1123–1131.

Berland, J. C., Rao, A. (eds.) 2004. *Customary Strangers: New Perspectives on Peripatetic Peoples in the Middle East, Africa and Asia.* Westport: Praeger.

Bhopal, K., Myers, M. (eds.) 2008. *Insiders, Outsiders and Others: Gypsies and Identity.* Hatfield: University of Hertfordshire Press.

Bogdan, M. et al. 2018. "Introducing the New Journal Critical Romani Studies." *Critical Romani Studies* 1 (1): 2–7.

Bourdieu, P. 1991. *Language and Symbolic Power.* Cambridge, Mass.: Harvard University Press.

Bourdieu, P. 2000. *Pascalian Meditations.* Cambridge: Polity Press.

Bourdieu, P. 2004. Gender and Symbolic Violence. In *Violence in War and Peace*, ed. N. Scheper-Hughes and P. Bourgois, 339–342. London: Blackwell.

Bourdieu, P., Wacquant, L. 1992. *An Invitation to Reflexive Sociology.* London: University of Chicago Press.

Brazzabeni, M. et al. 2015. Introduction. In *Gypsy Economy: Romani Livelihoods and Notions of Worth in the 21st Century*, ed. M. Brazzabeni et al., 1–30. New York/Oxford: Berghahn.

Brubaker, R. 2002. "Ethnicity without Groups." *European Journal of Sociology / Archives Européennes De Sociologie / Europäisches Archiv Für Soziologie* 43 (2): 163–189.

Brubaker, R. 2014. "Beyond ethnicity." *Ethnic and Racial Studies* 37 (5): 804–808.

Corradi, L. 2018. *Gypsy Feminism: Intersectional Politics, Alliances, Gender and Queer.* New York: Routledge.

Čada, K. 2012. Social Exclusion of the Roma and Czech Society. In *The Gypsy "Menace". Populism and the New Anti-Gypsy Politics*, ed. M. Stewart, 67–80. London: C. Hurst.

Červenka, J. 2000. Úloha české romistiky při poznávání Romů. In *Terénní výzkum integrace a segregace*, ed. S. Kužel, 267–270. Plzeň: Cargo.

Červenka, J. 2014. "Standardizace romštiny na území bývalého Československa." *Acta Universitatis Carolinae – Philologica* 3 (Slavica Pragensia XLII): 55–70.

Čulen, K. 2007. *History of Slovaks in America*. St. Paul, Minnesota: Czechoslovak Genealogical Society.

Davidová, E. 1965. *Bez kolíb a šiatrov*. Košice: Východoslovenské vydavateľstvo.

Dobruská, P. 2018. The Mobility of Roma from a Slovak Village and Its Influence on Local Communities. In *Remigration to post-socialist Europe: hopes and realities of return*. ed. C. Hornstein-Tomic et al., 285–318. Berlin: LIT Verlag.

Donert, C. 2017. *The Rights of the Roma: The Struggle for Citizenship in Postwar Czechoslovakia*. Cambridge: Cambridge University Press.

Elias, N. 1994. Introduction: A Theoretical Essay on Established and Outsider Relations. In N. Elias, J. L. Scotson. *The Established and the Outsiders*, xv–lii. London: Sage.

Elšík, V. 2003. "Interdialect contact of Czech (and Slovak) Romani varieties." *International Journal of the Sociology of Language* 162: 41–62.

Elšík, V., Beníšek, M. 2020. Romani Dialectology. In *Handbook of Romani Language and Linguistics*, ed. Y. Matras and A. Tenser, 389–428. Cham: Palgrave Macmillan.

Engebrigtsen, A. I. 2007. *Exploring Gypsiness: Power, Exchange and Interdpendence in a Transylvanian Village*. New York: Berghahn.

Eriksen, T. H. 2019. Beyond a Boundary. In *Ethnic Groups and Boundaries Today: A Legacy of Fifty Years*, ed. T. H. Eriksen and M. Jakoubek, 133–151. London: Routledge.

Eriksen, T. H., Jakoubek, M. (eds.) 2019. *Ethnic Groups and Boundaries Today: A Legacy of Fifty Years*. London: Routledge.

Fabian, J. 1983. *Time and the Other: How Anthropology Makes Its Object*. New York: Columbia University Press.

Fanon, F. 1955. Antillais et Africains. In F. Fanon. *Pour la revolution africaine. Ecrits politiques*, 22–23. Paris: François Maspero.

Fanon, F. 2008. *Black Skin, White Masks*. London: Pluto.

Fassin, D. et al. 2014. *Roms & riverains. Une politique municipale de la race*. Paris: La Fabrique.

Ferguson, Ch. A. 1959. "Diglossia." *Word* 15 (2): 325–340.

Fishman, J. A. 1967. "Bilingualism with or without Diglossia; Diglossia with or without Bilingualism." *Journal of Social Issues* 23 (2): 29–38.

Fishman, J. A. 2000. Who Speaks What Language to Whom and When? In *The Bilingualism Reader*, ed. L. Wei, 82–98. New York: Routledge.

Filčák, R. 2012. *Living Beyond the Pale: Environmental Justice and the Roma Minority*. Budapest: CEU Press.

Fotta, M. 2018. *From Itinerant Trade to Moneyleading in the Era of Financial Inclusion: Households, Debts and Masculinity among Calon Gypsies of Northeast Brazil*. New York: Palgrave Macmillan.

Fremlová, L. 2018. "Non-Romani Researcher Positionality and Reflexivity." *Critical Romani Studies* 1 (2): 98–123.

Gardner, K. 1993. "Desh-Bidesh: Silhety Images of Home and Away." *Man* 28 (1): 1–15.

Gay y Blasco, P. 1999. *Gypsies in Madrid: Sex, Gender and the Performances of Identity*. New York: Berg.

Gay y Blasco, P., Hernández, L. 2020. *Writing friendship: A Reciprocal Ethnography*. New York: Palgrave Macmillan.

Gažovičová, T. 2015. "Romani Pupils in Slovakia: Trapped between Romani and Slovak Languages." *ZEP: Zeitschrift für internationale Bildungsforschung und Entwicklungspädagogik* 38 (1): 18–23.

Grill, J. 2012. "'Going up to England': Exploring Mobilities among Roma from Eastern Slovakia." *Journal of Ethnic and Migration Studies* 38 (8): 1269–1287.

217

Grill, J. 2015a. 'Endured Labour' and 'Fixing up' Money: The Economic Strategies of Roma Migrants in Slovakia and the UK. In *Gypsy Economy: Romani Livelihoods and Notions of Worth in the 21st Century*, ed. M. Brazzabeni et al., 88–106. New York / Oxford: Berghahn.

Grill, J. 2015b. Historické premeny štruktúry medzikultúrnych vzťahov: Formy spolužitia v prípade Tarkoviec na východnom Slovensku. In *Čierno-biele svety: Rómovia v majoritnej spoločnosti na Slovensku*, ed. T. Podolinská and T. Hrustič, 146–171. Bratislava: Veda.

Grill, J. 2017. "'In England, They Don't Call You Black!' Migrating Racialisations and the Production of Roma Difference across Europe." *Journal of Ethnic and Migration Studies* 44 (7): 1136–1155.

Grill, J. 2018. "Re-Learning to Labour? 'Activation works' and new politics of social assistance in the case of Slovak Roma." *Journal of the Royal Anthropological Institute* 24 (2): https://doi.org/10.1111/1467-9655.12802.

Guy, W. 1977. "The Attempt of Socialist Czechoslovakia to Assimilate Its Gypsy Population." PhD diss., University of Bristol.

Guy, W. 1998 [1975]. Ways of Looking at Roma: The Case of Czechoslovakia. In *Gypsies: An Interdisciplinary Reader*, ed. D. Tong, 13–68. New York: Garland Publishing.

Gupta, A., Ferguson, J. 1992. "Beyond 'Culture': Space, Identity, and the Politics of Difference." *Cultural Anthropology* 7 (1): 6–23.

Hajská, M. 2015. *Gažikanes vaj romanes? Jazykové postoje olašských Romů jedné východoslovenské komunity ke třem místně užívaným jazykům.* In *Čierno-biele svety. Rómovia v majoritnej spoločnosti na Slovensku*, ed. T. Podolinská and T. Hrustič, 346–373. Bratislava: Veda.

Hajská, M. 2017. "Economic Strategies and Migratory Trajectories of Vlax Roma from Eastern Slovakia to Leicester, UK. " *Slovenský národopis* 65 (4): 357–382.

Halwachs, D. W. et al. 2013. *Romani, Education, Segregation and the European Charter for Regional or Minority Languages.* Graz: Grazer Romani Publikationen.

Halwachs, D. W. 2020. Languagre Policy and Planning in Romani. In *Handbook of Romani linguistic*, ed. Y. Matras and A. Tenser, 429–457. Cham: Palgrave Macmillan.

Hepworth, K. 2012. "Abject Citizens: Italian 'Nomad Emergencies' and the Deportability of Romanian Roma." *Citizenship Studies* 16 (3–4): 431–449.

Hojsík, M. 2008. *Evalvácia programu obecných nájomných bytov v rómskych osídleniach (Evaluation of municipal rental housing program in Roma settlements).* Bratislava: Nadácia Milana Šimečku.

Hojsík, M. 2012. Slovakia: On the Way to the Stable Social Housing Concept. In *Social Housing in Transition Countries*, ed. J. Hegedüs et al. New York: Routledge.

Horváthová, E. 1964. *Cigáni na Slovensku. Historicko-etnografický náčrt.* Bratislava: Vydavateľstvo Slovenskej akadémie vied.

Horváth, K. 2005. "Gypsy Work – Gadjo work." *Romani Studies* 15 (1): 31–49.

Horváth, K. 2012. Silencing and Naming the Difference. In *The Gypsy "Menace". Populism and the New Anti-Gypsy Politics*, ed. M. Stewart, 117–136. London: C. Hurst.

Howe, L. 1998. "Scrounger, Worker, Beggarman, Cheat: The Dynamics of Unemployment and the Politics of Resistance in Belfast." *The Journal of the Royal Anthropological Institute* 4 (3): 531–550.

Hrustič, T. 2011. Values and Ethnicity – Religious Conversions of Roma in Eastern Slovakia to the Watchower Society. In *Spaces and Borders: Young Researchers about Religion in Central and Eastern Europe*, ed. C. Rughiniş and A. Máté-Tóth, 23–32. Berlin: De Gruyter.

Hrustič, T. 2012. The Trends in the Participation of Romani Candidates in Elections in Slovakia. In *Roma Rights, Journal of the European Roma Rights Centre: Challenging of*

Representation – Voices on Roma Politics, Power and Participation. Budapest: European Roma Rights Centre.

Hrustič, T. 2014. The Rise and Fall of Romani Pentecostal Revivals in Eastern Slovakia – A Case Study of One Mission. In *Romani Pentecostalism: Gypsies and Charismatic Christianity*, ed. D. Thurfjell and A. Marsh, 193–214. Frankfurt am Main: Peter Lang.

Hrustič, T. 2015a. "Usury among the Slovak Roma: Notes on Relations between Lenders and Borrowers in a Segregated Taboris." In *Gypsy Economy: Romani Livelihoods and Notions of Worth in the 21st Century*, ed. M. Brazzabeni et al., 31–48. New York, Oxford: Berghahn.

Hrustič, T. 2015b. "'Záleží na nás ako sa dohodneme'. Prehľad rómskej politickej participácie na Slovensku (1990–2014)." In *Čierno-biele svety: Rómovia v majoritnej spoločnosti na Slovensku*, ed. T. Podolinská and T. Hrustič, 104–145. Bratislava: Veda.

Hrustič, T. 2020. "How Roma Mayors Penetrate the Municipal Power Structures: Resisting the Non-Roma Dominance in Slovak Local Governments." *Slovenský národopis* 68 (4): 397–411.

Hrustič, T., Poduška, O. 2018. Participácia a kolaborácia v akadémii a verejnej politike. (Úvod k tematickému číslu Romano džaniben). *Romano džaniben* 25 (2).

Hübschmannová, M. 1970. "Co je tzv. cikánská otázka?" *Sociologický časopis / Czech Sociological Review* 6 (2): 105–120.

Hübschmannová, M. 1972. "What Can Sociology Suggest about the Origin of Roms?" *Archiv orientální* 40: 51–64.

Hübschmannová, M. 1979. "Bilingualism among the Slovak Roms." *International Journal of the Sociology of Language* 19: 33–49.

Hübschmannová, M. 1993. *Šaj pes dovakeras – Můžeme se domluvit*. Olomouc: Vydavatelství Univerzity Palackého.

Hübschmannová, M. 1998. Economic Stratification and Interaction (Roma, an Ethnic Jati in East Slovakia). In *Gypsies: An Interdisciplinary Reader*, ed. D. Tong, 233–270. New York: Garland Publishing.

Hübschmannová, M. 1999. Několik poznámek k hodnotám Romů. In *Romové v České republice: 1945–1989*, 16–66. Praha: Socioklub.

Hübschmannová, M. 2000a. "Inspirace pro rozvoj romštiny." *Člověk a spoločnosť* 3 (1): 134–145.

Hübschmannová, M. 2000b. "Vztahy mezi Romy a Židy na východním Slovensku před druhou světovou válkou." *Romano džaniben* 7 (1): 17–23.

Hübschmannová, M. (ed.) 2005. *Po Židoch Cigáni: svědectví Romů ze Slovenska 1939–1945. I., 1939 – srpen 1944*. Praha: Triáda.

Hübschmannová, M., Kyuchukov, H. 2009. Asking for Favor in Two Romani Dialects. In *New Studies in Romology*, ed. H. Kyuchukov, 55–75. Sofia: Wini 1837.

Jenkins, R. 1997. *Rethinking Ethnicity*. London: Sage.

Jenkins, R. 2014. "Time to Move beyond Boundary Making?" *Ethnic and Racial Studies* 37 (5): 809–813.

Jakoubek, M., Hirt, T. (eds.) 2008. *Rómske osady na východnom Slovensku z hľadiska terénneho antropologického výskumu*. Bratislava: Nadácia otvorenej spoločnosti – Open Society Foundation.

Jensen, S. Q., Christensen A. 2012. "Territorial Stigmatization and Local Belonging: A Study of the Danish Neighbourhood Aalborg East." *City* 16 (1–2): 74–92.

Jovanović, J., Daróczi, A. C. 2015. Still Missing Intersectionality: The Relevance of Feminist Methodologies in the Struggle for the Rights of Roma. In *Roma Rights 2: Nothing about us Without Us? Roma Participation in Policy Making and Knowledge Production*, ed. M. Bogdan, 79–82. Budapest: European Roma Rights Centre.

Jurová, A. 2002. "Historický vývoj rómskych osád na Slovensku a problematika vlastníckych vzťahov k pôde („nelegálne osady")." *Človek a spoločnosť* 5 (4): 13–43.

Jurová, A. 2003. "Niekoľko poznámok k ozázkam rómskych osád („Kauza Letanovce")." *Človek a spoločnosť* 6 (1): 2–12.

Kandert, J. 2004. *Každodenní život vesničanů středního Slovenska v šedesátých až osmdesýtých letech 20. století.* Praha: Karolinum.

Kobes, T. 2009. *Tu zme šicke jedna rodzina, tu zme šicke jedna fajta: příbuzenství východoslovenského venkova.* Prešov: Centrum antropologických výskumov.

Kobes, T. 2010. "Fajta a povaha příbuzenství obyvatel východoslovenských romských osad." *Sociologický časopis / Czech Sociological Review* 46 (2): 235–255.

Kobes, T. 2012. "'Naši Romové' – difrakční vzorce odlišnosti východoslovenského venkova." *Romano džaniben* 19 (2): 9–34.

Kobes, T. 2017. "O lovcích a sběračích sociálních struktur a dominantních diskurzů." *Romano džaniben* 24 (1): 81–98.

Kovai, C. 2012. Hidden Potentials in 'Naming the Gypsy': The Transformation of the Gypsy-Hungarian Distinction. In *The Gypsy "Menace". Populism and the New Anti-Gypsy Politics*, ed. M. Stewart, 281–294. London: C. Hurst.

Kóczé, A. 2009. Missing Intersectionality: Race/Ethnicity, Gender, and Class in Current Research and Policies on Romani Women in Europe. *Center for Policy Studies Working Papers.* Budapest: CEU Center for Policy Studies.

Kubaník, P. 2015. *Hra na knížky: Poznámky k akvizici slovenštiny v Gavu.* In *Čierno-biele svety. Rómovia v majoritnej spoločnosti na Slovensku*, ed. T. Podolinská and T. Hrustič, 374–397. Bratislava: Veda.

Kubaník, P. 2017. "'Nebijte se, hádejte se'. Socializace asertivity v Gavu." Romano Džaniben 24 (2): 23–44.

Kubaník P. et al. 2013. *Romani Language Competence in an Intergenerational Transmission in the Czech Republic.* In *Romani V. papers from the Annual Meeting of the Gypsy Lore Society Graz 2011*, ed. B. Schrammel and B. Leber, 61–80. Graz: Treffpunkt sprachen, Plurilingualism Research Unit.

Kužel, S. (ed.) 2000. *Terénní výzkum integrace a segregace.* [Praha]: Cargo.

Lacková, I. 1999. *A False Dawn. My life as a Gypsy Woman in Slovakia.* Hertfordshire: University of Hertfordshire Press.

Majo, J. 2012. *Historicko-demografický lexikón obcí Slovenska 1880–1910.* Bratislava: Štatistický úrad Slovenskej republiky.

Mann, A. B. 1996. Zakladatelka romistiky na Slovensku Emília Horváthová (1931–1996). *Romano džaniben* 3 (1–2): 141–144.

Matras, Y. 2002. *Romani: A Linguistic Introduction.* Cambridge: Cambridge University Press.

Nečas, N. 1999. *The Holocaust of Czech Roma.* Praha: Prostor.

Malkki, L. 1995. *Purity and Exile: Violence, Memory, and National Cosmology among Hutu Refugees in Tanzania.* Chicago: University of Chicago Press.

Manrique, N. 2015. 'Give and Don't Keep Anything!' Wealth, Hierarchy and Identity among the Gypsies of Two Small Towns in Andalusia, Spain. In *Gypsy Economy: Romani Livelihoods and Notions of Worth in the 21st Century*, ed. M. Brazzabeni et al., 221–239. New York, Oxford: Berghahn.

Marušák, M., Singer, L. 2009. Social Unrest in Slovakia 2004: Romani Reaction to Neoliberal 'Reforms'. In *Romani Politics in Contemporary Europe: Poverty, Ethnic Mobilization, and the Neoliberal Order*, ed. N. Sigona and N. Trehan, 186–208. London: Palgrave Macmillan.

Mušinka, A. 2019. "Methodology of Three Statistical Surveys (So Called Atlas) of Roma Communities in Slovakia and Political Representation of Roma in Settlements of Prešov Self-Governing Region." *Annales Scientia Politica* 8 (2): 79–89.

Mušinka, A. et al. 2014. *Atlas rómskych komunít na Slovensku 2013.* Bratislava: UNDP.

Myers, M. 2015. Researching Gypsies and Their Neighbours: The Utility of the Stranger. In *Researching Marginalized Groups*, ed. K. Bhopal and R. Deuchar, 211–224. New York: Routledge.

Olivera, M. 2012. "The Gypsies as Indigenous Groups: the Gabori Roma Case in Romania." *Romani studies* 5 (1): 19–33.

Olivera, M. 2015. The Mechanisms of Independence: Economic Ethics and the Domestic Mode of Production among Gabori Roma in Transylvania. In *Gypsy economy: Romani Livelihoods and Notions of Worth in the 21st century*, ed. M. Brazzabeni et al., 145–162. New York: Berghahn.

Olivera, M., Poueyto, J. 2018. "Gypsies and Anthropology: Legacies, Challenges, and Perspectives." *Ethnologie Francaise* 172 (4): 581–600.

Oravcová, A., Slačálek, O. 2019. "Roma youth in Czech rap music: stereotypes, objectification and 'triple inauthenticity'." *Journal of Youth Studies*: https://doi.org/10.1080/13676261.2019.1645946.

Ort, J. 2017. "Mobilita Romů v kontextu lokálních vztahů. Případová studie z okresu Svidník na východním Slovensku." Master's thesis, Univerzita Karlova.

Ort, J. 2021. "Romové jako místní obyvatelé? Přináležení, cikánství a politika prostoru ve vesnici na východním Slovensku." *Sociologický časopis / Czech Sociological Review* 57 (5): 581–608.

Ort, J. 2022 [in print]. Belonging, Mobility, and the Socialist Policies in Kapišová, Slovakia. *Romani studies* 32 (1).

Ort, J., Dobruská, P. 2018. "Kontinuity a diskontinuity v transnacionálním sociálním poli na příkladu margovanských Romů." *Český lid* 105: 131–157.

Pattillo, M. 2009. "Revisiting Loïc Wacquant's Urban Outcasts." *International Journal of Urban and Regional Research* 33 (3): 858–864.

Piasere, L. 1985. *Mare Roma. Catégories humaines et structure sociale. Une contribution à l'ethnologie tsigane.* Paris: Paul-Henri Stahl.

Pintér, T. 2011. "Diglosia alebo funkčný bilingvizmus v jazykovej situácii Rómov na Slovensku a v Maďarsku." *Jazykovedný časopis* 62 (1): 3–18.

Podolinská, T., Hrustič, T. 2011. *Religion as a Path to Change? The Possibilities of Social Inclusion of the Roma in Slovakia.* Bratislava: Friedrich Ebert Stiftung, Institute of Ethnology SAS.

Podolinská, T., Hrustič, T. (eds.) 2015. *Čierno-biele svety: Rómovia v majoritnej spoločnosti na Slovensku.* Bratislava: Veda.

Powell, R., Lever, J. 2015. "Europe's Perennial 'Outsiders': A Processual Approach to Roma Stigmatization and Ghettoization." *Current Sociology* 65 (5): 680–699.

Powel, R., van Baar, H. 2019. *The Invisibilization of Anti-Roma Racisms: Securitization of the Roma in Europe*, ed. H. van Baar et al., 91–112, New York: Palgrave Macmillan.

Prokeš, M. et al. 2016. Korbany. In *Etnografie sociální mobility: etnicita, bariéry, dominance*, ed. J. Šotola and M. Rodrígez Polo, 185–236. Olomouc: Vydavatelství Filozofické fakulty UP.

Racleş, A. 2018. "Walking with Lina in Zamora. Reflections on Roma's Home-Making Engagements from Translocality Perspective." *Intersections* 4 (2): 86–108.

Sadílková, H. 2013. "Čí jsou to dějiny? Dosavadní přístupy k interpretaci poválečných dějin Romů v ČS(S)R." *Romano džaniben* 20 (2): 69–86.

Sadílková, H. 2016. "Poválečná historie Romů ve vzpomínkách pamětníků: Možnosti rekonstrukce poválečné migrace vybrané skupiny Romů ze Slovenska do českých zemí." PhD diss., Univerzita Karlova.

Sadílková, H. 2017. Resettling the Settlement: From Recent History of a Romani Settlement in South-Eastern Slovakia. In *Festschrift for Lev Cherenkov*, ed. K. Kozhanov and D. Halwachs, 339–351. Graz: Grazer Romani Publikationen.

Sadílková, H. 2019. Hledání místa romštiny ve školním prostředí a výuce na základních a středních školách – nejen na Slovensku. In *Inovácia – Rómsky jazyk – Inklúzia: Výučba rómského jazyka metodikou vyučovania cudzieho jazyka*, ed. J. Facuna and R. Lužica, 35–43. Bratislava: Štátný pedagogický ústav.

Sadílková, H. 2020. The Postwar Migration of Romani Families from Slovakia to the Bohemian Lands: A Complex Legacy of War and Genocide in Czechoslovakia. In *Jewish and Romani Families in the Holocauts and Its Aftermath*, ed. E. R. Adler and K. Čapková, 190–217. New Jersey: Rutgers University Press.

Sadílková, H. et al. 2018. *Aby bylo i s námi počítáno: Společensko-politická angažovanost Romů a snahy o založení romské organizace v poválečném Československu.* Brno: Muzeum romské kultury.

Scheffel, D. 2005. *Svinia in Black & White: Slovak Roma and Their Neighbours.* Toronto: University of Toronto Press.

Scheffel, D. 2015. "Belonging and Domesticated Ethnicity in Veľký Šariš, Slovakia." *Romani studies* 25 (2): 115–149.

Scott, J. 1985. *Weapons of the Weak: Everyday Forms of Resistance.* New Haven: Yale University Press.

Sigona, N., Trehan, N. 2011. The (Re)Criminalization of Roma Communities in a Neoliberal Europe. In *Racial Criminalization of Migrants in the 21st Century*, ed. S. Palidda, 119–132. London: Ashgate.

Silverman, C. 2018. "From Reflexivity to Collaboration. Changing Roles of a Non-Romani Scholar, Activist, and Performer." *Critical Romani Studies* 1 (2): 76–97.

Simmel, G. 1950. The Stranger. In *The Sociology of Georg Simmel*, ed. K. H. Wolff, 402–408. Glencoe: The Free Press.

Skupnik, J. 2007. "Svět se zrcadlem. Marginalizace a integrace z hlediska sociopsychologické dynamiky společnosti." *Sociologický časopis / Czech Sociological Review* 43 (1): 133–148.

Sloboda, M. et al. 2018. Language Planning in Slovakia: Nation-Building in the Context of European Integration. In *Language Planning in the Post-Communist Era*, ed. E. Andrews, 261–286. Palgrave Macmillan.

Sokolová, V. 2008. *Cultural Politics of Ethnicity: Discourses on Roma in Communist Czechoslovakia.* Stuttgart: Ibidem.

Solimene, M. 2015. 'I Go for Iron': Xoracané Romá Collecting Scrap Metal in Rome. In *Gypsy Economy: Romani Livelihoods and Notions of Worth in the 21st century*, ed. M. Brazzabeni et al., 107–126. New York: Berghahn.

Stewart, K. 1996. *A Space on the Side of the Road. Cultural Poetics in an "Other" America.* Princeton, NJ: Princeton University Press.

Stewart, M. 1997. *The Time of the Gypsies.* Boulder: Westview Press.

Stewart, M. 2012. Foreword: New Forms of Anti-Gypsy Politics: A Challenge for Europe. In *The Gypsy "Menace". Populism and the New Anti-Gypsy Politics,* ed. M. Stewart, xiii–xxxviii. London: C. Hurst.

Stewart, M. 2013. "Roma and Gypsy 'Ethnicity' as a Subject of Anthropological Inquiry." *Annual Review of Anthropology* 42 (1): 415–432.

Stewart, M. 2017. "Nothing about Us without Us, Or The Dangers of A Closed-Society Research Paradigm." *Romani studies* 27 (2): 125–146.

Škobla, D., Filčák, R. 2016. "Infrastructure in Marginalised Roma Settlements: Towards a Typology of Unequal Outcomes of EU Funded Projects." *Sociológia* 48 (6): 551–571.

Šotola, J., Polo, M. R. (eds.) 2016. *Etnografie sociální mobility: etnicita, bariéry, dominance*. Vydavatelství Filozofické fakulty Univerzity Palackého v Olomouci.

Šotola, J. et al. 2018. "Slovak Roma beyond Anthropological Escapism and Exotic Otherness. Concept of 'Whiteness' and the Structures of Everyday Life." *Slovenský národopis* 66 (4): 487–500.

Theodosiou, A. 2004. "'Be-longing' in a 'Doubly Occupied Place': the Parakalamos Gypsy Musicians." *Romani studies* 14 (2): 25–58.

Theodosiou, A. 2007. "Disorienting Rhythms: Gypsyness, 'Authenticity' and Place on the Greek-Albanian Border." *History and Anthropology* 18 (2): 153–175.

Uherek, Z. 2018. "Czech and Slovak Romani on the Path Abroad: Migration and Human Personality." *Romani Studies* 28 (1): 79–108.

van Baar, H. 2011. "Europe's Romaphobia: Problematization, Securitization, Nomadization." *Environment and Planning D: Society and Space* 29 (2): 203–212.

van Baar, H. 2012. "Socio-economic Mobility and Neo-Liberal Governmentality in Post-Socialist Europe: Activation and the Dehumanisation of the Roma." *Journal of Ethnic and Migration Studies* 38 (8): 1289–1304.

van Baar, H. 2014a. The Emergence of a Reasonable Anti-Gypsyism. In *When Stereotype Meets Prejudice*, ed. T. Agarin, 27–44. Stuttgart: Ibidem.

van Baar, H. 2014b. The Perpetual Mobile Machine of Forced Mobility: Europe's Roma and the Institutionalization of Rootlessness. In *The Irregularization of Migration in Contemporary Europe: Deportation, Detention, Drowning*, ed. Y. Jansen et al., 71–86. London: Rowman & Littlefeld.

van Baar, H. 2016. "Evictability and the Biopolitical Bordering of Europe." *Antipode: A Radical Journal of Geography*, 49 (1): 212–230.

van Baar, Huub et al. (eds.) 2019. *Securitization of the Roma in Europe*. New York: Palgrave Macmillan.

van Baar, H., Kóczé, A. 2020. The Roma in Contemporary Europe. Struggling for Identity at a Time of Proliferating Identity Politics. In *The Roma and Their Struggle for Identity in Contemporary Europe*, ed. H. van Baar and A. Kóczé, 3–45. Oxford: Berghahn.

van de Port, M. 1998. *Gypsies, Wars and Other Instances of the Wild*. Amsterdam: Amsterdam University Press.

Vaňko, J. D. 2007. "The Rusyn Language in Slovakia: Between a Rock and a Hard Place." *International Journal of the Sociology of Language* 183: 75–96.

Vrbová, B., Šotola, J. 2016. Šumvaldov. In *Etnografie sociální mobility: etnicita, bariéry, dominance*, ed. J. Šotola and M. Rodrígez Polo, 147–184. Olomouc: Vydavatelství Filozofické fakulty UP.

Wacquant, L. 1993. "Urban Outcasts: Stigma and Division in the Black American Ghetto and the French Urban Periphery." *International Journal of Urban and Regional Research* 17 (3): 366–383.

Wacquant, L. 2007. "Territorial Stigmatization in the Age of Advanced Marginality." *Thesis Eleven* 91: 66–77.

Walach, V. 2014. "Where Only the 'Decent People' Live: The Gypsy 'Menace' and Forging a Neoliberal Utopia in a Czech Postsocialist City." *Wschodnioznawstwo* 8: 71–88.

Wimmer, A. 2013. *Ethnic Boundary Making: Institutions, Power, Networks*. New York: Oxford University Press.

Wimmer, A., Glick-Shiller, N. 2003. "Methodological Nationalism and the Study of Migration: An Essay in Historical Epistemology." *International Migration Review* 37 (3): 576–610.

Wolff, H. 1959. "Intelligibility and Inter-Ethnic Attitudes." *Anthropological Linguistics* 3 (1): 34–41.

Zahra, T. 2016. *The Great Departure: Mass Migration from Eastern Europe and the Making of the Free World*. New York: W. W. Norton.

Zapletal, T. 2012. Přístup totalitního státu a jeho bezpečnostních složek k romské menšině v Československu (1945–1989). In *Sborník archivu bezpečnostních složek* 10, 13–83. Praha: Archiv bezpečnostních složek.

Závodská, M. 2021. "Vznik 'jazykové subkomise' Svazu Cikánů-Romů (1969–1973) pro standardizaci romštiny." *Romano džaniben* 28 (2): 123–154.

Index

A

Abu Ghosh, Yasar 27, 104, 117, 165, 177
'activation work' 135, 157, 163–165, 167, 175, 189
adaptation 29, 32, 41, 42, 59, 67, 68, 105, 121, 129, 136, 139, 140, 142, 156, 160, 172–174, 183, 189, 194, 195, 199, 200, 208
agency 16, 18, 24, 72–73, 97, 137, 159, 191, 193, 198, 203
alien 15, 37, 62, 64, 194, 204
alienation 213
Anderson, Benedict 35, 208
anonymisation 11, 22
anthropology 8–9, 16–19, 22, 31, 35, 47
anti-Gypsyism 23, 45–48, 61–62, 70, 73, 93, 101–102, 110, 117, 160, 177, 192–193, 196–197
assimilation 33, 46, 68, 80, 122–123, 127, 129, 159, 189, 194
assimilation policy 33, 122–123, 129

B

Baar, Huub van 38, 47, 76, 164, 174, 181, 191–193
'backwardness' 21, 34, 46–47, 56, 63, 69–70, 80, 83, 91, 98–99, 103, 106, 129, 150, 157, 159, 164, 169, 173, 182, 201, 205, 213
Bardejov 85, 89, 93, 184
Barth, Frederik 25
Belák, Andrej 17, 53, 56, 117
blackness 30, 32, 42, 56–58, 61, 74–76, 140, 196

blacksmithery 40, 84, 91, 106, 158, 161, 163, 171, 181, 204
Bohemian lands 45–46, 85, 90, 94, 112, 114, 125, 136, 157, 159, 161, 162, 178, 202
borders (*see also* boundaries) 12, 14, 27, 34, 36, 53–54, 62, 77, 83, 116, 160, 175, 187, 207, 208, 211
boundaries (*see also* borders)
 – concept of 25–26
 – cultural/social 54, 155, 197
 – territorial 35, 80, 83, 90, 93, 97, 107, 116–117, 169, 183, 188, 207, 212
 – political 45
Bourdieu, Pierre 75, 128, 130
Brazzabeni, Micol 27, 41, 76, 160, 174–75, 188–189
Brubaker, Rogers 25–26, 124

C

capital
 – capitalisation 143, 145, 182–183, 187, 189
 – economic 41, 53, 74, 171, 182, 189, 190, 199
 – *Gadžo* ('*gagikano*') 58
 – social 21, 41, 53, 74, 117, 171, 182, 183, 189–90, 199
 – symbolic 127, 143, 147, 184
 – migrant 182–183, 187, 189
capitalism 210
Christensen, Ann-Dorte 113, 115
cigánska robota 41, 156, 160, 163, 165–166,

168, 170, 172, 174, 176, 181–182, 188–189, 190

code-switching 39, 126, 128, 133–134, 136, 140, 144, 151–155, 170, 201

coexistence 31, 42, 153, 192, 196, 200
- conflictual 76
- harmonious 11, 40, 42, 96, 114, 194, 200, 214
- problematic 31, 49, 76

communism (communist era/period, *see also* socialism) 47, 49–50, 72, 91, 98, 129, 163, 164, 168, 179, 181

communist policies (*see also* socialist policies) 79

Communist Party 122

communist regime 13, 88, 122, 128, 139

competence/incompetence
- cultural 141, 145, 173
- language 19, 39–40, 121, 125, 127–128, 130, 139, 140–143, 145, 147–148, 150–151, 154–155, 157, 173, 201
- social 174, 183

conflict (*see also* coexistence – conflictual) 59, 63, 72, 96, 101, 110, 135, 152

council flats (*see also* low-grade council flats) 35, 44, 50, 53–54, 69, 79, 82, 95–99, 103–106, 108–109, 111–115, 118, 120, 130–131, 135–136, 140, 144, 157, 183, 212, 214

counter-narrative 73, 113, 194, 198

Critical Romani Studies (*see also* Romani studies) 24

cryptic code 39, 151–153, 155–156, 173, 199

Cunha, Ivone Manuela (*see* Brazzabeni, Micol)

Czech Republic (*see also* Bohemian lands) 19, 23–24, 43, 48, 57, 65, 69, 94, 112, 124, 129, 146, 149, 151, 157, 160, 162–163, 165, 167, 178–179, 182, 183–187, 202, 205–207

Červenka, Jan 18, 122–123, 125

D

darekana ('back in the day' – Romani concept) 71–72, 77, 150, 211

Davidová, Eva 17

degeša (Romani concept) 63, 66, 69–71, 150, 173, 201

demographic change 13, 33–34, 47, 54, 95, 143, 181, 190, 211–212, 214

depopulation (*see also* demographic change) 13, 162

deserving unemployed 188

deterritorialisation 89, 117

diglossia 124–125

'dispersal' policy 82, 85–86, 93, 98, 159, 210

displacement 114, 116, 193

Donert, Celia 47, 49, 82, 122, 159, 180–181

'doubly occupied place' 156

E

economic practices 40–41, 70, 160, 165, 167, 175–176, 178, 184, 189–190

economic strategies 33, 40–41, 156, 158, 160–163, 165, 172, 174–175, 177–179, 185, 188–191

economy
- informal 22, 52, 157, 163, 165, 167, 175–176, 179, 190
- formal 162, 174, 176, 179, 188, 190
- Gypsy (*see* Gypsy Economy)

education 14, 33, 50, 95, 97, 120–123, 127, 129–130, 136, 139, 141, 144, 156

Elias, Norbert 105, 117, 183, 188

Elšík, Viktor 124, 149, 150

employment (*see also* unemployment) 41, 50, 63, 71, 80, 86–87, 94, 104, 127, 132–133, 153, 161–163, 165–166, 175, 179, 190

Engebrigtsen, Ada I. 18

England 71, 186–187

Eriksen, Thomas Hylland 25

established vs. outsiders 105, 117, 183, 188, 190

ethnicity 25, 26, 27, 34, 75, 83, 197, 210

ethnography 16–17, 22–23, 26, 30, 35, 41, 76, 116, 188, 193, 210

European Charter for Regional and Minority Languages 123, 136

European Union 160, 166–167, 190

'evictability' 38, 181, 191, 193

F

Fabian, Johannes 29

Fanon, Frantz 30–32, 54, 57, 74–75, 140–141

Ferguson, James 116

Ferguson, Charles A. 124

Filčák, Richard 83, 87, 102

Fishman, Joshua A. 124, 126

Fotta, Martin (*see also* Brazzabeni, Micol) 193

G
Gardner, Katy 183
Gay Y Blasco, Paloma 23, 26, 35, 116
gender 21, 24, 40, 137, 128, 142, 145, 155, 185, 194, 203–206, 208
generations 19, 28, 54–55, 68, 71, 111, 124–125, 127, 129–130, 139, 141, 150, 154, 161–162, 168, 171
ghettoisation 193
Glick-Schiller, Nina 193
Greece 36, 54, 116, 149
Greek Catholic Church 13, 49, 51, 139
Grill, Jan 17, 27, 37, 46–48, 54, 56–58, 62, 63, 68, 71, 75–76, 104, 107, 159–160, 164–165, 167–168, 170, 174–175, 177, 182, 184–185, 187–189, 191, 206
Guy, Will 17, 45–47, 76, 82, 89–90, 93, 117, 159, 180–181, 187, 190–191, 203
Gadže 12, 15, 27, 42, 49, 52, 56, 57, 59, 60, 62, 63, 66–69, 71–74, 93, 101, 109, 113–114, 121, 132, 134, 141, 143–144, 147–149, 151–153, 175, 184–185, 190, 192, 198–199, 201, 205
  – 'amongst the *Gadže*' (Romani concept) 34–35, 69, 80, 83, 93, 95, 103–112, 117, 129–131, 147, 157, 169, 171, 182–184, 204, 207, 212, 214
  – 'amoral' *Gadže* 67–68, 175, 205
  – *Gadžo* cultural code 142
  – *Gadžo* customs 107, 143
  – *Gadžo* language (*see also* non-Romani language) 129–130, 132, 134, 173, 198, 201
  – *Gadžo* normality 199
  – *Gadžo* order 29, 68, 189, 199
  – *Gadžo* sense 93
  – *Gadžo* socio-economic networks 41, 49
  – *Gadžo* way of life (*see also* non-Romani way of life) 35, 41, 68, 71, 93, 117, 146, 150, 156, 194–195, 205–206
  – *Gadžo* world (*see also* non-Romani world) 68, 198, 205
  – 'our *Gadže*' (Romani concept) 44, 62, 64, 73, 76, 93, 148, 200–202
  – 'speak with the Gadže' (Romani concept) 173, 174, 189
  – 'to be one with *Gadže*' (Romani concept) 42, 58, 136
  – 'to live like a *Gadžo*' (Romani concept) 32, 34, 39, 56, 65, 68, 104, 107, 117, 131–132, 155, 177
  – 'to live with the *Gadže*' (Romani concept) 49, 143, 201, 207
  – 'to reach out to Gadženess' (Romani concept) 32, 69, 143, 201
  – 'so the *Gadže* don't say' (Romani concept) 60, 70, 72, 133–34, 152, 156, 174, 186, 197–200
  – 'to try to make out one is a *Gadžo*' (Romani concept) 32, 69, 143
Gadženess 32–33, 69
Gažovičová, Tina 122–123, 129, 136
Government Decree no. 502/1965 (*see also* 'dispersal' policy) 85, 93
Gypsies
  – 'backward' 21, 34, 46–47, 56, 63, 69, 70, 80, 83, 91, 103, 106, 150, 159, 173, 182, 201, 205, 213
  – 'lazy' 164, 183, 188, 189
  – 'Gypsy origin' 33, 46, 91, 92, 107, 159, 180, 204, 211
  – 'our Gypsies' (*see also* 'our Roma') 81, 204
  – 'problematic' 37, 42, 58, 63, 106, 117, 134, 168, 196, 197
Gypsy Economy 41, 157, 160, 165, 174–175, 177, 189
'Gypsy settlement' (*see also* Romani settlement) 34, 80, 85, 89, 117
  – 'liquidation of' 89, 117
Gypsy Work (*see cigánska robota*)
Gypsy worker 161
Gypsy-Roma Union (*see Zväz Cigánov-Rómov*)
Gypsyness
  – 'silencing' 30, 32–33
  – '(not) naming' 31–32, 117, 196
  – 'escaping' 42, 80, 83, 108, 169, 174, 177
  – 'exaggerated' 32

H
Hajská, Markéta 17, 124–125, 168
Halwachs, Dieter W. 123
Hojsík, Marek 81–83, 97, 115
Horváth, Kata 27, 31–34, 51, 60, 61, 69–70, 75, 77, 103, 118, 165, 168, 196, 198–199, 211

Horváthová, Emilia 17, 158
housing 14, 33–35, 46, 79–83, 85–88,
    90–92, 94–99, 101, 103–106, 108, 110–112,
    116, 117, 120, 122, 138, 159, 165, 169, 177,
    178, 180, 187, 204, 206, 210, 212
Howe, Leo 169, 170, 188
Hrustič, Tomáš 17, 23, 48, 104, 176
Hübschmannová, Milena 16–18, 23, 28, 37,
    45–46, 57, 62–63, 81, 122–125, 129, 136,
    144–145, 158, 161
Hungary 31–35, 46, 51, 60, 64, 68–70, 77,
    103, 137, 198
Hungarians 31–33, 61, 70
Hungarian language 124–125

I

identity – 16, 26–27, 29, 31, 35–37, 39, 68,
    116, 118, 124–125, 132, 174, 191, 204,
    208–209
imagined community 35, 36, 208, 209
'inappropriate/d others' (see Others
    – inappropriate/d)
inferiority 29–30, 32, 57, 62, 66, 75, 93, 118,
    129–130, 158–159
intelligibility 60, 133–134, 148, 151–153,
    174, 196
inter-ethnic marriage 50, 65, 207

J

Jakoubek, Marek 12, 17, 25
Jenkins, Richard 25–26
Jensen, Sune Qvotrup 113, 115
Jews 14, 38, 90, 161

K

Kandert, Josef 163
kinship 37, 40, 69, 92, 94–95, 105–106, 194,
    206–209
Kobes, Tomáš 17, 28, 36–37, 40, 48, 62, 92,
    132, 184, 187, 191, 206, 210
Kovai, Cecilia 27, 31, 32–34, 46, 51, 60–61,
    69, 70, 75, 77
Kubaník, Pavel 17, 125–127, 129, 133, 147

L

Lacková, Elena 38, 57, 93
language
    – acquisition 126–128, 130, 131, 144
    – domains 120, 123, 124, 131, 132, 136,
        138–139, 142

– choice 25, 126, 130, 133, 134, 136
– competence (incompetence) 19, 39, 40,
    121, 125, 127–128, 130, 139, 140–143,
    145, 147–148, 150–151, 154–155, 157,
    173, 201
– planning 121, 123, 136–139
– policy 120, 122, 136–139
– prestige 121, 124–125, 130, 141, 145
– standardisation 122–123, 139
– transmission 124, 130, 139, 141, 154
– transparency 60, 135–136, 142, 151–155,
    169
Law no. 74/1958 (see also nomadism) 159,
    180–182
local authority (see also municipal authori-
    ty/office) 35, 38, 46, 79, 81–82, 89, 91, 99,
    116–117, 120, 127, 132–133, 136–138, 148,
    157, 176, 180, 191, 196, 204, 207, 212
local committee 80, 85, 87, 89, 94, 97, 99,
    107, 180–181
local culture 15, 49, 142, 150, 197
local way of life (see local culture) 15, 39,
    48, 72
low-grade council flats (see also council
    flats) 21, 35, 50, 82, 96, 99

M

Malkki, Lisa 128
marginality 13, 16, 33–34, 47–48, 70, 82,
    101–103, 142, 160, 163, 165–166, 168–69,
    176, 181–182, 190–191, 196–197, 202, 211
media 11, 15, 23, 40, 42, 59, 96, 114, 126,
    139, 195, 214
methodological nationalism 193
migration 41, 47–48, 71, 76, 94, 107, 108,
    124, 149, 158–162, 178–187, 189–191, 197,
    202–203, 205–206
Minh-ha, Trinh T. 36, 132
mobility
    – social (socio-economic) 23, 46, 70,
        71, 97, 107, 120–121, 141, 178, 182,
        186–187, 191, 207
    – spatial 36, 94, 103, 107, 112, 116, 117,
        159, 182, 187
morality 41, 67–68, 160, 188, 205
municipal authority/office (see also local
    authority) 14, 80, 121, 122, 137, 138, 164
musicianship 36–38, 40, 54, 59, 67, 146,
    157–158, 161, 163, 204
Mušinka, Alexander 12, 83, 108, 118

N

neoliberalism 47, 160, 164, 193
newcomers 29, 102, 119, 195,
nomadism 35–36, 116, 159, 180, 193, 203
nomadisation 193
non-conflict (*see* conflict)
non-Romani normality (*see also* normality) 194
non-Romani world (*see also* Gadžo world) 21, 27, 32, 42, 58, 66–68, 71–72, 74–75, 124, 129, 132, 150, 168, 170, 175, 199
non-Romani way of life 34–35, 38, 45, 64, 105, 107, 115, 145, 150, 156, 174, 199–202
non-Romani dominance 20, 29, 42, 101, 107, 108, 110, 118, 135, 144, 160, 190, 194, 197–199, 202
non-Romani language 27, 60, 69, 141–145, 151–152, 155–156
normality 27, 30, 32, 57, 59, 138, 159, 181, 191, 194, 196, 198–199

O

odd jobs (*see also* economy – informal) 52–53, 55, 71, 109, 111, 128, 135, 152, 157, 163–164, 165, 167, 170–173, 175–176, 179, 183, 189, 200, 204
Olivera, Martin 16, 27, 38–39, 50, 58, 119, 156, 193
Other 25, 204, 207, 209
  – colonial 24
  – excluded 194
  – European 193
  – Gypsies 201
  – 'inappropriate/d' 36, 132
'our Roma' 34, 36–37, 44, 61–62, 64, 92, 94, 103, 181, 187, 196, 198, 200, 202–203, 213
outsiders 61, 65, 92, 193
  – locals vs. 13, 15, 26, 37, 92, 102, 142, 145
  – 'eternal' 29, 38, 197, 202
  – 'perennial' 193
  – established vs. 105, 117, 183, 188, 190

P

paternalism 55, 73, 186, 206
pativ ('respect, honour' – Romani concept) 143, 150
participation (of the Roma)
  – political 47, 49, 95, 133
  – social 46, 48–50, 60, 70–71, 152, 155, 159, 162, 168, 198, 204

patron / client 31, 40, 62, 73–74, 97, 103, 141, 158
Pattillo, Mary 115, 118
Piasere, Leonardo 58
Pintér, Tibor 125
Podolinská, Tatiana 17, 48
Poland 12–14, 90, 114, 149, 208
Poles 15, 26, 28, 61, 64, 75
Polish language 15, 208
Polish Roma 149, 208
politics of space 33, 34, 38, 79–119, 201
Port, Mattijs van de 54
post-marital residence 40, 94, 155, 204
pre-war period 13, 84, 161, 163, 186
precarity 33, 41, 98, 165, 186

R

race 24, 75, 46, 47, 48, 54–56, 58, 63, 67, 70, 76, 161, 195–197, 205, 210
racial discrimination (*see also* racism) 196–197
racial/racialised hierarchy (*see also* social hierarchy) 45, 54, 56, 58, 74, 76, 106, 139, 190, 192, 195–196, 205
racialisation 30, 45, 48, 55, 57–58, 61, 65–66, 74–76, 106, 118, 128, 139, 140, 188, 190, 192, 195–196, 198, 210, 211
racism 42, 73, 110, 164, 174, 181, 186, 192, 194, 196, 199
  – internalised racism 56, 75
  – excaping racism 184
racial segregation (*see also* segregation) 48, 63, 76, 98
relocation (*see also* resettlement) 13, 35, 47, 68, 81–83, 85–86, 90, 100, 114, 116
resettlement 90, 181
resistence 72–73, 80, 93, 97, 114, 116, 118, 133, 172, 188, 194, 198, 212
residential structure 87, 95, 114
'Romani butji' 168
Romani language 12, 14–16, 18–19, 27, 39, 40, 50, 61, 63, 69, 120–156, 172–174, 189, 198, 200–201, 208
Romani studies 16–19, 24
Romani settlement (*see also* Gypsy settlement) 12, 14, 17, 20–21, 32, 34–35, 39, 42, 44, 50, 54, 67, 69, 78–79, 81–83, 90, 94–96, 101, 112, 114, 116–118, 150, 182, 201
Romanian Roma 18, 149, 151, 156, 208–209
Rusyn language 14–15, 19, 39, 40, 69,

120–121, 124–128, 130–140, 142, 144–146, 149–156, 170, 172–173, 201, 208
Rusyn Roma 28, 39, 43, 120, 132, 137
Rusyns 13–14, 26, 28, 31, 121, 127–128, 145

S
Sadílková, Helena 17, 22, 46, 49, 76, 81, 89, 116–117, 122–123, 125, 159, 191, 193
Scheffel, David 12, 17, 37, 38, 48, 59, 76, 81, 93, 116, 118, 154, 193
Second World War 13–14, 36, 38, 45, 49, 62, 78, 80–82, 84, 91, 158, 161, 178
segregation (*see also* racial segregation) 12–13, 15, 21, 42, 46–48, 50, 56, 63–64, 76, 81–83, 86, 90, 98, 114, 118, 127, 149, 150, 210
selfexclusion 60, 117
Simmel, Georg 193
skin colour 30–31, 42, 45, 57–58, 63, 75, 196, 206
Sloboda, Marián 123, 128, 137, 139
Slovak language 14–15, 19, 27, 39, 69, 120–121, 124–146, 149, 152–154, 158–159
Slovaks 13–14, 19, 26, 28, 31, 37–38, 59, 74, 185, 192
smithery (*see* blacksmithery)
sociability 11, 194, 198–199
social hierarchy 15, 30, 33, 38, 45, 54–56, 58, 74, 76, 106, 121, 128–129, 131, 133, 136, 139, 142, 154, 178, 182, 190, 192, 195, 196, 205
social mobility (*see* mobility – social)
socialism 27, 31, 33, 46, 49, 57, 80, 98–99, 113, 123, 127, 129, 159, 162, 168, 180, 210–211
socialist policies (*see also* state policies) 79, 89, 95, 98, 159
socialist worker 159
Sokolová, Vera 27, 107, 181, 203, 210–211
spatial mobility (*see* mobility – spatial)
state policies 33, 35, 41, 47, 79, 82–83, 85, 86, 89, 91, 93, 95, 98–99, 105, 117, 122–123, 128–129, 138–139, 159, 167, 191, 193, 203, 210
Stewart, Michael 16, 23–24, 26, 31, 35, 68, 75, 116, 168
Stewart, Kathleen 156
stigma/stigmatisation (*see also* territorial stigmatisation) 16, 21, 31–32, 57, 64, 67,

70, 75, 83, 97, 99, 104, 109, 110, 111–115, 118, 123, 136, 146, 154, 169, 177, 183, 195, 199
stranger 193
subversion 41, 156, 169, 173–174, 188–189, 194, 198–199
superiority 29, 42, 61, 67–68, 73–74, 104, 160, 183, 196, 198, 205
Svidník 79–80, 87, 89, 95, 112, 114, 133, 140, 151, 159, 162–163, 167–168, 171, 175–176, 180, 184–185
symbolic violence 75
Šotola, Jaroslav 15, 17, 23, 24, 29, 48

T
temporality 29, 34, 77, 210
territorial hegemony 83, 90, 99, 117, 213, 214
territorial stigmatisation 83, 97, 99, 109, 112–114, 118, 169, 183
territorialisation 77, 81–83, 88–89, 91, 93, 99, 101–102, 104, 113, 116–118, 210
Theodosiou, Aspasia 26, 35–40, 54, 116, 118, 132, 149–150, 156, 191, 193, 202–203

U
unemployment (*see also* employment) 47, 55, 127, 157, 164, 165–167, 169, 170, 175, 188
United Kingdom (*see* England)
urbanisation 82, 191
usury 176

V
Vaňko, Juraj 95

W
Wacquant, Loïc 75, 83, 99, 113, 118
'welfare scroungers' 188
whiteness 15, 30, 32, 41–42, 54, 57–59, 61, 75, 196
Wimmer, Andreas 25, 193
work ethic 158, 160, 163–165, 168–170, 173, 175, 188

Z
Zväz Cigánov-Rómov (Gypsy-Roma Union) 49, 86, 90, 122
Závodská, Milada 122